Modern Chinese Parts of Sp

What is the essence of a part of speech? Why is it difficult to classify parts of speech? What are the bases and criteria for classifying them? How should they be classified? In doing so, how should a conversional word be dealt with? How should nominalization be treated? These are just some of the questions answered in this book.

The classification of parts of speech in Chinese is a tough job due to the language's lack of morphological differences. Based on the analysis of nearly 40,000 Chinese characters, this book proposes that, essentially, a part of speech is not of a distributional type and that its intrinsic basis is an expressional function and the semantic type. Essentially, large categories such as substantive words, predicate words and modification words are classes of words classified according to their expressional functions. Basic categories such as nouns, verbs and adjectives are classes that combine semantic types with syntactic functions. In classifying parts of speech, the book pays attention not to identifying a single distributive characteristic that is internally universal and externally exclusive but to clustering the grammatical functions that have the same classification value through the "reflection-representation" relationship among distribution, expressional function and semantic type (distribution reflects expressional function and semantic type, which are, in turn, represented as distribution), thereby identifying the classification criteria. It uses distributional compatibility and the correlation principle to analyze which distributional differences represent differences in parts of speech and which do not. In this way, grammatical functions that have equal classification values are collected into one equivalent function cluster, each of which represents one part of speech. The book uses four strategies to classify parts of speech, namely the homogeneity strategy, the homomorphical strategy, the priority homomorphical strategy and the consolidation strategy. It will be a valuable reference for Chinese linguistic researchers and students as well as Chinese learners.

Guo Rui is a professor in the Department of Chinese Language and Literature, Peking University. His main research lies in Chinese grammar and semantics.

Chinese Linguistics

Chinese Linguistics selects representative and frontier works in linguistic disciplines including lexicology, grammar, phonetics, dialectology, philology and rhetoric. Mostly published in Chinese before, the selection has had far-reaching influence on China's linguistics and offered inspiration and reference for the world's linguistics. The aim of this series is to reflect the general level and latest developments of Chinese linguistics from an overall and objective view.

Titles in this series currently include:

Prosodic Syntax in Chinese
History and Changes
Feng Shengli

Modern Chinese Parts of Speech
Classification Theory
Guo Rui

Modern Chinese Parts of Speech
Systems Research
Guo Rui

The Experiential Guo in Mandarin
A Quantificational Approach
Ye Meng

Research on Functional Grammar of Chinese
Information Structure and Word Ordering Selection
Zhang Bojiang and Fang Mei

Research on Functional Grammar of Chinese
Reference and Grammatical Category
Zhang Bojiang and Fang Mei

For more information, please visit https://www.routledge.com/
Chinese-Linguistics/book-series/CL

Modern Chinese Parts of Speech

Classification Theory

Guo Rui

Routledge
Taylor & Francis Group
LONDON AND NEW YORK

The Commercial Press

First published 2019 by Routledge

2 Park Square, Milton Park, Abingdon, Oxfordshire OX14 4RN

52 Vanderbilt Avenue, New York, NY 10017

Routledge is an imprint of the Taylor & Francis Group, an informa business

First issued in paperback 2020

British Library Cataloguing-in-Publication Data
A catalogue record for this book is available from the British Library

Library of Congress Cataloging-in-Publication Data
Names: Guo, Rui, 1962– author.
Title: Modern Chinese parts of speech : classification theory / Guo Rui.
Other titles: Xian dai Han yu ci lei yan jiu. English
Description: London ; New York, NY : Routledge, 2019. |
Series: Chinese linguistics | Includes bibliographical references and index.
Identifiers: LCCN 2018039608 (print) | LCCN 2018046278 (ebook) |
ISBN 9781351269209 (ebook) | ISBN 9781138576711 (hardcover)
Subjects: LCSH: Chinese language–Parts of speech. |
Chinese language–Syntax. | Chinese language–Grammar.
Classification: LCC PL1231.5 (ebook) |
LCC PL1231.5 .G8613 2019 (print) | DDC 495.15–dc23
LC record available at https://lccn.loc.gov/2018039608

ISBN: 978-1-138-57671-1 (hbk)
ISBN: 978-0-367-66107-6 (pbk)

Typeset in Times New Roman
by Newgen Publishing UK

MIX
Paper from
responsible sources
FSC
www.fsc.org   FSC™ C013985

Printed in the United Kingdom
by Henry Ling Limited

Contents

Figures

Tables

Foreword to the Chinese Edition

Lu Jianming

Modern Chinese Parts of Speech: Classification Theory by Guo Rui finally meets its audience today. The book comes up with several revisions on the basis of his doctoral thesis and is the encouraging outcome of his devoted exploration of modern Chinese parts of speech over more than a decade.

Chinese parts of speech have always been very difficult problems. What are the problems? Why have these problems not been solved? Guo Rui has summarized, analyzed and disentangled them very well in his book. He has summed them up in the following five questions:

1. Does Chinese have parts of speech?
2. What is the nature of a part of speech?
3. What are the bases and criteria for classifying parts of speech?
4. How can parts of speech be determined (how to classify them)?
5. How can conversional words be dealt with?

These questions are occasionally discussed in academic circles but fall short of in-depth investigation and exploration. Guo Rui has analyzed the causes of this in his book: first, our understanding of parts of speech comes from Western Indo-European linguistics. The words of Indo-European languages have morphological markers and changes when used in a sentence, and the bases for classifying the parts of speech in Indo-European languages are these morphological markers and changes. On this basis, it is thought that parts of speech are classified according to word forms, but Chinese words have neither morphological markers nor changes. Therefore, Chinese words do not have parts of speech.

Second, Indo-European languages essentially have a one-to-one correspondence between their parts of speech and syntactic constituents. For example, a noun functions as a subject or object; a verb functions as a predicate; an adjective as an attributive; an adverb as an adverbial and so on. Accordingly, it is thought that parts of speech are classified according to a word's capability of functioning as sentence constituents. But Chinese essentially has a one-to-many correspondence between its parts of speech and sentence constituents; a word can often function as either subject, object, predicate, attributive or adverbial and so on. The multiple functions of a Chinese word are a headache for some scholars in Chinese academic circles who use sentence constituents as the basis for classifying Chinese parts of speech. They also create another problem in that it is difficult to decide the syntactic relations of a good many syntactic structures. For example, is 容易掌握 (easy to command) a predicate-object relation or an "adverbial-headword" modifier and a modified relation? Is 便于掌握 (convenient to command) a predicate-object relation or an adverbial-headword modifier and modified relation? Is 决心干到底 (determined to fight to the end) a predicate-object relation or an adverbial-headword modifier and a modified relation? It is difficult to decide. The difficulty in deciding the syntactic relations of these constructions may affect understanding of the parts of speech of such words as 容易 (easy), 便于 (convenient) and 决心 (determined).

Third, words in the synchronic hierarchy of any language actually have different historical and field hierarchies. Indo-European languages have morphological changes, and the morphological changes of words are very small and basically not affected by historical and field hierarchies. Because Chinese words do not have morphological changes, the use of words in different historical and field hierarchies may vary greatly, undoubtedly creating many troubles for the classification of Chinese parts of speech. However, in the past, we always lacked an understanding of them.

Fourth, an even more fundamental reason why Chinese parts of speech have always been a very difficult problem is that when they were discussed in the past, only some typical examples were cited, but no one has actually examined one by one the uses of tens of thousands of modern Chinese words. Thus, everybody can only engage in idle theorizing.

The above analyses all show keen insights; however, I must add one more: fifth, what is the intrinsic nature of a part of speech? Since structuralist language views have been prevalent in the world, the intrinsic nature of a part of speech has been distribution, that is, a part of speech belongs to a distribution type. These views are universally accepted. Chen Wangdao expressed these views in the discussions on grammatical innovation in the 1940s. Then, starting in the 1960s, Zhu Dexi emphasized and expounded on these views again and again (see Zhu Dexi, Lu Jiawen & Ma Zhen 1961; Zhu Dexi 1982a; Zhu Dexi 1985a respectively). Furthermore, these views by Zhu Dexi are considered "extremely enlightening new views" proposed through "breaking away from the interference and constraint of the traditional Indo-European language views and looking at Chinese in a plain light". From the present perspective, this view does not have a deep understanding of the essence of a part of speech. Therefore, the Chinese part-of-speech problem has still not been solved satisfactorily.

In my opinion, the prominent contributions of Guo Rui's *Modern Chinese Parts of Speech: Classification Theory*, first and foremost, lie in the fact that he has proposed his brand-new and more profound views on the essence of a part of speech: "The essence of a part of speech is not distribution. Therefore, it is difficult to succeed in any attempt to classify Chinese parts of speech through seeking the internally universal and externally exclusive distribution characteristics." A part of speech is the type of a word's grammatical meaning, which we call an expressional function, namely the meaning type of a word in its combination, such as the main types of statement, reference and modification, and the small types of entity, position, measurement unit, quantity and demonstration. Therefore, "a part of speech is actually the classification of words that uses their expressional functions at lexical level as intrinsic basis". He figured out his views not just by racking his brains but through conducting actual investigations and devoted analyses of more than 40,000 modern Chinese words. He figured them out through his profound analyses of a variety of loopholes of the distribution theory, the similarity theory and the prototype theory in the Chinese part-of-speech classification. More importantly, he figured them out through his thorough examination of this question: the grammatical position or combinatory position has selectional restriction on the words that enter into the position. The selectional restriction definitely needs certain bases. Then what are its bases? By using his ample perceptual knowledge gained through the actual investigation of more than 40,000 words and long-term and repeated research, he discovered that the bases for the selectional restriction of a grammatical position on words are not distribution itself but certain properties at deeper levels, namely the expressional functions of words. The concepts of word properties such as the so-called substantive word and predicate word actually reflect expressional functions such as reference and statement at the lexical level. It is a pity that people did not realize this in the past. Zhu Dexi was the earliest person to propose the two concepts of "reference" and "statement" (see "Self-Reference and Transfer Reference – Grammatical Functions and Semantic Functions of Chinese Nominalization Markers such as de (的), zhe (者), suo (所), zhi (之)", in *Dialect*, Issue 1, 1983). But Guo Rui's understanding goes deeper.

First, Zhu Dexi only classified expressional functions into reference and statement, whereas Guo Rui has classified them into four basic types: A. A statement denotes an assertion; B. A reference denotes an object; C. Modification restricts a statement or reference; D. An auxiliary function denotes regulation.

Second, Guo Rui thinks that expressional functions can be classified into two levels: intrinsic expressional function and extrinsic expressional function. The intrinsic expressional function of a word is inherent; the external expressional function is the one realized by a word in its certain grammatical position. Under usual circumstances, the expressional functions at the two levels are consistent, for example, 小王黄头发 (Little Wang has yellow hair), where 小王 (Little Wang) is a reference at either level. But sometimes they may not be consistent. For example, 黄头发 (yellow hair) is a reference as far as intrinsic expressional function is concerned; however, it is a statement in terms of extrinsic expressional function because it can be modified at its front by some adverbs, for instance, 小王也黄头发 / 小王的确黄头发 (Little Wang also has yellow hair; Little Wang indeed has yellow hair).

It must be pointed out that Guo Rui's expressional function is also a kind of grammatical meaning of a word. The intrinsic basis for classifying words into, for example, nouns or verbs is actually the distinction between such expressional functions as a reference and a statement. The distribution difference and morphological difference among parts of speech are simply the external exhibitions of differences in expressional functions. Just like expressional functions have layers, Guo Rui correspondingly classifies parts of speech into two layers – the parts of speech that correspond to intrinsic expressional functions are at the lexical level, and those corresponding to extrinsic expressional functions are at the syntactic level. The part of speech at the lexical level is a word's inherent one, which is labeled in a dictionary, while that at the syntactic level results from the use of words, which can be controlled by syntactic rules. The part of speech of 黄头发 (yellow hair) cited in the above example is nominal at the lexical level, but in the above example sentence, it is a predicate at the syntactic level. One can easily understand that "expressional functions are specified by a language's internal composition and reflect the relationship among language signs, thereby having their grammatical meanings. They do not reflect the relationship between language sign and the real world, thus having no conceptual meaning; they also do not reflect the relationship between language sign and its user, thereby having no pragmatic meaning".

Readers may ask, since an expressional function is also a kind of grammatical meaning, why shouldn't one directly say that "parts of speech should be classified according to a word's grammatical meaning"? Theoretically speaking, this is true, but grammatical meanings themselves have or can be understood at different levels. Therefore, Guo Rui uses the expressional function to illustrate the nature of a part of speech.

Guo Rui's views on parts of speech are obviously a great breakthrough in traditional views and have universal linguistic theoretical meanings. Classifying parts of speech on the intrinsic bases of the expressional function at the lexical level of a word or not regarding distribution but the expressional function as the essence of a part of speech "can explain why it is comparable with different languages in different eras," and why words distribute differently in different eras and languages yet belong to the same part of speech. Just as Guo Rui illustrated, the words 看 (see) in modern Chinese and 视 (watch) in classic Chinese distribute differently. The former can take a numeral plus a measure word object, but cannot be modified by a numeral, such as 看三次 (see three times), but not 三看 (three sees), whereas the latter cannot take a numeral plus a measure word object and can be modified by a numeral, such as *视三 / 三视 (*watch three/three watch). But both are verbs. The English word "stone" can be modified by a numeral, for example "two stones", and can function as the object of a preposition indicating a place, for instance, "on the stone", whereas the Chinese word 石头 (stone) does not have these functions. But both are nouns. The view that the essence of a part of speech is its expressional function can produce a reasonable explanation: because a part of speech has the same expressional function. A part of speech is a category; the same part of speech must have commonality of its properties; different parts of speech must have differences in their properties. The commonality and difference in property are those of expressional functions and the bases of language comparison.

Guo Rui's views on part of speech may not be approved of by all my colleagues; nevertheless, I hope these colleagues will not immediately oppose or suspect them. There is no harm in seriously pondering his new views on parts of speech. Likewise, there is no harm in knowing the operational procedures for his classification of Chinese parts of speech, and then deciding whether to agree or object, to completely or partially agree, or to completely or partially object.

The second contribution made by Guo Rui's *Modern Chinese Parts of Speech: Classification Theory* is that it proposes new operational procedures and methods for classifying parts of speech. Namely, the book calculates the degree of compatibility among grammatical functions to reveal the relationship between grammatical function and part of speech. In what sense? As mentioned earlier, Guo Rui considers an expressional function as the essence of a part of speech. The essential bases for classifying parts of speech are the expressional function of a word, which is, however, invisible and impalpable. In reality, it is not operative to classify the parts of speech of a word in direct accordance with its expressional function. We must find observable and specific classification criteria that can truly reflect the essence of a part of speech. Then how should we determine classification criteria? Guo Rui points out in his book that different grammatical functions have different values for classifying different parts of speech: some have distinctive values, whereas others have non-distinctive values. Therefore, the various grammatical functions expressed by a part of speech should not be put on a par and treated equally. We only select those distinctive grammatical functions for part-of-speech classification. In order to classify parts of speech effectively with those distinctive grammatical functions, Guo Rui created the concepts of "equivalent function" and "heterovalent function". Some differences among the functions demonstrate the differences in the properties of a part of speech. For example, the pair of grammatical functions 不 (not) ~ and ⟨attributive⟩ ~ demonstrates different properties of a part of speech and can be regarded as a heterovalent function, whereas the grammatical functions that reflect such identical properties as functioning as subject or object can be regarded as an equivalent function. Guo Rui points out that, theoretically speaking, if we can identify all the functions of a word, determine which functions are equivalent and form them into clusters of equivalent functions, then we identify the distinctive grammatical functions of all the parts of speech and largely classify all the words into different parts of speech. Therefore, the determination of equivalent functions is the key to identifying classification criteria and determining how many parts of speech a language has. Obviously, the determination of equivalent functions is the key to classifying parts of speech. Then how should we determine equivalent functions? Guo Rui suggests that the compatibility of grammatical functions is useful in this regard. The compatibility is manifested in (A) whether several different grammatical functions can be regarded as equivalent function and (B) whether the different grammatical functions are valuable for classifying parts of speech. If we can calculate the degrees of compatibility among grammatical functions, we can identify the equivalent functions that can distinguish between parts of speech and can use the degrees as specific classification criteria. For example, a word that can function as a subject can also function as an object, and vice versa. Then, functioning as a subject and object is a set of compatible grammatical functions. For another example, if a word that can enter 很 (very) ~ can also enter ~ 极了 (extremely) and ~ 得很 (nicely), and if a word that can enter ~ 极了 (extremely) and ~ 得很 (nicely) can also enter 很 (very) ~, then 很 (very) ~, ~ 极了 (extremely) and ~ 得很 (nicely) are a set of compatible grammatical functions. But the compatibility of grammatical functions between 不 (not) ~ and 〈numeral〉, and that between 〈numeral and measure word〉 ~ and 〈functioning as adverbial〉 is extremely small. As mentioned before, the fundamental bases of selectional restriction of a grammatical position on a word are its expressional functions, and their extrinsic manifestations are the grammatical functions of the word. Obviously, the grammatical functions that have a rather big compatibility often reflect the same selectional restriction of the two different grammatical positions on words and also the common properties of a part of speech, thus being an equivalent grammatical function. The two grammatical functions that have a rather small or no compatibility degree reflect different properties of a part of speech and are generally heterovalent functions. Hence, we can use the compatibility of grammatical functions to determine their values for classifying parts of speech. In his book, Guo Rui has proposed not only the concept of "compatibility between grammatical functions of a word" but also the methods and formulae for calculating their compatible degrees. Undoubtedly, this advances one step forward to the demonstration of part-of-speech classification. Superficially, it seems that Guo Rui still classifies parts of speech of a word according to its distribution and grammatical functions, but he does it fundamentally differently from what others did previously, and goes deeper and further, as it were. This may be profoundly understood as long as a reader carefully reads the whole book.

As mentioned previously, Guo Rui's new views on Chinese parts of speech were figured out not just by racking his brains but also through undertaking actual investigation and devoted analyses of more than 40,000 modern Chinese words. This can be considered a prominent merit of the book. This may also be said to be one of its features compared with other monographs of the same kind on Chinese parts of speech. Reading through the whole book, a reader can easily discover that it utilizes massive and detailed statistical figures to do all the following: analyze the paradoxes of the overall similarity clustering view, the prototype theory, the partial distribution view, the overall distribution view and so on; explain the calculation of the compatible degrees among grammatical functions of parts of speech and the compatible degrees among the major grammatical functions of Chinese; demonstrate Chinese conversional words and homographs belonging to different parts of speech; describe specific criteria for classifying parts of speech and specific cases; expound the correlation between word frequency and grammatical function, and clarify the common grammatical functions and other characteristics of various parts of speech. You may as well look at his explanations of common grammatical functions and other characteristics of adjectives:

1. 99.47% of adjectives can function as a predicate.
2. 98% of adjectives can be modified by absolute degree adverbs represented by 很 (very).
3. 94% of adjectives can be negated by 不 (not), but many fewer of them can be negated by 没有 (no).
4. 97% of adjectives can be modified by other adverbials.
5. 83% of adjectives can take complements.
6. 69% of adjectives can function as complements. 67% of adjectives can function as compound complements; 8% of adjectives can function as conglutinate complements.
7. Only ten adjectives can take real objects but must be followed by quantitative quasi-objects that generally denote comparison and occurrence, for example, 高他一头 (one head higher than he), 大他两岁 (two years older than he), 熟了一个 (ripe one piece).
8. 72% of adjectives can take auxiliary words such as *le* (了), *zhuo* (着) or *guo* (过), but few of them can take *zhuo* (着).
9. 93% of adjectives can function as a subject or object. Similar to the verb that functions as a subject or object, an adjective that functions as a subject or object also has the following two cases. One case is that the adjective in the position of a subject or object still retains its properties, for example:

(16)   a.   认真不好 (Being serious is not good)
      b.   不认真不好 (Not being serious is not good)
      c.   太认真不好 (Being too serious is not good)
      d.   办事认真不好 (Doing things seriously is not good)

The second case is that an adjective that functions as a subject or object reflects the properties of a noun, for example:

(17)   a.   追求幸福 (Pursue happiness)
      b.   *追求很幸福 (*Pursue very happiness)
      c.   追求自己的幸福 (Pursue one's own happiness)
(18)   a.   保持平衡 (Keep one's balance)
      b.   *保持很平衡 (*Keep very balance)
      c.   保持身体的平衡 (Keep one's bodily balance)

The adjectives in the second case that function as a subject or object are still called adjectives, and we do not treat them as conversional words, instead calling them "nominal adjectives".

10. 32% of adjectives can be modified by attributives; this also has two cases. One is that adjectives modified by attributives retain their properties; at this time, the attributive takes "de (的)", for example:
(19) a. 形势的稳定有利于经济发展 (The stability of situation favors economic development)
      b. 形势的不稳定不利于经济发展 (The instability of situation is adverse to economic development)
      c. The rapid stability of situation favors economic development (形势的迅速稳定有利于经济发展)

Another case is that the adjective reflects only the properties of a noun (0.43%), for example: economic difficulty (经济困难), 生命危险 (life danger). The adjectives in the second case are all nominal adjectives.

11. Many adjectives can function as attributives, but their number is far fewer than imagined in the past, accounting for only 29% of the total.
12. 12% of adjectives can directly function as adverbials. Although some adjectives cannot do so, they can do so after adding "di (地)" (40% of adjectives). Because not a high proportion of adjectives can function as adverbials, it works to treat those adjectives that can function as adverbials as conversional words that function as adjectives and adverbs.
13. 2.73% of adjectives are separable phrasal characters, whose adjectives have only one form of verb-object, for example, 吃惊 – 吃了一惊 (taken aback – taken one aback), 称心 –称他的 心(satisfied – satisfy his heart).
14. 15% of adjectives have their corresponding reduplicated forms.

This fully reflects his solid academic discipline.

Of course, we cannot say that Guo Rui's theory and methods for classifying parts of speech can thoroughly solve once and for all the problems of classifying Chinese parts of speech; neither can we require him to do so. The reasons are twofold: on the one hand, it is not so easy to really carry out the classification; on the other hand, just as Guo Rui himself said, "we do not know sufficiently the status of quite special words such as onomatopoeia in a part-of-speech system. We are not clear how to demonstrate it with the methods presented in this book". Any researcher should cherish this matter-of-fact attitude toward his or her academic research.

In conclusion, Guo Rui's *Modern Chinese Parts of Speech: Classification Theory* provides readers with new spirits and thoughts on classifying Chinese parts of speech. Of course, everybody should pay attention to his conclusions, or his brand-new views on parts of speech, but I think his way of thinking and analysis strategy deserve more attention. The advancement of science relies on new ideas, theories, methods and strategies constantly proposed by researchers on the basis of their practice. The life of science consists in innovation on the basis of seeking truth. This serves as my Foreword.

Lu Jianming
December 29, 2001

1 Introduction

1.1 The questions that must be answered to explore Chinese parts of speech

The issue of parts of speech is fundamental for grammar; the study of the grammar of a language requires the classification of its parts of speech. However, the issue has never had a satisfactory solution; many questions have not been answered and remain discrepant and controversial. The major questions are as follows:

1. Does Chinese have parts of speech? The question was debated in the 1950s, and in the 1990s some scholars questioned the existence of Chinese parts of speech.
2. What is the nature of a part of speech? Currently, it is universally accepted that its nature is distribution, but we cannot identify the grammatical function of any part of speech that is internally universal and externally exclusive. Can we say that the essence of a part of speech belongs to some other factors besides distribution?
3. What are the bases and criteria for classifying parts of speech?
4. How can parts of speech be determined at an operation level? With what standards should we classify various Chinese parts of speech? In the past, we relied on our language sense to identify the distribution norms for the parts of speech existing in our mind and did not provide proof for why we should identify these norms. We might even have skipped over the distinctions between some parts of speech. Is there any method for determining the distinctions between parts of speech according to the distribution of words before they are classified into parts of speech?
5. How can we deal with conversional words? For example, is a word such as 研究 (study) a verb and concurrently noun? This book aims at answering these questions. The author started to ponder these part-of-speech questions in 1986. Zhu Dexi and Lu Jianming undertook the National Seventh Five-year (1986–1990) Plan Key Social Science Research Project named "Exploring Modern Chinese Parts of Speech", in which the author participated as a research team member. Later, he cooperated

with the research team of the National Seventh Five-year Plan's Key Natural Science Project named "Modern Chinese Grammatical Information Database", undertaken by the Institute of Computational Linguistics at Peking University. The team members include Professors Yu Shiwen and Zhu Xuefeng, and they examined the functions of over 30,000 words. During the Eighth Five-year Plan, from 1991 to 1995, we continued to collaborate with the Institute of Computational Linguistics and increased the number of words and their functional examination scope on the basis of the Seventh Five-year Plan Research Project. The research team members included Zhang Yunyun and Wang Hui. The present book is based on the corpus of over 40,000 words examined, written, revised and proofread by many scholars, including Zhu Dexi and Lu Jianming, for more than a decade.

1.2 Difficulties in classifying Chinese parts of speech

For a long time, there have been no good solutions for the Chinese part-of-speech issue; the causes include both subjective and objective ones. Subjectively, in the past, we talked much about theory and did little actual work. As a result, we did not have a deep understanding of the real situation of parts of speech. (This book is based on the examination of over 40,000 words and is supported by plentiful actual materials.) Objectively, the Chinese language's own characteristics make it difficult to classify its parts of speech. These features include the following:

1. Words do not have formal tags or morphological changes. 2. The constituents of modern Chinese are mixed at different hierarchies in different historical stages, making the grammatical functions and syntactic rules of a word complicated. 3. In general, words are multi-functional; this makes it more difficult to classify parts of speech according to their grammatical functions when words have no morphological changes. 4. The difficulties in parsing words make us unable to tell whether a certain usage belongs to a word or a word-formation. 5. It is difficult to judge the grammatical relations of a syntactic structure. Without morphological change, it is difficult to judge what function a word plays in its combinations; thus, it is difficult to use grammatical functions as criteria to classify parts of speech. For example, there are different opinions on whether 决心/完成任务 (determined to complete a task) is a predicate-object construction or a modifier-head construction.

To sum up, there is only one key cause for the difficulty of classifying Chinese into parts of speech, namely Chinese has no morphological changes.

Fortunately, previous and current scholars' work paves a solid foundation for us. Based on past studies, the book will explore further in detail how to classify parts of speech in Chinese that has no morphological change.

1.3 An overview of studies of Chinese parts of speech

1.3.1 The formation and development of the framework of parts of speech

According to Yao Xiaoping (1999), Georg von der Gabelentz, a German who wrote *Chinesische Grammatik*, was the first to establish the complete Chinese grammar system. He classified Chinese notional words into nine parts of speech: noun, some relative (roughly equivalent to locative), numeral, adjective, verb, negative, pronoun, onomatopoeia and interjection. The *Chinesische Grammatik*, however, did not have much influence on China's academic circle; rather, what greatly influenced the later Chinese grammar studies is *Ma's Grammar*, by Ma Jianzhong (1898). Inspired by Western grammar, he classified the words of classical Chinese into the following nine parts of speech: noun, pronoun, verb, static word, state word, preposition, conjunction, auxiliary word and interjection. This system provided the basic pattern of Chinese parts of speech, and did not change greatly after that. After quite a long time, only numerals are separated from static words; modal particles were separated from auxiliary words; measure words and onomatopoeias were added.

Li Jinxi's *A New Chinese Grammar* (1924) was the first of its kind because it was influential and studied systematically modern Chinese grammar. It classified Chinese words into five major parts of speech and nine basic classes: entity word (noun and pronoun), narrative word (verb), distinctive word (adjective and adverb), relative (preposition and conjunction), modal word (auxiliary word and interjection). Its basic classes, whose names are slightly different, are the same as those in *Ma's Grammar*.

Lv Shuxiang's *Chinese Grammar Synopsis* (1942–1944) classified modal particles (the scope is larger than the modal particles referred to generally, including the modal particle referred to subsequently, the modal adverb and interjection), while Wang Li's *Modern Chinese Grammar* (1943, 1944) classified words into numeral and modal particle.

Modern Chinese Lecture by Ding Shengshu et al. (1952, 1953) classified measure word and onomatopoeia (including interjection), and pointed out the special classes of time word, place word and locative.

The Temporary Chinese Teaching Grammatical System (1956) classified Chinese words into 11 parts of speech: noun, measure word, pronoun, verb, adjective, numeral, adverb, preposition, conjunction, auxiliary word and interjection. The system was revised into *The High School Teaching Grammatical System Synopsis* (1984) and onomatopoeia was added to it. This system of 12 parts of speech had a rather big influence and has been adopted by most of the current dictionaries that tag parts of speech, except for a few dictionaries that separate modal particles from auxiliary words.

Zhao Yuanren's *Spoken Chinese Grammar* (1968) has distinctive word as a part of speech, which includes demonstrative distinctive word (this, that), fractional distinctive word (each, all, another), quantitatively distinctive word (one, ten) and measurable distinctive word (integral, half, numerous).

Chen Wangdao's *A Synopsis of Grammar* (1978) classifies copula, copulative and demonstrative.

Zhu Dexi's *Grammar Handouts* (1982b) separated distinctive words from adjective; place word, locative and time word from noun; and modal particles from auxiliary words, totaling 17 parts of speech. *Modern Chinese* (1993), produced by the Department of Chinese Language at Peking University, classified state adjectives into state word, but returned place word, locative and time word to the category of a noun, totaling 15 parts of speech.

On the basis of the 17 parts of speech proposed by Zhu Dxi (1982b) and the 15 parts of speech proposed by *Modern Chinese*, compiled by the Department of Chinese Language at Peking University, the present book adds numeral, measure word and demonstrative, for a total of 20 parts of speech (see Section 1.5).

1.3.2 Two core issues for studying Chinese parts of speech

The first core issue is the relationship between part of speech and syntactic constituent; the second core issue is the criteria for classifying parts of speech. Almost all controversies stem from the two issues, and the reason why they trigger controversies has something to do with the fact that Chinese has no morphological change in the strict sense.

1.3.2.1 The relationship between part of speech and syntactic constituent

Because Chinese has no morphological change, which, therefore, cannot be used to classify parts of speech, we can only use the grammatical functions of a word. One of the characteristics of Chinese is that a word can function as many syntactic constituents. For these reasons, we have the questions of the relationship between part of speech and syntactic constituent: how does a part of speech correspond to its syntactic constituent? Specifically, there are three questions: (1) Does a part of speech correspond to its syntactic constituent directly or indirectly? (2) Is the correspondence one-to-one or complicated? (3) What syntactic constituents can a part of speech function as? The methods for answering the first two questions include the double-line system, the one-line system and the three-layer system.

The double-line system: This refers to the part of speech level and the syntactic constituent level. However, because a Chinese word is generally multi-functional, there are slots between part of speech and syntactic constituent. To resolve the slots, scholars use various methods, including the change in part of speech and the addition of functions.

The change in part of speech establishes the simple one-to-one correspondence between part of speech and syntactic constituent. For example, a noun should function as subject or object; a verb should function as predicate or complement; an adjective attributive; an adverb adverbial. If a word occurs at the position of different characteristics, it may be deemed to have changed its part of speech. Most of earlier works on Chinese grammar adopted this method. For instance, *Ma's Grammar* proposed the theory that a part of speech functions in the guise of various syntactic constituents. If a verb occurs at the position of subject or object, then it functions in the guise of a noun; if it occurs at the position of attributive, then it functions in the guise of an adjective (static word). Chen Chengze's *An Initial Start of Chinese Grammar* (1922) and Jin Zhaozi's *Studies of Chinese Grammar* (1922) proposed the flexible use of parts of speech. Li Jinxi's *A New Chinese Grammar* (1924) proposed distinguishing between parts of speech according to sentences. All these works use the change in part of speech to resolve the slot between part of speech and syntactic constituent. *The Temporary Chinese Teaching Grammar System* (1956) proposed the "nominalization theory". In sentences such as 他的来使大家很高兴 (His coming makes everybody happy) and 狐狸的狡猾是很出名的 (The slyness of a fox is famous), 来 (coming) and 狡猾 (slyness) do not contain the meaning of substantial action or properties but regard them as "things". They lose the properties, or some properties, of their verb and adjective forms, while acquiring some properties of a noun. We call this the nominalization of an adjective. "Nominalization" is a vague expression and does not clearly say that there is a change in part of speech, but in essence it is the same as the loaned part of speech and its flexible use. Because most Chinese words can function as many syntactic constituents without morphological change, although the method of changing parts of speech assigns certain syntactic constituents to a part of speech, it makes Chinese parts of speech changeable (Zhu Dexi, 1982c). As a result, words do not have their definite parts of speech, and we may even reach] the conclusion that "there is no part of speech without a sentence".

The function addition method holds that there is a complicated correspondence between part of speech and syntactic constituent. A part of speech is multifunctional: so long as the meaning of a word does not change, the word belongs to the same part of speech even if it occurs at different positions. Although this method causes a word to have its definite part of speech, it causes a part of speech to have no definite syntactic constituents. In essence, it openly admits the slot between part of speech and syntactic constituent instead of denying it. During the debate on grammar innovation at the end of the 1930s and the early 1940s, Fang Guangdao proposed classifying parts of speech according to a generalized morphology, while Chen Wangdao proposed classifying them based on integrated structural functions. In doing so, they used the function addition method. Lv Shuxiang and Zhu Dexi's *Talks on Grammar and Rhetoric* (1951) proposed that if the meaning of a word does not change, then its part of speech does not change. Later, what was meant by Zhu Dexi's saying that a part of speech is multifunctional, was narrowed down slightly. 批评 (criticism) and 研究 (study) and so on, which are directly modified by nouns and function as the quasi-objects of predicate verbs such as 做 (do), 进行 (carry out), 加以 (conduct) and 有 (have) are considered nominal verbs. In this case, they are considered to be nominal. But Zhu Dexi still thought that 出版 (publication) in 这本书的出版 (the publication of the book) and 去 (going) in 去是应该的 (Going is obliged) have the properties of a verb.

The one-line system: This notion was put forward by Fu Donghua in the 1930s. Because a Chinese word is multifunctional, the simple correspondence between part of speech and syntactic constituent must use loaned parts of speech. He held that it would be better just to presume that it is impossible to classify words into parts of speech and said that "if a word is not used in a sentence, there is no way to know its part of speech". Therefore, parts of speech should be combined with sentence constituents. For example:

张三 (Zhang San)　作 (writes)　文 (an essay)
subject-noun　　　predicate　　object-noun

Actually, this view is a natural development of "distinguishing between parts of speech according to a sentence" and "there being no parts of speech without a sentence". During the debate on Chinese parts of speech in the 1950s, Gao Mingkai also thought that Chinese had no parts of speech mainly because they should be classified according to the morphology of a word. Chinese has no morphological change and therefore has no parts of speech. Later, he changed his point of view and thought that "the morphological changes of a word, its combination capacity and syntactic functions etc. are all the external marks of its part-of-speech meaning". Chinese has no morphological change, and its parts of speech can only be classified according to the use of a word. But because Chinese parts of speech are multifunctional, "a word can be used simultaneously as noun, adjective and verb" (meaning a notional word can appear at the positions of subject, predicate and attributive). Therefore, every notional word belongs to several parts of speech, implying that Chinese has no parts of speech (Gao Mingkai, 1960). Xu Tongqiang (1994b) thought that the parts of speech in Indo-European languages have a one-to-one correspondence to sentence constituents, thus causing the necessity to classify them. Now that one Chinese part of speech corresponds to many sentence constituents, this implies that Chinese does not have parts of speech at all. With regard to the theory that Chinese has no parts of speech, Zhu Dexi (1960) thought that, although the classification of parts of speech according to sentence constituents takes grammatical functions into consideration, "because selectional criteria are too loose and the method is too simple, parts of speech cannot be classified this way, instead reaching the conclusion that a word has no definite parts of speech. The entire error of this method lies in the fact that it assumes that there is a one-to-one correspondence between part of speech and sentence constituent . . . but as a matter of fact, the relationship between part of speech and sentence constituent is complicated". If the one-line system is taken to the extreme, however, it cannot solve Chinese syntactic problems and instead causes more troubles, and few people accept this theory.

The three-layer system: This system comes into existence by combining the change in part of speech with the addition of functions. It adds an intermediate layer between part of speech and syntactic constituent so as to close the slot between the two, assuming that there are some changes in the properties of a word at its intermediate layer at the syntactic position of different characteristics. This thinking not only maintains the point of view that if the meaning of a word does not change, then its part of speech does not change, but also explains that the same part of speech can appear at different syntactic positions. Scholars who use the three-level system have very different opinions and therefore quite different effects.

Wang Li (1943, 1944) and Lv Shuxiang (1942, 1944) borrowed Otto Jespersen's three-level theory and set up the intermediate word level, as Lv called it. A word level is classified into the first level (the words at the positions of subject and object), the secondary level (the words at the positions of predicate and attributive) and the last level (the words at the positions of adverbial and complement). Parts of speech are classified according to the meaning of a word and are unchangeable, and when a word is used at different syntactic positions, its level changes. But word level is a vague concept and distinguished according to the importance of a word in its combination. Therefore, it is more correct to say that it classifies the syntactic constituents of a word. There is no substantial distinction between saying that a word can function as different word levels, and that it can function as different syntactic constituents. It is not effective to use the three-level theory to connect a part of speech with a syntactic constituent in order to close the slot between the two.

Chen Aiwen (1986) assumed that there are two types of part-of-speech concept. The first type is equivalent to the classification between part of speech and mental structure, and has the properties of noun, verb and adjective respectively; the second type is equivalent to the classification between part of speech and objective world, and has the properties of a basic noun, verb and adjective respectively. The first type of part of speech is actually classified according to grammatical properties; the second type is actually classified according to the meaning of a word. The first type may change with different usages; the second type does not. For example, the word 出版 (publish) has the properties of a verb in 同意出版 (agree to publish), but has the properties of a noun in 图书出版 (book publication). In both cases, they are basic verbs. Chen Aiwen proposes the two types of part-of-speech concept for the purpose of understanding the correspondence between part of speech and syntactic constituent. He is aware that adherence to the concept that the meaning of a word does not change and then its parts of speech do not change cannot explain that its properties may change at different positions. Therefore, it is necessary to establish the two types of part-of-speech concept and form the three-layer system of "part of speech (X basic word) – properties of a word – syntactic constituent", taking word properties as the intermediate layer that connects a part of speech with a syntactic constituent. This approach actually classifies parts of speech according to the meaning of a word and then decides its properties, only making a clear-cut classification between the two types of part-of-speech concept but making no substantial difference from the change in parts of speech in the double-line system.

Xiao Guozheng (1991) and Xiang Mengbing (1991) thought that some verbs and adjectives at the positions of subject and object have denotation, namely using their expressional functions to denote the change in their properties at different positions.

This book proposes that the nature of a part of speech is the type of expressional function in the large categories of substantive word, predicate word and modification word. According to the two levels of expressional function, we can classify parts of speech into the part of speech at the lexical level and that at the syntactic level. The part of speech at the lexical level is the inherent property of words and expressions that are labeled in a dictionary; the part of speech at the syntactic level is generated by using words and expressions and governed by syntactic rules. Most of the covert and flexible uses of a part of speech pointed out by previous scholars belong to changes in parts of speech at the syntactic level. The three-layer system of "part of speech at the lexical level – part of speech at the syntactic level – syntactic constituent" is thus formed. There are two situations in which a word appears at different syntactic positions: (1) a word has its properties at multiple lexical levels, for example, 出版 (publish) has the properties of a verb in 出版两本书 (publish two books), but has the properties of a noun in 图书出版 (book publication); (2) there are some changes in part of speech at the syntactic level, for example, 出版 (publish) still has the properties of a verb at lexical level in 这本书的出版 (the publication of the book) but has the properties of a noun at the syntactic level. The changes in part of speech at the syntactic level essentially have covert core constituents.

Although both the three-level theory and the viewpoints of this book on the relationship between part of speech and syntactic constituent belong to the three-layer system, they are different. The intermediate layer "word class" established between part of speech and syntactic constituent by the three-class theory is not identical with the intermediate layer "the properties of a word at the syntactic level" established by this book. The word "class" is classified into the first class (subject and object), the secondary class (predicate and attributive) and the last class (adverbial and complement). The parts of speech at the syntactic level refer to extrinsic expressional functions such as reference, statement and modification. Subject and object generally belong to reference; predicate belongs to statement. In this regard, the two are identical. But attributive corresponds to modification; complement corresponds to statement. In this regard, the two are different. The root cause for the difference between the two is their own different starting points. The three-class theory emphasizes the importance of a syntactic constituent, but an expressional function emphasizes a word's method of meaning expression in use.

The third question is to which syntactic constituent a part of speech corresponds. This is the most difficult question. If the question is answered, the specific criteria for classifying parts of speech will be available. We shall discuss them in Chapter 6.

1.3.2.2 Criteria for classifying parts of speech

The criteria for classifying parts of speech include the meaning of a word, its morphology and its grammatical function.

In one case, parts of speech are classified purely according to the meaning of a word. Two important grammar works, *Chinese Grammar Synopsis* by Lv Shuxiang and *Chinese Modern Grammar* by Wang Li in the 1940s did so without prior consultation. There are two lethal problems for the classification of parts of speech according to the meaning of a word: (1) its meaning does not correspond completely to its grammatical properties, and the parts of speech classified according to the meaning are not closely related to syntax; (2) the meaning of a word itself is not clearly observable and therefore not operable. In another case, the parts of speech are classified according to the meaning of a word, but its part-of-speech conversion is judged according to the position of a word in a sentence, like *Ma's Grammar* by Ma Jianzhong and *A New Chinese Grammar* by Li Jinxi. This approach actually creates two systems of parts of speech. One system is classified according to the meaning of a word; the other system is classified according to syntactic constituent. Since the second system can be classified according to syntactic constituent, classifying the first system according to the meaning of a word is then unnecessary, while classifying the system according to syntactic constituent establishes a one-to-one correspondence between part of speech and syntactic constituent. Thus we can reach the conclusion that a word has no definite parts of speech.

Some Western languages have plentiful morphological changes, which can be used to classify their parts of speech, but Chinese has no morphological change, which, therefore, cannot be used to classify its parts of speech. In the early 1950s, Gao Mingkai regarded morphology as the nature of a part of speech and arrived at the conclusion that Chinese has no parts of speech.

Chen Chengze (1922) pointed out that "a part of speech cannot be decided according to the form of a word or the word itself and can only be decided according to the position of the word in a sentence". Jin Zhaozi (1922) observed that "Chinese characters do not show word properties and rely on their positions to show them". That is to say, parts of speech are decided according to the grammatical functions of a word. He did not come up with the criteria and operational procedures for classifying parts of speech. Because he thought there was a one-to-one correspondence between part of speech and syntactic constituent, he had to use the method for flexible use of parts of speech, not fixing their use. Lu Zhiwei proposed two types of structural relationship in his *Single-Syllable Vocabulary in Beijing Dialect* (1938): (1)

attached relation: red flower (attachment + thing attached); (2) approxima-tion relation: eat a meal (approximator + thing approximated). The two types of structural relationship provide three kinds of basic parts of speech: a noun that occupies the position of the thing attached or approximated, a verb that occupies the position of approximator and an adjective that occupies the position of attachment. This is equivalent to classifying parts of speech according to sentence constituents. Because a word is multifunctional, if this is strictly implemented, then certainly it will have no definite parts of speech. For the first time, the discussion on grammar innovation explicitly proposed classifying parts of speech according to the overall grammatical functions of a word. Fang Guangdao proposed classifying parts of speech according to generalized morphology, namely according to the combination capacity of a word. Based on Ferdinand de Saussure's syntagmatic and paradigmatic relations, Chen Wangdao proposed classifying parts of speech of a word according to its syntagmatic relation. But he just discussed this theoretically and did not propose a set of operating criteria. In his *Elementary Chinese* (1948), for the first time, Zhao Yuanren made a systematic use of grammatical functions to classify parts of speech and proposed a set of operating criteria. For example, a noun can be modified by a quantitative phrase; a verb can be modified by "不 (not)" and followed by "le (了)". In 1968, he performed a systematic classification of Chinese parts of speech more entirely according to grammatical functions. Zhu Dexi (1960, 1982b, 1985a) emphasized several times that the essential basis for classifying parts of speech is the distribution of a word, and that this is true not only to Chinese but also to other languages. Due to the lack of morphological change, Chinese can only use the grammat-ical functions of a word to classify its parts of speech. This came to be agreed upon after discussions on Chinese parts of speech in the 1950s. However, because of the complicated relationship between part of speech and gram-matical function, how to identify the part of speech of a word according to its grammatical functions becomes a prominent issue. The question, in essence, is still the relationship between part of speech and syntactic constituent: Is the correspondence between part of speech and syntactic constituent one-to-one or complicated? If it is one-to-one, then nearly all the members of noun, verb and adjective are conversional words. If it is complicated, then how complicated? One point of view is that the same generalization word that occurs at any position belongs to the same part of speech. In this way, there is no conversional word whose meaning is the same. The two extreme points of view are now scarcely acceptable. Most people think something in between: there is no one-to-one correspondence between part of speech and syntactic constituent; the same generalization word that occurs at any pos-ition may have different parts of speech.

The subsequent question is how to determine the correspondence between part of speech and grammatical function. Once the question is figured out, the criteria for classifying parts of speech will be worked out, because the question is the key to the current studies of Chinese parts of speech. However, in most of the studies of Chinese parts of speech since the 1980s, parts of speech have been classified subjectively as a first step, and the criteria for classifying them have been found as a next step. Due to the lack of clear demonstration, it is difficult to achieve agreement among various scholars on classifying, grouping and annexing the parts of speech of a word.

To work out the relationship between part of speech and grammatical function, the Chinese grammar circle has tried various approaches. One approach is to regard a part of speech as a prototype category or a fuzzy category. Mo Pengling and Wang Zhidong (1988) proposed the fuzzy clustering analysis method. Shi Youwei (1994) proposed the flexible approach to Chinese parts of speech and tried to calculate the membership degrees of words to deal with the relationship between part of speech and grammatical function. Yuan Yulin (1995, 1998) used the prototype theory to deal with the relationship between distribution and part of speech. Lu Yingshun (1998) also tried to calculate the approximation degrees of words to determine the attribution of the parts of speech he analyzed. The problem with these methods is that there is no way to demonstrate the determination of a prototype, thereby being difficult to classify parts of speech.

1.3.3 The question of conversional words

There is a heated discussion on this question. The following three factors are involved in whether a word is a conversional word: (1) the identity of a word; (2) whether a word has the properties of several parts of speech or its part of speech is multifunctional; (3) what strategy is used to classify parts of speech.

The general view on the relationship between word identity and a conversional word is that the different senses of a polyseme or the different usages of the same generalization word belong to different parts of speech and are reckoned as a conversional word, whereas the homonyms whose meanings are not associated belong to different parts of speech, are not reckoned as conversional words, and are treated as two independent words. Xu Shu (1991) and Lu Jianming (1994) thought that only the same generalization word that belongs to different parts of speech can be called a conversional word, whereas different generalization words that belong to different parts of speech are two words belonging to utterly different parts of speech. As a matter of fact, it is only a matter of name to regard the polyseme that belongs to different parts of speech as a conversional word or only to regard the same generalization word as a conversional word. The key question here is whether these words have properties of only one or several parts of speech. In our view, the term "conversional word" should be used in its broad sense. To distinguish two cases, the conversional word whose meaning is identical is called a homonymous conversional word, and a polyseme that belongs to different parts of speech is called heteromorphic conversional word. The conversional word in its narrow sense refers to homonymous conversional word; the generalized conversional word includes both homonymous and heteromorphic conversional words.

The difficulty lies in determining the identity of a word. If different generalization words have the properties of different parts of speech, they must be regarded as different parts of speech. The same generalization word that has the properties of several parts of speech need not necessarily be treated as a conversional word. Whether a word is treated as a conversional word has something to do with what strategy is used to classify parts of speech. Because of the discrepancy in judging a word's identity, there is a difference in the range of heteromorphic conversional words. For example, if 研究 (study) is not identical in 研究问题 (study a problem) and 社会研究 (social study), then it should be treated as two parts of speech, namely a verb and concurrently a noun. Likewise, if 木头 (wood) is not identical in 木头断了 (the wood is broken) and 木头桌子 (wooden desk), then it should be treated as a noun and concurrently a distinctive word (see Yang Chengkai, 1991). There is not much discussion on how to determine word identity. Currently, we mainly rely on our language sense to do this and have no strict operational procedures. Although in most cases we can reach agreement, rather big discrepancies on some difficult questions still remain.

Another question is whether a word at different positions has the properties of several parts of speech or whether its part of speech is multifunctional. The question is related to the correspondence between a part of speech and a grammatical function. Zhu Dexi (1982b) thought that 调查 (investigation) in 社会调查 (social investigation) and 进行调查 (conduct investigation) is different in property from 调查 (investigate) in 调查问题 (investigate a problem). The latter can take an adverbial and a complement and so forth, having the properties of a verb, whereas the former can only take an attributive, having the properties of a noun. Hu Mingyang (1996b) also performed a detailed examination of similar issues. This book suggests that the compatibility of grammatical functions can be used to determine the relationship between grammatical function and a part of speech, namely in what case a word has the properties of several parts of speech and in what case a part of speech is multifunctional.

Zhu Dexi (1982b, 1985a) and Lu Jianming (1984) discussed what strategy should be used to classify parts of speech. We shall discuss this in detail in Chapter 7.

1.3.4 Operational procedures for classifying parts of speech

The study of Chinese parts of speech before the 1980s rarely discussed the concrete operational procedures for classifying parts of speech. Since the 1980s, a good many scholars have paid attention to these processes. In his *Re-investigation of Chinese Part-of-speech Classification Issues* (1980), Shi Anshi tried to classify parts of speech layer by layer, using only one criterion one time. The upper layer of criteria is a bit broader than the lower layer. This method offers progress in making criteria for classifying parts of speech stricter and enhancing the operability of classifying them. Lu Jiawen

(1982), Lu Chuan (1991), Lu Jianming (1994) and Gao Gengsheng (1995) also proposed operational procedures for classifying parts of speech layer by layer. The layer-by-layer classification reveals the hierarchical nature of parts of speech in more detail than the past major classification into only a notional word and a functional word. The present book not only uses the hierarchical classification method but also identifies the criteria for classifying each part of speech layer by layer.

Xing Fuyi (1981) concentrated his discussion on the grouping of words and proposed grouping methods such as direct decision, exclusion and analogy.

1.3.5 Other studies

In addition to the above, scholars also studied Chinese parts of speech from various angles. Mo Pengling and Shan Qing (1995) did a statistical calculation of the grammatical functions of noun, verb and adjective in their actual corpus and provided valuable statistical data. Chen Ningping (1987) used a continuous statistical model to analyze the drift of verb to noun. Li Yuming (1996) and Zhang Bojiang (1994) tried to explain the properties of distinctive words and the flexible use of parts of speech, starting from the spatiality of a noun and the temporality of a verb. Shen Jiaxuan (1997) used Croft's tagging theory to discuss the major functions of Chinese adjectives. These studies that apply new theories are very heuristic.

1.4 Outline of chapters

The book mainly covers two parts.

Part 1 (Chapter 2) discusses the prerequisites for classifying parts of speech, including word parsing, word identity and the internal hierarchies of modern Chinese. To parse words, we can use their two basic characteristics – standby application and independent application – to distinguish between word and phrase. In terms of standby application, words should have finite length and number; as an independent application unit, the rules for combining words are different from those for combining morphemes, and the difference should be used to parse words.

Modern Chinese is an inhomogeneous system mixed with different hierarchical constituents. Analyze its internal hierarchies, and we can deal with the system well. It mainly has the historical hierarchy and the field hierarchy. A language may have different grammatical systems at different historical and field hierarchies; the grammatical functions of its words may also be different, and the criteria for classifying their parts of speech should be different too. The classification of modern Chinese parts of speech should consider these different hierarchies and treat the constituents at different hierarchies differently.

The determination of word identity involves whether a word has a certain grammatical function, thereby influencing its classification results. Therefore, it is one of the issues to be solved first in order to classify parts of speech. To determine the word identity, we need to distinguish between constituent meaning and structural meaning, lexical transfer reference and syntactic transfer reference, lexical transfer reference and lexical self-reference, word-formation, morphology and syntax.

Part 2 (Chapters 3 through 7) discusses the theoretical issues for classifying parts of speech. Chapter 3 discusses the possibility and purpose of classifying parts of speech and points out that words are combined not randomly but in a certain order. The orderliness indicates that a grammatical position has selectional restrictions on words, and that different grammatical positions allow different words to enter. This shows that we can classify words into different parts of speech according to their different properties. From the perspective of natural taxonomy, parts of speech are generalized from syntactic structures, not artificially postulated beforehand for the sake of grammar. The purpose of classifying parts of speech is to reveal the properties of a word and establish its general reference system. In other words, we think that language is not desultory but systematically organized, and has its natural order independent of linguists. Words have their own positions in such a natural order.

Chapter 4 discusses the nature of parts of speech. Since US descriptive linguistics came into being, it has been generally believed that a part of speech is of the distribution type. Words that have the same distribution form a part of speech. The "distribution" here has three possibilities: (1) individual distribution, (2) population distribution, (3) fractional distribution. No matter in what sense the distribution is, the viewpoint that a part of speech is of the distribution type is not justifiable. The prominent issue is that we cannot use the distribution characteristics themselves to answer why we select these distribution characteristics instead of others as the criteria for classifying parts of speech. If factors other than distribution characteristics are not considered, we cannot classify parts of speech purely according to distribution characteristics. In our opinion, the nature of a part of speech is not of the distribution type. The nature of classifying parts of speech according to distribution is to classify them according to the selectional restriction of grammatical positions on words. There must be some bases used as conditions for selectional restrictions. Then, what are the bases for such selectional restrictions? We think that the expressional function and the semantic type of a word are the intrinsic causes for constraining its distributions. Like morphological change, distribution is only the extrinsic exhibition of the properties of a part of speech. The intrinsic basis for distinction among words, for example, the large categories of parts of speech such as a substantive word, a predicate word, a substantive modification word, a predicate modification word, is actually the distinction between such expressional functions as reference, statement, substantive modification and predicate modification. The distributional difference and morphological difference among parts of speech are simply the external exhibitions of differences in expressional functions. Expressional functions can be classified into intrinsic expressional function and external expressional function. We can also classify parts of speech into the parts of speech at the lexical level and the syntactic level. Syntactic combination is a series of expressional functions rather than a series of parts of speech. The selectional restriction of a grammatical position on a word is based on its expressional function, which is the nature of parts of speech such as a substantive word, a predicate word and a modification word.

The essence of basic parts of speech such as nouns, adjectives, state words, measure words, locatives, distinctive words, numerals and measure words is the semantic type that combines with grammatical function. Only when the semantic type of a word is in agreement with its difference in syntactic distribution is it necessary to classify its parts of speech. Therefore, at the level of basic parts of speech, the essence of a part of speech is the type that combines the semantic type with the grammatical function.

The expressional function is a word's pattern of meaning expression; the semantic type is the categorized semantic meaning. The two belong to grammatical meaning; thus, we can say that grammatical meaning is the intrinsic cause for restricting the distribution of a word.

Chapter 5 discusses criteria for classifying parts of speech, which must satisfy the three conditions: reflecting the properties of a part of speech, being observable and being comprehensive. Theoretically speaking, a word's morphological change, expressional function, grammatical meaning or intrinsic expressional function all can be used as criteria for classifying parts of speech. But in Chinese, only the grammatical function (a word's distribution) can satisfy these conditions and be used as criteria for classifying parts of speech.

The grammatical position occupied by a word is called its distribution. The capability of a word to occupy a certain grammatical position is the word's grammatical function. Two factors define a constituent's distribution: (1) the grammatical relationship between the immediate constituent and its grammatical role; (2) the larger environment in which the structural whole made up of the two immediate constituents can appear. The grammatical function has different generalization levels. A word's capability of occupying the grammatical position defined in the environment of evaluating it and its parts of speech is a rather specific grammatical function; the capability of functioning as a syntactic constituent is a rather abstract grammatical function. We can use a word's distribution characteristics to infer the properties of its parts of speech. The grammatical meaning of a word is the main intrinsic cause for restricting its distribution and basically determines its grammatical distribution. Although distribution is not the nature of a part of speech, the words that belong to the same part of speech have a roughly similar distribution. Like morphological change, distribution is only an extrinsic exhibition of grammatical meaning. That is to say, there is a "reflection-exhibition" relationship between distribution of a word and its grammatical meaning: distribution reflects the grammatical meaning, which in turn exhibits distribution. We can use the properties of parts of speech reflected by a word's distribution to classify its parts of speech.

However, the relationship between distribution and a part of speech is complicated, as exhibited in the following: (1) what determines the properties of a part of speech is not just the distribution of a word; its lexical and pragmatic meanings, word-formation, prosodic characteristics, and other factors may also influence distribution; (2) some grammatical positions reflect the same properties, and then the above-mentioned distributional difference cannot reflect the difference in properties; for example, 很 (very) ~ and 极 (extremely) ~ have the same requirements for words to enter into their grammatical positions, but the difference in the two functions of the two words does not reflect different properties of their parts of speech; (3) it is possible that some grammatical positions allow several parts of speech to enter. For example, either a noun, a verb, an adjective or a distinctive word and so on can appear at the position of a subject; either a verb, an adjective, a state word or a noun and so on can appear at the position of a predicate. Therefore, the properties of a part of speech cannot be inferred entirely according to word distribution. We should not only rely on word distribution to infer the properties of a part of speech but also use some other means to eliminate the factors that influence the nongrammatical meanings of word distribution and the interference caused by an incomplete correspondence between properties and grammatical position. The correspondence between a part of speech and word distribution should be sought from the complicated relationship between the properties of a part of speech and word distribution, thereby reasonably and justifiably classifying parts of speech according to the distribution.

Chapter 6 discusses how to classify parts of speech according to distribution. Not all differences in distribution reflect the difference in the properties of a part of speech; different functions of different parts of speech have different values for classifying them: some functions are distinctive; some are not. Therefore, we cannot treat equally all the functions of a part of speech and only select those distinctive functions to classify parts of speech. We can use the compatibility of functions and the relevant rules to determine the values of functions for classifying parts of speech, thereby identifying the functions that distinguish between word properties and selecting among them the criteria for classifying parts of speech. The compatibility of functions refers to the property that the same group of words shares two or more grammatical functions, for example, the word that can function as a subject can also function as an object and vice versa. But the compatibility of some other functions is extremely small, for instance, 不 (not) ~ and (numeral) ~. Functions that have a rather big compatibility often reflect the same selectional restriction of the two different grammatical positions on words and also the common properties of a part of speech; thus, they are equivalent-value functions. The functions that have a rather small or no compatibility reflect different properties of a part of speech and are generally hetero-value functions. An equivalent-value function is transferable. If the equivalent-value functions of a language are gathered into clusters, then we come up with the correspondence between a part of speech and a grammatical function; an equivalent-value function cluster represents a part of speech.

Chapter 7 discusses conversional words and nominalization. The same generalization word that has the properties of several parts of speech is not necessarily treated as a conversional word in its narrow sense. Whether it is treated as a conversional word has something to do with the strategy for classifying parts of speech. To classify Chinese parts of speech, we mainly use the two strategies: (1) the homogeneous strategy; namely, starting from the properties of a part of speech, all the properties of the part of speech of a generalization word are treated equally to create the one-to-one correspondence between a part of speech thus classified and its properties. If a generalization word has the properties of several parts of speech, then we treat it as conversional word. (2) The priority homomorphic strategy; namely, starting from a generalization word, we give priority to the properties of certain parts of speech and do not treat as a conversional word the word that has the properties of several parts of speech. Instead, we treat it as having a priority part of speech, thus creating a correspondence between a part of speech and the properties of a priority part of speech. In fact, different strategies for classifying parts of speech cause a good many controversies in Chinese parts of speech. Strategies are not right or wrong but only good or bad. Which strategy for classifying parts of speech is the best depends on specific circumstances. To select a strategy for classifying parts of speech, the following two factors should be taken into consideration: (1) the total numbers of parts of speech, and conversional words in their narrow sense should be as few as possible; (2) the fewest possible syntactic rules: there should be as few as possible grammatical functions of different words in the same part of speech. The two factors are exactly contradictory: the fewest number of parts of speech is in conflict with the fewest number of syntactic rules and vice versa. Therefore, in selecting a strategy for classifying parts of speech, we should consider both factors, reducing the numbers of both parts of speech and syntactic rules to the lowest degree as possible, specifically:

1. If there are large numbers of words that have two or more parts of speech or can be controlled by rules, then we use the priority homomorphic strategy; if not, we use the homogeneous strategy. If the homogeneous strategy is used for the large number of words that have two or more parts of speech, a massive number of conversional words may appear. Although there are a few syntactic rules, there are too many parts of speech, and a massive number of conversional words have to be identified before syntactic processing. If something goes wrong with the conversional word identification, something may also go wrong with syntactic processing.
2. If the priority homomorphic strategy is used for a few words that have two or more parts of speech, there will be too many syntactic rules, although there are not too many parts of speech. This is because more

syntactic rules are needed to deal with the use of a conversional word. The use of the homogeneous strategy may reduce the numbers of not only syntactic rules but also parts of speech. Therefore, in general, we should use the homogeneous strategy. However, if words that have two or more parts of speech can be controlled by rules, then the priority homomorphic strategy is desirable.

Based on this justification, according to the priority homomorphic strategy, Chinese words that have the properties of both a verb and a noun should be treated as a verb instead of a conversional word.

There are two types of nominalization: (1) the reference of external expressional function and the nominalization at the syntactic level; nominalization still has the general characteristics of a verb or an adjective, and does not change its properties at the lexical level; (2) some words that have the properties of a verb (or an adjective) and a noun embody the properties of a noun at the position of subject or object. They no longer have the general characteristics of a verb when functioning as subject or object but those of a noun. We can reckon that their intrinsic expressional functions have changed; that is to say, the properties of a part of speech at the lexical level have changed, but we do not treat them as conversional words according to the priority homomorphic strategy.

1.5 The methods and main conclusions in the book

1.5.1 Methods and main viewpoints in the book

In our opinion, the nature of a part of speech is not distribution. Therefore, it is difficult to succeed in any attempt to classify Chinese parts of speech through seeking internally universal and externally exclusive distribution characteristics. The large category of a part of speech (substantive words, predicate words and modification words) belongs to the type of expressional function; the basic category of a part of speech (nouns, measure words, verbs, adjectives, state words, numerals and measure words ...) is the type that combines the semantic type of a word with its grammatical function.

To operate part-of-speech classification, the book calculates the compatibility degree among grammatical functions to reveal the relationship between a grammatical function and a part of speech. The book suggests that there is compatibility among some grammatical functions. For example, a word that can function as a subject can also function as an object and vice versa. Different grammatical functions that have a rather large degree of compatibility reflect the same properties of a part of speech, have equivalent correspondence to it and can be clustered together. A cluster of equivalent grammatical functions is actually the distinctive function of a part of speech. The identification of distinctive functions of all parts of speech is, in effect, the classification of all the words into different parts of speech. This method, in our opinion, moves one step forward toward the demonstration of part-of-speech classification.

1.5.2 Overview of the part-of-speech system in the book

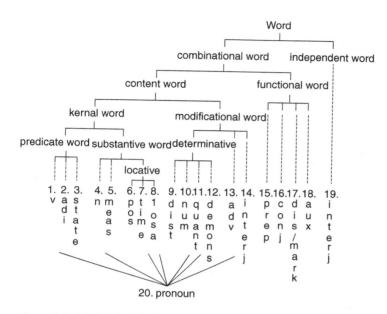

Figure 1.1 A brief description of modern Chinese part-of-speech system

Chinese parts of speech are classified according to their hierarchies. There are 20 basic parts of speech, 19 of which are classified according to their grammatical functions. A pronoun is special and is not classified according to its grammatical functions, which are equivalent to a verb, a noun, a time word, a place word, a numeral, a measure word and an adverb. The part-of-speech examples are given as follows:

1. Verbs: 吃 (eat), 洗 (wash), 跑 (run), 休息 (rest), 想 (think), 病 (fall ill), 坐 (sit), 有 (have), 是 (be), 来 (come), 能 (can), 可以 (may), 完成 (accomplish), 思考 (ponder)…
2. Adjectives: 高 (high), 短 (short), 大 (large), 晚 (late), 干净 (clean), 认真 (serious), 伟大 (great), 不幸 (unlucky), 有趣 (interesting), 可笑 (laughable), 结实 (sturdy), 相同 (identical)…
3. State words: 雪白 (snow-white), 甜丝丝 (happy), 黑咕隆咚 (pitch-dark), 轰轰烈烈 (vigorous), 优良 (good), 酷热 (extremely-hot), 瘦高 (thin and tall), 旖旎 (graceful)…
4. Nouns: 石头 (stone), 文化 (culture), 国家 (country), 人民 (people), 船只 (boat), 时间 (time), 钟头 (hour), 长江 (Changjiang), 泰山 (Mount Tai), 孔子 (Confucius), 学校 (school)…

5. Measure words: 个 (piece), 张 (sheet), 斤 (jin), 次 (time), 天 (day), 年 (year), 分钟 (minute), 点 (point), 些 (some), 种 (type), 团 (regiment), 滴 (drop), 杯 (cup), 瓶 (bottle), 批 (batch), 套 (set) ...

6. Locatives: 前 (front), 上 (above), 里 (inside), 左 (left-side), 南 (south), 下面 (below), 后头 (back-end), 以前 (before), 周围 (ambient), 旁边 (aside), 附近 (near), 对面 (opposite-side) ...

7. Time words: 今天 (today), 去年 (yesteryear), 上午 (morning), 刚才 (just), 过去 (past), 春节 (Spring Festival), 正月 (first month of a lunar year), 最近 (recently), 拂晓 (daybreak), 星期天 (Sunday) ...

8. Place words: 当地 (local), 街头 (street), 门口 (doorway), 野外 (field), 一旁 (on one side), 乡下 (countryside), 民间 (folk), 原处 (original place), 远处 (distant), 基层 (grass-root level), 头里 (front) ...

9. Distinctive words: 高等 (high-class), 公共 (public), 亲爱 (dear), 民用 (civil), 日常 (routine), 随机 (random), 袖珍 (miniature), 现行 (current), 野生 (wild), 业余 (amateur), 男 (male) ...

10. Numerals: 一 (one), 二 (two), 三 (three), 五 (five), 十 (ten), 百 (hundred), 千 (thousand), 万 (ten thousand), 亿 (hundred million), 半 (half), 几 (several), 数 (several), 多 (multiple), 诸 (all) ...

11. Measure words: 一切 (each and all), 大量 (bulk), 不少 (good many), 所有 (all), 大批 (large batch), 部分 (some), 个把 (one or two), 少许 (a little), 俩 (both), 片刻 (a while), 许久 (long time) ...

12. Demonstratives: 这 (this), 那 (that), 每 (each), 其他 (other), 任何 (any), 另 (another), 唯一 (only), 上 (above), 下 (below), 前 (previous), 后 (rear), 头 (first) ...

13. Adverbs: 很 (very), 都 (totally), 只 (only), 也 (also), 又 (again), 就 (just), 不 (not), 赶紧 (speedily), 常常 (often), 正在 (be doing), 亲自 (personally), 难道 (surely), 究竟 (on earth) ...

14. Onomatopoeia: 啪 (bang), 叮当 (dingdong), 哗啦 (crash) ...

15. Prepositions: 被 (by), 从 (from), 对 (versus), 在 (at), 按照 (according to), 比 (than), 跟 (with), 向 (to), 由 (via), 凭 (on) ...

16. Conjunctions: 和 (and), 或者 (or), 而 (but), 不但 (not only), 而且 (but also), 虽然 (although), 但是 (however), 即使 (even though), 况且 (besides) ...

17. Modal words: 吗 (ah), 呢 (well), 来着 (only), 罢了 (just) ...

18. Auxiliaries: 了 (le), 着 (zhuo), 过 (guo), 的 (de), 地 (di), 得 (de), 所 (suo), 等 (etc.), 似的 (like) ...

19. Interjections: 啊 (ah), 唉 (alas), 喂 (hello), 哎哟 (oh), 哼 (hum), 哎呀 (gosh) ...

20. Pronouns: 我 (I), 你 (you), 他们 (they), 谁 (who), 什么 (what), 哪里 (where), 几 (several), 多少 (how many), 怎样 (how), 怎么样 (what about), 这儿 (here) ...

2 Basic issues concerning classification of parts of speech

2.1 Parsing of words

The parsing of words is not discussed in detail here.

It is difficult to divide the boundary line between word and phrase in Chinese; hence, a good many scholars have raised the question of continuity[1] between word and phrase (see Wang Hongjun, 1994; Shen Yang, 1996). Perhaps we should not emphasize the continuity between word and phrase but instead emphasize that there is indeed a boundary line between them, although it is difficult to divide the line.

The parsing of words requires an understanding of their properties. Functionally speaking, a word is the smallest sentence-making unit. From the perspective of properties, it is the smallest applicable linguistic constituent.

A word has the following three properties:

1. Integrity: A word is a whole or integral, and is not separable.
2. Independent application: As a sentence-making unit, a word may be used independently or combined with other linguistic constituents temporarily but not fixedly.
3. Stand-by application: A word is a standby linguistic unit for language application, which is kept in stock in a word bank rather than generated temporarily.

Taking into consideration the properties of a word, we can propose the following three principles to determine its boundary line.

2.1.1 The integrity principle

A word has its integrity, and as a whole it is not separable or incomplete. The integrity principle can be described with the following two criteria:

2.1.1.1 Expansion criteria

A word usually cannot be expanded. In principle, an expandable segment is a phrase; a segment that cannot be expanded is a word.

Expandable: 手疼 (hand pain) → 手很疼 (The hand is very painful); 手上 (on hand) → 我的手/上(on my hand)

Not expandable (word): 肉麻 (disgusting) →*肉很麻 (*The flesh tingles); 身上 (body) → 我的/身上 (on my body)

手很疼 (The hand is very painful) and 手上 (on hand) are expandable and therefore are phrases; 肉麻 (disgusting) and 身上 (body) are not expandable and therefore are words.

2.1.1.2 *Integrity criteria*

A word usually must be integral. In principle, a segment without integrity is a phrase; an integral segment is a word.

Not integral: 急性肠炎和慢性肠炎 (acute enteritis and chronic enteritis) → 急性和慢性肠炎 (acute and chronic enteritis); 火车上汽车上 (in train and in automobile) → 火车汽车上 (in train and automobile)

Integral: train and automobile (火车和汽车) →*火汽车

桌子椅子 (desk and chair) →*桌椅子

地上身上 (on the ground and on one's body) →*地身上

急性肠炎 (acute enteritis) and 火车上 (in train) can be separable and therefore are phrases; 火车 (train), 桌子 (desk) and 身上 (body) are not separable and therefore are words.

2.1.2 *The transparency principle*

As a temporary combination unit, a word has its structural and functional transparency and transparent meaning when combined with other constituents, whereas the morphemes inside a word are often not transparent. The transparency principle has the following three criteria:

2.1.2.1 *Structural transparency criteria*

A word has a transparent structure when combined with other words or phrases, whereas the structure inside a word may not be transparent. The structural transparency is manifested as follows:

(1) Whether a structural relation is apparent or not. A segment whose internal structural relation is not apparent is usually a word.

The structural relation is apparent: 新书 (new book), 桌子椅子 (desk and chair), 吃完 (eat up), 白菜 (celery cabbage), 提高 (raise high) (phrase).

The structural relation is not apparent: 天真 (naive), 个别 (individual), 若干 (some), 冬烘 (pedant) (word).

(2) Whether the type of structural relation exists or is in agreement with a typical phrase or not.

Not existing in a typical phrase: 纸张 (paper), 船只 (boat), 马匹 (horse), 人口 (population) (word).

Not in agreement with the structural relational type of a typical phrase: 枣红 (claret) (noun + adjective = attributive and headword construction consisting of modifier and headword) (word).

The above two cases should be regarded as words.

(3) Whether there is structural reanalysis or not:

The segment that causes structural reanalysis should be regarded as a word: 等于 (equal), 善于 (skillful), 所以 (therefore), 不仅 (not only), 毫不 (no), 之一 (among), 之前 (before), 加以 (conduct), 有所 (somewhat).

2.1.2.2 *Functional transparency criteria*

Functional transparency means that the function of the segment combined in a certain mode is the same as that of the typical phrase combined in the same mode. The segment whose function is not transparent should be regarded as word.

Transparent function: 手疼 (hand pain) →*很手疼 (*very hand pain); 很新 (very new) →*很新衣服; 加水 (add water) →* add water cup (加水杯子)

Nontransparent function: 头疼 (headache) → 很头疼 (terrible headache); 很多 (many) → 很多衣服 (many clothes); 加工 (process) → 加工木材 (process timber)

The functions of 手疼 (hand pain) and 加水 (add water) are transparent, and therefore they are phrases, whereas those of 头疼 (headache), 很多 (many), and 加工 (process) are not transparent, and therefore they are words.

2.1.2.3 *Transparent meaning criteria*

Transparent meaning denotes that the meaning of the segment as a whole can be inferred from its component constituent. The segment whose meaning is not transparent should be regarded as word.

Transparent meaning: 白鞋 (white shoe), 白云 (white cloud), 白发 (white hair) (phrase or word).

Non-transparent meaning: 白菜 (cabbage), 痛快 (delighted), 丈夫 (husband) (word).

2.1.3 *The finite principle*

As a standby unit, a word has a finite number and length.

Finite criteria: the segment whose length and number of constituents of the same kind should be regarded as a phrase.

The length of segments such as "3245" can be expanded infinitely, and the number of constituents of their same kind is infinite; therefore, they should be regarded as phrases.

2.2 Internal hierarchies of modern Chinese

To divide parts of speech, the first thing to do is distinguish whether a constituent is a word or not. But sometimes it is hard to tell whether a constituent is a word or not. Lv Shuxiang (1979) pointed out that it is easy to tell whether some constituents are words or not, but that it is complicated to tell some others. For example, 叶 (leaf) does not form a word in most cases but can do so in botany; 时 (time) does not form a word in speech but can do so in writing. If 叶 (leaf) and 时 (time) are recognized as words, then an important fact is obliterated: these morphemes cannot form words in most cases. Furthermore, which part of speech a word belongs to sometimes depends on different occasions. For example, 杯 (cup) should be regarded as a measure word in spoken Chinese but can be used as noun in writing, for example, 杯中 (in a cup). 金 (gold) is a distinctive word in everyday spoken Chinese but a noun in scientific and technical Chinese. In the past, modern Chinese was considered to be homogeneous, thereby having no way to deal with this phenomenon. In reality, modern Chinese is an inhomogeneous system mixed with different hierarchical constituents. By analyzing its internal hierarchies, we can deal with the phenomenon well.

Modern Chinese mainly has its historical hierarchy and field hierarchy (in other words, a two-hierarchy system). Its writing is actually a mixture of different historical hierarchies and can be largely classified into two hierarchies (systems): modern colloquial Chinese hierarchy and classical Chinese hierarchy. Written modern Chinese is based on modern colloquial Chinese and mingled with some expressions of classical Chinese. In written modern Chinese, the classical Chinese hierarchy mainly manifests itself in the following two forms:

1. The classical Chinese words that are mingled with the modern colloquial Chinese. For example, 国 (country), 时 (when, e.g., 来时 (when coming)), 战 (war, e.g., 站前 (before war)), 该 (the, e.g., 该同志 (the comrade)), 本 (this, e.g., 本校 (this school)), 虽 (though, e.g., 虽难 (though difficult)), etc.

2. The classical Chinese usage mingled with modern colloquial Chinese. Although some words exist in modern colloquial Chinese, they can still be used in classical Chinese, for example:

(31) 在一个"关于儿童对物体运动速度"的认知研究中,实验人员让儿童比较两个小汽车运动的速度是否一致(事实上两车运动的速度是一致的),其目的是要看看儿童是怎样理解求速度的公式的. (《儿童的心理世界》,方富熹、方格主编,北京大学出版社) (To study children's cognition of an object's motion speed, the experimental personnel let them compare whether the motion speeds of

two vehicles are the same or not (in fact, their speeds are the same), so as to understand how children solve formulae for speed. (*The Psychological World of Children*, compiled by Fang Fuxi and Fang Ge, Peking University Press)

(32) 一些人纪律和全局意识淡化,搞上有政策,下有对策,有令不听,我行我素,导致小团体主义和无政府主义滋长. (《人民日报》1995年6月27日) (Some people have a weak discipline and weak global awareness; the inferior have their own countermeasures when the superior have their policies. They do not obey their superior and act according to their own wishes, thus giving rise to the spread of factionalism and anarchism.) (*The People's Daily*, June 27, 1995)

(33) 于1993年8月8日举办新兴公司成立两周年的盛大庆典,宴开137桌,发给与会千余来宾每人288元的"红包". (《人民日报》1995年12月4日) (The second grand anniversary celebration ceremony for the Xinxing Company foundation will be held on August 8, 1993; the banquet consists of 137 tables; each of around thousands of participants will receive their own "red envelope" of 288 yuan.) (*The People's Daily*, December 4, 1995)

The word 车 (vehicle) in Example (31) is in the modern colloquial Chinese hierarchy, but is directly modified by a numeral without a measure word, thus being used as classical Chinese. The words 上 (superior) and 下 (inferior) in Example (32) are also in the modern colloquial Chinese hierarchy, but here they are used as subjects independently, just like classical Chinese words. Before the numeral 千 (thousand) in Example (33), there is no measure word, which is used as a classical Chinese word.

The constituents in the classical Chinese hierarchy primarily occur in verse, title, four-word phrase, parallel format, and in front of monosyllable locatives such as 前 (front), 后 (rear), 内 (in), 外 (outside), 中 (middle), military language, journalistic language, official document language, and scientific and technical language.

The constituents in different historical hierarchies have three possible grammatical differences:

1. **Whether being a word or not:** For example, 国 (state), 校 (school), 敌 (enemy), 鸭 (duck), 应 (should), 该 (this), 置 (put), 共 (total) and 俩 (both) do not form words in the colloquial modern Chinese hierarchy but do so in the classic Chinese hierarchy. For example:

(34) 冷战结束后,西方国家在对外政策中突出了经济因素,在处理国与国关系时,对本国经济利益的考虑往往多于对政治的考虑. (《人民日报》1995年1月1日) (After the end of the Cold War, the foreign policies of the Western countries emphasized economic factors; in handling the relationship between their countries and other countries,[2] they often considered their economic interests more important than their politics.) (*The People's Daily*, January 1, 1995)

(35) 十多年来,该校共培养了2.7万名干部,超过了同期该校普通高等教育培养的人数. (《人民日报》1995年1月4日) (For more than a decade, the school has trained a total of 27,000 cadres, which exceeds the number of people who received higher education by the school in the same period.) (*The People's Daily*, January 4, 1995)

(36) 左手一只鸡,右手一只鸭. (歌词) (A chicken in the left hand; a duck in the right hand.) (a song)

(37) 运用观察法时,应使被观察者始终处于日常教学或生活的情景之中,尽量避免外来干扰. (《儿童的心理世界》,方富熹,方格主编,北京大学出版社) (In applying the observation method, the observed should always be in an everyday teaching or living context; every effort should be made to avoid extraneous interference.) (*The Psychological World of Children*, compiled by Fang Fuxi and Fang Ge, Peking University Press)

(38) "抓两头",就不能一头热,一头冷,更不能"嫌贫爱富",置贫困村于不顾. (《人民日报》1995年1月4日) ("To take charge of two ends", you cannot just emphasize one end but ignore another, not to mention that "you like the rich but dislike the poor", ignoring the poor villages.) (*The People's Daily*, January 4, 1995)

(39) 他先以一部兵力围攻徐水,伺机诱歼来援之敌. (《人民日报》1995年4月28日) (He first uses part of his military force to lay siege to Xushui County and then waits for his chance to seduce and annihilate the enemy reinforcements.) (*The People's Daily*, April 28, 1995)

2. **Grammatical functions:** Namely the differences between the classical Chinese usage and the general usage that are mingled in modern colloquial Chinese, as mentioned above.

3. **Parts of speech:** For example, the words like 杯 (cup), 盘 (plate), 拳 (fist) and 口 (mouth) belong to measure words in the modern colloquial Chinese hierarchy like 一杯酒 (a cup of wine), 一盘菜 (a plate of vegetable), 打一拳 (hit a fist) and 咬一口 (give a bite) but belong to nouns in the classical Chinese hierarchy like 杯中 (in a cup), 盘中 (on a plate), 挥拳 (shake one's fist), and 口中 (inside a mouth). The word 依然 (still) belongs to an adverb in modern colloquial Chinese, for example, 国际形势依然不稳定 (The international situation is still unstable). But it belongs to state words in the classical Chinese hierarchy, like 风采依然 (The charm is still the same).

The field hierarchy is mainly classified into everyday language hierarchy and specialized language (including scientific and technical language) hierarchy. For example, 叶 (leaf) and 鳄 (crocodile) are not words in the everyday Chinese hierarchy, but are words in biological Chinese. 胸 (chest) and 肩 (shoulder)[3] are not words in the everyday Chinese hierarchy but are words in the physiological and medical Chinese hierarchies. For another example, the word 金 (gold) is a distinctive word in the everyday Chinese hierarchy, but is a noun in the scientific and technical Chinese hierarchy. The word 热 (hot) is an adjective or a verb in the everyday Chinese hierarchy, but can be a noun in the scientific and technical Chinese hierarchy.

Some dictionaries only recognize the universal hierarchies of the words that form words in different hierarchies and have different parts of speech (modern colloquial Chinese and everyday Chinese hierarchies). Those that do not form words in the universal hierarchy are treated as morphemes and labeled into parts of speech according to the universal hierarchy.[4] Other dictionaries recognize both the universal hierarchy and the specialized hierarchy, but do not divide their parts of speech.[5] However, the two types of dictionaries are too simple; it is better to recognize the constituents in various hierarchies and label their hierarchies. For example, the constituents in modern colloquial Chinese and everyday Chinese hierarchies are not labeled, but the constituents in the classical Chinese and specialized Chinese hierarchies are labeled as follows: 国 (country: [classical Chinese], noun; 口 (mouth): measure word, [classical Chinese], noun; 金 (gold): distinctive word; [chemistry], noun.

A language may have different grammatical systems at different historical and field hierarchies; the grammatical functions of its words may also be different, and the criteria for classifying their parts of speech should be different too. The classification of modern Chinese parts of speech should consider these different historical hierarchies and treat the constituents in different hierarchies differently. The ideal way of dealing with this is to separate the two hierarchies completely and establish a set of criteria for classifying the parts of speech for them separately. However, there is no clear-cut boundary between modern colloquial Chinese and classical Chinese hierarchies, and it is difficult to completely divide the two hierarchies. Moreover, there are more grammatical similarities between the two hierarchies than differences. Since the purpose of our study is to parse all the words in written and spoken modern Chinese, we consider the colloquial modern Chinese and classical Chinese hierarchies jointly together and establish the same criteria for classifying their parts of speech. For example, only a word that meets the criterion of "numeral ~∧* subject or object" is a measure word.

2.3 The identity of words

2.3.1 Individual words and generalization words

Each appearance of a word is a token (individual word); several individual words that have the same sound form and meaning can be grouped into the same type (generalization word). The determination of a generalization word is to determine whether the word that appears in different places is the same word that appears several times or a different word, namely determining its identity. The object of classification is type (generalization word). Therefore, words must be grouped before classification, and grouping is a precondition for classification (see Zhu Dexi, Lu Jiawen & Ma Zhen, 1961).

What we mean by classifying parts of speech is to take a generalization word as the unit to divide its parts of speech. For this reason, if the individual words that appear at different grammatical positions are identical, then all their functions should be regarded as different functions of the same word; however, if not, they should be regarded as different generalization words.

The determination of word identity involves whether a word has certain grammatical functions and thereby may influence grouping results. Besides, it may influence whether a word should be included in a dictionary. Therefore, it is one of the issues to be solved first in order to divide parts of speech. For example, if 木头 (wood) in 木头桌子 (wooden desk) is regarded as not identical with 木头 (wood) in 买木头 (buy wood), then it should be treated as a noun and concurrently as an adjective (non-predicate).

2.3.2 Case studies

The principles for word identity determination are homophony and synonymy, but how to use the principles is a tricky question. In the following, we will explain in some detail several cases of word identity determination with regard to the classification of parts of speech.

2.3.2.1 Constituent meaning and structural meaning

In determining the identity of meaning, we should distinguish between the meaning possessed by a word itself (constituent meaning) and the structural meaning. Some grammar books hold that the meaning of 死 (die) in 他死了 (he died) and 他死了父亲 (he died his father) (in Chinese grammar) is different and regard them as two generalization words. The former is intransitive, while the latter is transitive. In our view, the difference in meaning between 他死了 (he died) and 他死了父亲 (he died his father) is not caused by 死 (die) itself but by its grammatical structure. They belong to the same generalization word.

Then, how should we tell whether a certain meaning belongs to a word's own meaning or its structural meaning? Our answer is that the systematic and analogical meaning is the structural meaning and, if not, the constituent meaning. For example, 死 (die) is a verb with univalent change. We can place its only argument element at the position of subject or object, taking the above 他死了 (he died) and 他死了父亲 (he died his father) for examples. The majority of or almost all verbs and state verbs with one syllable and univalent change can behave like this. Other examples are the following:

(1) a. 腿断了 (A leg breaks).   b. 桌子断了条腿 (The desk breaks one of its legs).

(2) a. 眼睛瞎了 (The eye is blind).   b. 他瞎了一只眼睛 (He blinds one of his eyes).

(3) a. 钱丢了 (Money is lost).   b. 我丢了钱 (I lose money).

(4) a. 第一段漏了 (The first paragraph leaves out).   b. 漏了第一段 (the first paragraph is left out)

(5) a. 电线杆倒了 (The electric pole falls).   b. 倒了一根电线杆 (fell an electric pole).

The verbs in the above five examples should be regarded as the identical generalization words in Groups *a* and *b* respectively. Other examples are the following:

(6) a. 他很高 (He is very tall).   b. 他高我一头 (He is one head taller than me).

(7) a. 他很小 (He is young).   b. 他小我两岁 (He is two years younger than me).

(8) a. 他很大 (He is older).   b. 他大我半岁 (He is half a year older than me).

(9) a.他很矮 (He is short).   b. 他矮我一寸 (He is one inch shorter than me).

In these examples, the adjectives in Groups *a* and *b* are systematically different. The comparative meanings in Group *b* should be understood as structural meanings and not possessed by the adjectives themselves. The adjectives in both groups should be regarded as generalization words.

Let us analyze the following groups of examples:

(10) a. 文化生活丰富 (The cultural life is rich).   b. 丰富文化生活 (enrich cultural life)

(11) a. 思想统一 (Thoughts are unitary).   b. 统一思想 (unify thoughts)

(12) a. 制度完善 (The system is complete).   b. 完善制度 (complete the system)

(13) a. 关系密切 (The relation is intimate).   b. 密切与群众的关系 (establish close relations with the masses)

(14) a. 队伍壮大 (The army is strong).   b. 壮大队伍 (strengthen the army)

(15) a. 生活充实 (Life is rich).   b. 充实生活 (enrich life)

The above examples show that the "make-do" meaning in the type of word in 丰富文化生活 (enrich cultural life) is systematic and analogical and should be regarded as structural meaning. That is to say, this type of word has the "make-do" meaning when it is used in the "~ (object)" environment. The "make-do" meaning is grouped into the structural meaning brought about by the "adjective + object" construction. But so long as we enlarge the scope of examination, we may find three facts: (1) there is only a limited number of adjectives that have the so-called "make-do" usage; (2) many adjectives that are synonymous or near-synonymous with the type of words such as 丰富 (rich) and 统一 (unitary) have no "make-do" usage. For example, 丰盛

(rich), 一致 (consistent), 完备 (complete), 紧密 (close), 强大 (powerful) and 实在 (actual) are nearly synonymous or synonymous with 丰富 (rich), 统一 (unify), 完善 (complete), 密切 (close), 壮大 (strengthen) and 充实 (enrich) but have no "make-do" usage. (3) The so-called "make-do" meaning appears not only when adjectives have objects but also on other occasions, for example, 基础得到巩固 (the foundation is consolidated), 对制度加以完善 (perfect a system), 使《纲要》提出的原则不断得到丰富和发展 (continuously enrich and develop the principles raised in the program), 意见不能统一 (opinions cannot be unified). In these examples, the "make-do" meanings of 巩固 (consolidate), 完善 (perfect) and 统一 (unify) can only be regarded as the meanings possessed by these words themselves, not their structural meanings. Hence, we have to admit that the "make-do" meaning of the type of words such as "rich" is possessed by the words themselves.

We have another reason to regard the "make-do" meaning as the words' own meanings instead of their structural meanings. Namely, if we regard the "make-do" meaning as the structural meaning, then we have to admit that it is a syntactic means in modern Chinese. As a result, we can only group the type of words such as 丰富 (rich) and 完善 (perfect) into adjectives instead of conversional words that function as adjective and verb, thus making syntax unnecessarily complicated. In fact, on the whole, no one thinks that modern Chinese has the "make-do" syntactic means. In dealing with word identity, we should coordinate words with syntax. Since we think that there is no "make-do" usage in Chinese syntax, we can only group the "make-do" meaning of the type of word 丰富 (rich) into its own meaning. Therefore, words such as 丰富 (rich), 统一 (unitary), 完善 (perfect), 密切 (intimate), 壮大 (strong) and 巩固 (consolidated) should belong to identical generalization words.

2.3.2.2 *Lexical transfer reference and syntactic transfer reference*

The type of words such as 领导 (leader), 导演 (director), 锁 (lock), 铲 (shovel), 练习 (exercise), 报告 (report), 典型 (representation) and 内行 (expert) has the two uses of predicate and noun. The two uses of 领导 (leader) and 导演 (director) have the relationship between action and its doer; the two uses of 锁 (lock) and 铲 (shovel) have the relationship between action and instrument; the two uses of 练习 (exercise) and 报告 (report) have the relationship between action and content; the two uses of 典型 (representation) and 内行 (expert) have the relationship between attributive and subject. In these examples, when used as noun, these words have a reference meanings; what they refer to are not action, behavior and attribute themselves but other objects related to them. This reference is what we call transfer reference. The transfer reference of the above words is a kind of fixed usage. A dictionary should take them as independent senses, and we call this type of transfer reference lexical transfer reference. Therefore, the lexical transfer reference should be regarded as an independent generalization word and should differ from a generalization word's predicate usage.

Opposite to lexical transfer reference is syntactic transfer reference, which refers to the temporary transfer reference when some words appear at the position of subject or object. Because syntactic transfer reference has no fixed meaning, we regard syntactic transfer reference and its corresponding non-transfer reference as the same generalization word, for example:

(16) a. 很大/很小 (very big/very small)   b. 有大有小 (have a big or small thing)

(17) a. 很肥/很瘦 (very fat/very thin)   b. 有肥有瘦 (have fat and thin)

The 大 (big) and 小 (small) in Example (16 b) refer to a big or small thing; 肥 (fat) and 瘦 (thin) in Example (17 b) refer to fat meat or thin meat respectively. In both cases, there is a syntactic transfer reference. We group all of them in both groups into the same generalization word respectively.

The syntactic transfer reference of a predicate is very rare in modern Chinese but very common in classical Chinese, for example:

(18) 见贤思齐,见不贤而内自省(《论语·里仁》) (When we see a man of virtue and talent, we should think of equaling them; when we see a man of a contrary character, we should turn inward and examine ourselves.) (*Confucian Analects*)

(19) 然则小故不可以敌大,寡故不可以敌众,弱故不可以敌强 (《孟子·梁惠王上》) (However, the small naturally cannot rival the big; the few, of course, are no match for the many; the weak cannot rival the strong.) (*Book One on Lianghuiwang, Mencius*)

(20) 失所长则国家无功,守所短则民不乐生.以无功御不乐生,不可行于齐民(《韩非子·安危》) (With lack of the meritorious, the state is powerless; if keeping the unmeritorious, the people do not enjoy their life. Under these circumstances, it is impossible for the Qi people to live without merit.) (*Chapter on Safety and Danger* in *Han Fei Zi*)

(21) 将军身披坚执锐,伐无道,诛暴秦,复立楚国之社稷,功宜为王 (《史记·陈涉世家》) (The general is well armed to the teeth, combats the brutal and the tyrannical Qin state and reestablishes the Chu state. His merit makes him deserve to be a king.) (*Chen She's Story* in *Historical Records*)

(22) 今梁赵相攻,轻兵锐卒心竭于外,老弱罢于内   (《史记·孙子吴起列传》) (Now the Liang and Zhao states attack each other; the light-armed and well-protected soldiers aspire to fight outside, and the old and weak rest inside.) (*The Biographies of Sun Zi and Wu Qi* in *Historical Records*)

The syntactic transfer reference of a modification word is common in modern Chinese, for example:

(23) a. 急性肠炎好治,慢性肠炎不好治 (Acute enteritis is easy to cure, but chronic enteritis is not easy).

    b. 急性好治,慢性不好治 (The acute are easy to cure, but the chronic are not easy).

(24) a. 打一个长途电话 (make a long-distance phone call)

    b. 打一个长途 (call a long distance)

(25) a. 许多苹果都坏了 (Many apples get rotten).   b. 许多都坏了 (Many get rotten).

(26) a. 没收一切财产 (confiscate all property)   b. 没收一切 (confiscate all)

The distinctive words such as 急性 (acute), 慢性 (chronic) and 长途 (long-distance) in Group *b* of Examples (23) and (24), and the measure words 许多 (many) and 一切 (all) in Group *b* of Examples (25) and (26) are all syntactic transfer references and grouped into the same generalization words with those in Group *a* respectively.

2.3.2.3 Lexical transfer reference and lexical self-reference

Some predicates can be used for a reference but have no transfer reference meaning except self-reference, namely referring to action, behavior or attribute itself. For example:

(27) a. 研究问题 (study a problem)   b. 进行研究 (carry out study)

(28) a. 答复对方 (answer the other party)   b. 给对方一个答复 (give the other party an answer)

(29) a. 收支不平衡 (Income and payment are not balanced).   b. 保持平衡 (keep one's balance)

(30) a. 很不幸 (very unfortunate)   b. 遭受不幸 (suffer from misfortune)

研究 (study), 答复 (answer), 平衡 (balanced) and 不幸 (unfortunate) in Group *a* of Examples (27) through (30) are used as predicates, but in Group *b* they are used as nouns and have self-reference meanings. The self-reference has its fixed meaning and is called lexical self-reference. We regard the lexical self-reference and its corresponding predicate use as the same generalization word. For example, the above words belong to the same generalization words in Groups *a* and *b* respectively.

Although there is an evident distinction between typical lexical self-reference and typical lexical transfer reference, the boundary line between lexical self-reference and transfer reference is still rather indistinct. We will specify the distinction between the two in the following.

The relationship between action and reference is as follows:

1. The relationship between action and its doer, for example, 代表 (representative), 领导 (leader), 编辑 (editor), 导演 (director), 指挥 (commander).

2. The relationship between action and tool, for example, 锁 (lock), 锯 (saw), 铲 (shovel).
3. The relationship between action and its object, for example, 摆设 (furnish), 储蓄 (save), 花费 (expenditure), 建筑 (building), 武装 (armament).
4. The relationship between action and content. The content means the things existing in the form of substance or abstract things, for example, 通知 (information), 报告 (report), 补助 (subsidy), 练习 (exercise), 要求 (requirement), 计划 (plan), 忠告 (advice), 根据 (basis), 感觉 (perception), 命令 (order), 建议 (suggestion), 定义 (definition), 主张 (claim).
5. The relationship between action and source or credential, for example, 区别 (difference), 趋向 (tendency), 仇恨 (hatred), 依据 (basis), 病 (disease), 梦 (dream).
6. The use as a noun purely means the action itself, for example, 研究 (research), 调查 (investigation), 生产 (production), 解决 (solution), 改革 (reform).

Among the above six cases, we regard the first five cases as transfer reference and treat them as verb and concurrently noun (see Chapter 7); the sixth case is regarded as self-reference.

2.3.2.4 Word-formation, morphology and syntax

In the above, we discussed the word identity caused by meaning. In the following, we will discuss the identity caused by changes in form.

Morphology and word-formation come from the Indo-European languages, where the changes in a word's form bring about two results, taking English for example:

a. Changes in lexical meaning: work - worker (addition), sing - song (inflection)
b. Changes in grammatical meaning (no change in lexical meaning): work - worked (addition), sing - sang (inflection)

Group *a* belongs to word-formation, namely the change in a word form creates a new word (derivative); Group *b* belongs to morphological change. That is to say, the morphological change does not create a new word, only a different form of the same word. In other words, the constituents represented by the two forms in Group *a* are not identical and should be regarded as two words, but the constituents represented by the forms in Group *b* are identical and should be regarded as one word.

It is generally held that Chinese has no morphological changes like those in Indo-European languages but has its morphology, which is achieved by reduplication and addition of -zi (子), -er (儿), -tou (头) and -hua (化). But they are very likely to belong to neither morphology nor word-formation but to syntax. The so-called syntax means that the changes in form can be regarded as a kind of word combination. For example, "走 (going) + le (了)" does not belong to word-formation or morphology but belongs to a syntactic combination. If the changes in form are syntactic, then the original form and the varied form belong to the same generalization word. We will distinguish between word-formation, morphology and syntax based on the following six criteria:

A. System: it can be analogized in a certain scope. A system does not necessarily mean a big quantity; under certain conditions, most changes in form are systematic.
B. Compulsion: whether it must be so as long as conditions are met.
C. Functional identity: whether the grammatical functions of a varied form are the same as the original form or still have the basic functions of the original form.
D. Whether there is a systematic difference in meaning between varied form and original form.
E. Whether the original form is a word: English has the word "porter", but its original form "port" is not the word from which "porter" is derived.
F. Whether the root part and the part to be used to change form are words.

In the following, we will analyze reduplication. There are three types of reduplication: morphological reduplication, word-formation reduplication and syntactic reduplication.

Zhang Shoukang (1985) listed the word-formation and morphology of noun, verb, adjective, measure word, numeral, pronoun and so on, and thought that the reduplication of verb, adjective and measure word belongs to morphology. We will analyze them one by one according to the six criteria.

1. VERB REDUPLICATION

There are two forms of verb reduplication: ABAB and AABB.

The ABAB reduplication form: 商量商量 (consult), 讨论讨论 (discuss). They are systematic; their grammatical functions are basically the same and have no compulsion; both parts are words. Therefore, they should be regarded as not morphological reduplication but syntactic reduplication.

Table 2.1 The distinctions among morphology, word formation and syntax

	System	Compulsion	Functional identity	Systematic difference in meaning	A word in its original form	Two independent words	Systematic difference in meaning
Morphology	+	+	+	+	+	−	−/+
Word formation	?	−	?	?	?	−	−/+
Syntax	+	−	+	+	+	+	+

Note: + denotes the existence of the characteristic; - denotes the non-existence of the characteristic; ? denotes no requirement for the characteristic, which is optional.

The AABB reduplication form: a. 比比划划 (gesticulate), 拉拉扯扯 (pull and push): they are not systematic, have different grammatical functions and belong to word-formation reduplication. b. 走走停停 (walk and stop), 说说笑笑 (josh): their order can be changed into 停停走走 (stop and walk), denoting that the two actions alter in turn (or both actions happen). They should be regarded as the reduplication of the two verbs 走 (walk) and 停 (stop). This is syntactic reduplication.

2. ADJECTIVE REDUPLICATION

In the past, the reduplicated form of an adjective was called the vivid form and regarded as identical.

The adjective reduplication is systematic (a good many adjectives can be reduplicated). But the original form that is not a word has no functional identity:

a. The original word is not a word: 堂堂正正 (dignified and imposing), 风风火火 (rash and too much in haste), 密密麻麻 (close and numerous, very dense); the reduplicated form is not a word: 胖胖 (fat), 红红 (red), 圆圆 (round)

b. The original form and the reduplicated form have different functions in the following ways:

Compare:

	Not ~	*very ~*	*combined complement*	*~ complement*
干净 (clean)	+	+	+	+
干干净净 (very clean)	-	-	-	-

A reduplicated adjective no longer has the basic functions of an adjective 很 (very) ~; it has the properties of a state word.

On the other hand, some original forms belong to other parts of speech.

The original form is a verb: 比划 (gesticulate), 勾搭 (gang up with), 跟跄 (stagger), 商量 (consult), 溜达 (stroll), 哆嗦 (tremble)
The original form is a noun: 疙瘩 (knot), 枝节 (branch and knot)[6]
The original form is an adverb: 切实 (earnestly)
The original form is a numeral and measure word: 半拉 (half)

Thus we can see that the AABB form that has the properties of a state word belongs to word-formation reduplication.

Furthermore, some adjective reduplications mean "either A or B", for example, 好好坏坏 (either good or bad), 大大小小 (either big or small). This belongs to syntactic reduplication.

3. STATE WORD REDUPLICATION

For example: 雪白雪白 (snow-white), 笔直笔直 (very straight), 通红通红 (red through), 乌黑乌黑 (pitch dark), 喷香喷香 (extremely delicious-smelling). They are systematic, have the same functions (all have the properties of a state word) but no compulsion; both parts are words. They should be regarded as syntactic reduplication.

4. MEASURE WORD REDUPLICATION

For example, 个个 (piece by piece), 条条 (sections after sections of), 天天 (day by day), 次次 (time and time again)

The reduplication is systematic; the grammatical function of a measure word changes. The reduplicated form has the functions of both a numeral and a measure word, for example:

Measure word: 一条条道路 (sections after sections of a road)
Numeral and measure word: 九条道路 (nine sections of a road)
Measure word: 一次次摔倒 (fall over time and time again)
Numeral and measure word: 九次摔倒 (fall over for nine times)

However, because the basic functions of a measure word are kept (being able to be modified by numerals, and the functions of increased numerals and measure words are incomplete, the reduplicated measure words are not regarded as word-formation reduplication. Because there is no enforceability, both reduplicating and reduplicated parts are words, and they should be regarded as syntactic reduplication.

5. NUMERAL REDUPLICATION

For example, 三三两两 (in twos and threes), 千千 (thousands after thousands), 万万 (ten thousands after ten thousands), 许许多多 (many many)

The reduplication of a numeral is not systematic and has some changes in function. For example, the reduplicated numeral cannot modify a measure word, and there is no systematic difference in meaning, thus being ought to be regarded as word-formation reduplication.

6. NOUN REDUPLICATION

For example, 风风雨雨 (hardships), 方方面面 (respects after respects), 恩恩怨怨 (grievances after grievances), 条条框框 (regulations and restrictions), 瓶瓶罐罐 (bottles and cans). Their reduplication is not systematic; some nouns before reduplication have no word form and should be regarded as word-formation reduplication.

7. LOCATIVE REDUPLICATION

For example, 上上下下 (up and down), 前前后后 (front and rear), 里里外外 (inner and outer), 左左右右 (left and right). Their reduplication is systematic; their function does not change fundamentally but has no enforceability; both reduplicating and reduplicated parts are words, belonging to syntactic reduplication.

8. ADVERB REDUPLICATION

For example, Type A: 刚刚 (just), 常常 (very often), 白白 (fruitlessly), 早早 (very early). 渐渐 (gradually), 悄悄 (silently), 偏偏 (unexpectedly), 隐隐约约 (faintly), 的的确确 (very indeed), 陆陆续续 (successively)

Type B: 最最 (the very most), 永远永远 (forever and forever), 非常非常 (very much and very much)

Type A cannot be reasoned by analogy and has no uniform grammatical meaning; some adverbs before reduplication are not words. This type can only be regarded as word-formation reduplication. In fact, Type B does not belong to reduplication but to repetition: it can be repeated for more than two times: very very good, ignore you forever forever forever. Repetition is neither word-formation nor morphological formation but the use of words.

Yang Chengkai (1991) thought that there is no need to group the reduplicated form of a word as a part of speech and to distinguish between word-formation reduplication and syntactic reduplication. Indeed, there is no need to classify syntactic reduplication as a word into a part of speech, but word-formation reduplication should be stored in a word bank as independent words.

Chinese essentially has no attached word-formation. "X + zi (子), er (儿), tou (头), hua (化)" are used to form words, such as 竹子 (bamboo), 尖子 (tip), 兔儿 (rabbit), 石头 (stone), 看头 (worth seeing), 液化 (liquefy), 淡化 (play down). le (了), zhuo (着), guo (过) and men (们)[7] form phrases (see Chen Baoya, 2000) and are syntactic. But their functions are like word-formation, and the words thus formed should be regarded as identical units. For example, 来了一个人 (a person comes) should be regarded as 来 (come) having its object 一个人 (a person).

2.3.2.5 With de (的)/di (地) or without de (的)/di (地)

In examining the grammatical functions of a word, a good many studies that discuss parts of speech suggest that a word that takes de (的) or di (地) has the grammatical function of the word itself. We do not agree with this.

Grammatically speaking, de (的) or di (地) can be analyzed into the suffix of adverb de[1] (的), the suffix of state word de[2] (的) and the attached constituent of a noun-like phrase de[3] (的) (see Zhu Dexi, 1961). A constituent that takes de[1] (的) or de[3] (的) has quite different grammatical functions. For example, 逻辑 (logic) and 历史 (history) cannot function as adverbial originally, but can function as adverbial after taking de[1] (的). Moreover, they can no longer be used as subject or object. 急躁 (irritable), 狡猾 (sly), 谦虚 (modest) cannot function as adverbial originally, but can do so as adverbial after taking de[1] (的). However, the addition of de[3] (的) to 吃 (eat), 买 (buy), 做 (do) brings about changes in not only the grammatical function but also meaning. Therefore, in our opinion, words that take de[1] (的) and de[3] (的) or not, are not identical at all, and we cannot reckon that these words have the grammatical function of de (的).

de[2] (的) is rather special. Under usual circumstances, the functions of the constituent before de[2] (的) are basically the same, both having the properties of a state word, for example, 干干净净 (very clean), 干干净净的 (very clean plus de (的)). Only a constituent that is the reduplicated form of a monosyllable adjective has different properties from de[2] (的). There are two cases: (a) the monosyllable adjectives such as 胖胖 (fat fat), 红红 (red red), 长长 (long long) do not form words, but the constituent with de[2] (的) thus formed has the properties of a state word; (b) the reduplicated forms of monosyllable adjectives such as 好好 (good good), 慢慢 (slow slow), 大大 (big big) have the properties of an adverb, but the constituent with de[2] (的) thus formed has the properties of a state word. We regard "胖胖 (fat fat) plus de (的)" and "大大 (big big) plus de (的)" wholly as one word; the reduplicated forms of monosyllable adjectives such as 胖胖 (fat fat) are regarded as not being a word; the reduplicated forms of monosyllable adjectives such as 大大 (big big) are regarded as adverbs and different generalization words of "大大 (big big) plus de (的)". Other constituents with de[2] (的) and the constituents before de[2] (的) are regarded as one generalization word.

2.3.3 Brief summary

In classifying parts of speech, why should we discuss the identity of words? The fundamental reason is that part-of-speech classification aims at generalization words, as shown in the following two respects:

1. All the functions of the same generalization word belong to its own and cannot be classified into different units.
2. Different generalization words should be classified into different units, their grammatical functions should be examined respectively, and they should not be regarded as one combined unit.

2.4 Investigating the functions of a word

2.4.1 The materials used to investigate the functions

In investigating the functions of a word, we mainly rely on our language sense, the written materials after the foundation of New China and contemporary audio language materials such as radio broadcasting, movies and television.

For a few words that rarely occur in materials after the New China foundation, we use the materials that appeared after 1919. The materials before 1919
are not used to investigate the functions of a word.

Language is constantly changing; new usages and coinages may arise at
any time. If new usages and coinages are extensively used, strongly acceptable
and rather stable, then we use the new usages and some coinages to investigate
their functions. Otherwise, new usages and coinages are not used to investigate
their functions. For example, 投入 (input) is fundamentally a verb and cannot
be modified by 很 (very), but recently there is the expression 很投入 (very
input), whose meaning is different from the verb 投入 (input). The expression is extensively used and stable. Therefore, we determine that 投入 (input)
should be a verb and adjective concurrently. 专业 (profession) can only be
used as attributive and take de (的), thus being a distinctive word. However,
recently the expression 很专业 (very profession) has arisen, but it is not extensively used and is not stable. This is only a flexible use, and we do not use it to
investigate its function. 太业余了 (too amateur) is not a fixed expression and
cannot be used to investigate its function.

2.4.2 Dealing with special uses

Some words have their special uses in addition to their ordinary uses. We
divide their parts of speech according to their ordinary uses, not according to
their special uses. The special uses include the following cases:

(1) Syntactic transfer reference as discussed previously. It is a temporary use
and thus is not used to investigate the functions of a word.
(2) An obvious elliptical use. For example, sometimes an adverb can function
as a predicate, which, however, obviously omits the head word. We thus
do not reckon that the use of an adverb as a predicate is its function. For
example, 我不 (I do not), 你赶快 (You hurry up!)
(3) A word is used as quotation. Any word if used as quotation may change its
function and behave like a noun, therefore not being usable to investigate
its function. For example, the auxiliary word de (的) cannot be used as
subject; however, when used as quotation, it can function as subject, for
example, "de (的)" is an auxiliary.
(4) A word is used to denote numerical conversion and calculation. Conversion
and calculation are special expressions and have their own methods of
expression, which are different from those of everyday Chinese, thus not
being usable to investigate their functions. For example, 两个五是十 (two
times five is ten); 把斤换算成克 (convert jin into gram).
(5) A word is used as a fixed expression, and then we do not use it to
investigate its function. For example, the fixed expression 不男不女 (not
man not woman) cannot be used to claim that the words 男 (man) and
女 (woman) can be modified by 不 (not). The fixed expression 硬着头皮
(brave all rebuff) also cannot be used to treat 硬着 (brave) as verb.

(6) A few exceptions. Some words are historical legacies; some have no clear source. For example, 忽然之间 (suddenly), 短期内 (within a brief period) and 很 (very) are used as complements.

Notes

1 In fact, it is difficult to divide the boundary line between the compound word formed by combining root words and phrases not only in Chinese but also in other languages such as English. For example, "airmail" and "air mail". In the same dictionary such as *Webster's Ninth New Collegiate Dictionary*, the following pairs are correct: full moon/half-moon, back stroke/breaststroke, morning coat/tailcoat, water buffalo/watermelon.

2 Here, 国 (country) in classical Chinese collocates 与 (and) in classical Chinese; if 和 (and) in modern Chinese is used to replace 与 in classical Chinese, then the sentence will be ungrammatical.

3 The technical language hierarchy often uses classical Chinese elements; 叶 (leaf), 鳄 (crocodile), 胸 (chest), 肩 (shoulder) are also words in the classical Chinese hierarchy used in the everyday Chinese.

4 See *The Modern Chinese Learning Dictionary*.

5 See *The Modern Chinese Usage Dictionary*.

6 It means 支支吾吾 (hem and haw). For example, a line by Chen Jinfu: 枝枝节节, meaning somewhat hesitant to say something (Hong Shen's drama: *Wukui Bridge*). It also means fragmentary, for example: What I love about Peking is not something 枝枝节节 (fragmentary) but a whole portion of history that unites my soul (*Missing Peking* by Lao She).

7 A few combinations such as 为了 (for), 除了 (except), 人们 (people) and 他们 (they) are words; except for these, others should be regarded as phrases.

3 Possibilities and purposes of classifying parts of speech

3.1 Possibilities of classifying parts of speech

3.1.1 Controversy on the existence of Chinese parts of speech

Traditional Chinese linguistics does not deal with grammar and, of course, not parts of speech. Though traditional Chinese linguistics makes distinctions between notional words and functional words, motional words and still words, dead words and living words, these are only semantic distinctions and are not the strictly grammatical classification of parts of speech. The real classification of Chinese parts of speech began with *Ma's Grammar* (1898) by Ma Jianzhong. Drawing on the Western grammars, he classified the ancient Chinese parts of speech into nine parts of speech as follows: nouns, pronouns, motional words, still words (adjectives), descriptive words (adverbs), prepositions, conjunctions, auxiliary words, interjections.

But in the 1950s, Gao Mingkai (1953) put forward his opinion that there is no classification of parts of speech in Chinese; thus, a debate was triggered by *On Chinese Language* (1952), written by a former Soviet Union scholar named Н. И.КоHрад (see Gong Qianyan, 1997). КоHрад maintained that it was wrong that Н. я. Mapp of the Soviet Union and the Western linguists N. Maspero and B. C. Karlgren believed that Chinese was a primitive language. He pointed out that Chinese has a rich vocabulary, is expressive and is one of the most developed languages in the world. Maspero maintained that Chinese has no grammatical categories and parts of speech; his main evidence was that Chinese has no morphology. Other Soviet Union scholars and Karlgren had similar viewpoints. However, КоHрад refuted them from the starting point that it is proved that Chinese has a rich morphology and, hence, has its parts of speech.

1. Affixation: prefixes or suffixes: -zi (子), -er (儿), -tou (头), -jia (家), for example, 资本家 (capitalist); di- (第-), wu- (无-), for example, 无条件地 (unconditionally); zong- (总), for example, 总领事 (councilor general); fan- (反-), for example, 反革命 (counterrevolutionary).

2. Stress: when the latter syllable of a double-syllable word is stressed, it is a verb; if the former syllable is stressed, it is a noun, for example, 写字 (write), 道路 (road).
3. Change in tone: for example, 好 (hǎo, adjective, meaning "good"), 好 (hào, verb, meaning "like, love").
4. Lexicalization of grammatical forms: The analytical form of possible voices: 笑 (laugh), 可笑 (laughable), 可笑的 (laughable).
    The lexicalization of passive voice: 拘留 (detain), 被拘留 (be detained), 被拘留的 (detainable).
    The morphology of cases of a noun: 桥 (bridge, MOCT), 桥的 (of the bridge, MOCTa)
    臂 (arm, КИСТЬ), 用臂 (with the arm, КИСТЬю).
    他 (he, OH), 给他 (give him, eMy, dative).
    The morphology of tenses of a verb: 来 (come), 来了 (has come); 来 (come), 要来 (will come).

In addition to the above morphological evidence, a syntactic marker also serves as evidence that Chinese has parts of speech because it signifies the capability of a word to occupy a certain syntactic position in a sentence.

Therefore, КоНрад concluded the following

1. The modern Chinese language, the language of the Han nationality, is famous for its incomparably rich vocabulary.
2. Chinese vocabulary consists of words formed by morphology, whereas the word formation methods are diverse.
3. Chinese words can be classified into various parts of speech and contain all the concepts needed by a language. Chinese has its own special word formation methods.
4. When words are combined into speech, their grammatical forms come into being and have rich and diversified characteristics and meanings.
5. Chinese syntactic structure has its own precise rules, which reveal all the relations among words and phrases in a sentence.
6. Such highly developed vocabulary and grammatical structures enable Chinese to express any ideas of the people at the highest cultural level.

Gao Mingkai supported Maspero's view that "Chinese has no parts of speech" and objected to КоНрад's view. He proved his idea in the following way:

Major premise: the classification of parts of speech is based on the morphology of a word.
Minor premise: a Chinese notional word has no morphology (or its morphology is not enough to classify parts of speech).
Conclusion: therefore, there is no way to classify the parts of speech of a Chinese notional word.

Gao Mingkai proved that Chinese has no morphology in the following way:

1. Affixation is no morphology. Indo-European languages use word roots to express their forms. For example, *lego* (I'm reading now), *legis* (You're reading now) and *legit* (He's reading now) in Latin. In these examples, word roots and morphology are combined; the word root leg- cannot be independent. Latin has its genitive case: liber (book, subjective case), -libri (of the book/the book's, genitive case), but French uses the preposition "de", for example, de le livre, meaning "of the book", to express the same meaning. However, "de" is not in the genitive case, for it is separable from "livre". The affixation elements in Chinese like zhe (者), men (们), de (的) also belong to this type of constituent.

2. Changes in tone do not belong to morphology because they can only differentiate varied meanings rather than parts of speech. For example, 好 (hǎo, adjective, meaning "good"), 好 (hào, verb, meaning "like or love"), 钉 (ding, noun, meaning "nail"), 钉 (dìng, verb, meaning "put a nail into"), 背 (bēi, verb, meaning "carry on the back"), 背 (bèi, noun, meaning "back"; verb, meaning "recite").

Gao Mingkai summarized that for four reasons, Chinese has parts of speech; however, none of them is valid.

First, if Chinese had no parts of speech, then Chinese would be regarded as a kind of low-level language. However, whether there is classification of parts of speech or not is not an adequate basis for judging the level of a language. Though Chinese has no classification of parts of speech, its speakers have the notions of "noun, verb, adjective". The only thing is that these concepts are expressed by words rather than by grammar. Language development facts show that the morphology of Indo-European languages tends to be simplified, but we cannot say that they are low-level languages.

Second, the statement that Chinese has parts of speech is based on the meaning of a word instead of its form. But Chinese has no special forms to show its parts of speech, so the conclusion is that it surely has no parts of speech.

Third, when somebody believes that Chinese has parts of speech, their belief is based on the evidence that Chinese has a morphology. However, they are not clear about what morphology is, thinking that whatever constituent that follows or precedes a word root is morphology. As a matter of fact, zhe (者), de (的), le (了) and so forth in Chinese are just grammatical means (syntactic means); they are merely functional words rather than morphology.

Fourth, when somebody believes that Chinese has its parts of speech, their belief is based on the fact that it has changes in tone. But the changes in tone represent different meanings, and the reason why they think there is a difference in parts of speech after changes in tone is still based on the meaning of a word.

КоНрад's belief that Chinese has a morphology actually reveals that he looked at Chinese from the perspective of Indo-European languages. For example, he regarded 给他 (give him) as the dative form of a noun, and 用臂 (with the arm) as the instrumental case of a noun. In Gao Mingkai's opinion, most of the reasons why Chinese has no morphology are valid. But what a morphology is, is still a question that is difficult to answer. Judging from the criteria that a word root is part of a morphological form, "books", and "looked" cannot be regarded as a morphology, either. The difference between Gao Mingkai and КоНрад lies in whether Chinese has a morphology or not, and the common point is that both agreed that the nature of a part of speech is morphology. Because the nature of a part of speech is attributed to morphology and there are no definite criteria to judge what morphology is, it is hard to decide whether Chinese has parts of speech or not.

The publication of Gao Mingkai's essay resulted in a series of criticisms. His critics maintained the following views:

A. They agreed that the basis for classifying parts of speech is morphology (in other words, they agreed with the major premise), but they believed that Chinese has a morphology. Therefore, it has parts of speech. Such critics are represented by Lu Zongda (1955) and Yu Min (1955). Yu Min's Chinese morphology is shown in the following table:

Original word	Reduplication pattern	Change	Number of words	Meaning produced by reduplication	Part of speech
人 (rén, meaning person)	人人 (rén'rén, meaning each person)	Stress is shifted and a non-syllabic "r" is suffixed to noun and sometimes verb	1	every, each	noun
好 (hǎo, meaning good)	好好儿 (hǎohâo, meaning very good)	Stress is shifted and a non-syllabic "r" is suffixed to noun and sometimes verb, and there is change in tone	1	very	adjective
飞 (fêi, meaning fly)	飞飞 (fêifei, meaning fly one time)	weakened tone	1	one time	verb
三 (sân, meaning three)	三三 (sânsân, meaning many	zero	2	multiple	numeral

According to Yu Min and Lu Zonda, the table shows that nouns, adjectives and verbs have their respective rules of change. Therefore, they used these rules to classify the parts of speech of the three types of words:

B. They agree that the basis for classifying parts of speech is morphology in its narrow and broad senses, and that it can be used to classify parts of speech accordingly. Such critics are represented by Wen Lian and Hu Fu (1954), Б. Г. Мудроb (1954).

Morphology in its narrow sense: affix. For example, -zi (子), -er (儿), -tou (头) and reduplication.

Morphology in its broad sense: the capability of words to combine with each other. For example, 人 (person), 一个人 (one person), 笔 (pen), 三只笔 (three pens), 笑 (smile), 不笑 (not smile), 会笑 (can smile), 快 (fast), 很快 (very fast).

C. The function of a word is the basis for classifying parts of speech, and its meaning should be taken into account at the same time. This is represented by Cao Bohan (1955), who pointed out that "we feel that the criteria for classifying parts of speech must be decided by the function of a word in a sentence, and that the classification must be based on its meaning". Why must it be done in this way? The main reason is that parts of speech and the constituents of a sentence do not fit well with each other (namely, they do not correspond well with each other). In such a case, word meaning is needed to help classify parts of speech. For example, it is unnecessary to classify words that function as subject and object into two parts of speech because nouns functioning as subject and object all mean the names of things, whose attributes are the same.

Moreover, some scholars like Wang Li (1955) held that meaning, morphology and syntax should be jointly used to classify parts of speech.

Gao Mingkai (1954, 1955) refuted this as follows:

1. The function of a word and its capability to combine with other words cannot be used to classify parts of speech. Grammar can be classified into morphology and syntax, but parts of speech belong to morphology. The so-called parts of speech are the classification of words functioning as the building block of a language (in a word-bank, words are not combined into sentences); they do not refer to the position or function of a word in a sentence. If we classify parts of speech according to morphology in its broad sense, then we may commit the following mistakes:

a. The borderline between morphology and syntax is not clear. Morphology in its broad sense and the function of a word fall into the category of syntax rather than morphology. The part of speech of a word and its function in a sentence are two different concepts. For instance, in the past, wood was often used as the beam of a house, but now steel bars are used instead; thus, steel functions as wood, but steel is not wood. A part of speech is similar to the distinction between wood and steel, which has a static nature, but a subject and a predicate are similar to the distinction among a pillar, a beam and a wall, and have a dynamic nature. A part of speech refers to the attribute type of a word itself rather than its functional type. Wood, brick and steel are different from each other when they are stored in a warehouse and before they are put into use. They do not need to come into use for their distinction. If that is the case, it is just like what Li Jinxi observed, "The part of speech of a word should be judged by sentence, and without sentence, there is no part of speech".

b.   Because parts of speech of a word do not correspond to its functions, it is impossible to classify them according to the functions. For example, in English, a noun, the present participle of a verb and an infinitive can serve as the subject of a sentence. In Chinese, the problem is even more serious, not only the so-called noun, verb and adjective can occur at the position where a subject can do, but also the so-called morphology in its narrow sense cannot work effectively. For instance, 不去 (not go) is a so-called verb, while 不红 (not popular) is a so-called adjective.

2. Morphology in its narrow sense cannot be used to classify parts of speech. The existence of a morphology in Chinese should be recognized, but it is not enough to classify parts of speech. Morphology can be classified into two types: (1) word formation type (new words are formed by inflections); (2) inflectional type (changes in a word form are special signs for changes in parts of speech or express a particular grammatical category). Only the inflectional type can distinguish between parts of speech. But Chinese morphology belongs to the word-formation type: 者 (zhe), 子 (zi), 儿 (er) are all word-formation affixations, which have nothing to do with the classification of parts of speech. Words like 了 (le) and 们 (men) are functional words rather than a morphology.

Gao Mingkai stressed that the statement that Chinese has no parts of speech is based on grammar; however, Chinese speakers use concepts to tell difference between things, actions and properties. The old Slavic language has the category of even numbers, but Russian does not. However, Russian speakers also have the concept of even numbers.

The apparent reason why Gao Mingkai held that Chinese has no parts of speech is that he looked at the issue from the perspective of Indo-European languages, believing that parts of speech can be classified only according to a morphology. But the fundamental reason is that he failed to realize the nature of parts of speech. Their nature is not the morphological type, just like male and female are not distinguished by their physical features or their clothing. The critics of Gao Mingkai also failed to realize the nature of parts of speech, either continuing to regard morphology as their nature, insisting on finding some examples of Chinese morphology (Lu Zongda, Yu Min), or regarding the essence of a word as the function of a word (including the combination of words and syntactic constituents) (Wen Lian, Hu Fu, Cao Bohan). Actually, function (relations and positions in combination) is not the nature of parts of speech, either. Judging from this point of view, Gao Mingkai's viewpoint is correct: the part of speech and the function of a word in a sentence are different concepts; a grammatical function is not the nature of a part of speech. It is exactly for this reason that he was not convinced.

As Lv Shuxiang (1954) summed up, "if one thing or several things can be used to classify parts of speech, what does it matter if morphology cannot be used? In other words, we can put Gao Mingkai's minor premise aside for a while and change his major premise to do experiments".

Later, Gao Mingkai (1960) changed his viewpoint in a certain way and held that a "part of speech is, in essence, a matter of grammatical meaning; it is the grammatical meaning expressed by form" (p. 37). "Morphology and the combination capability of a word (including the syntactic combination capability, namely the syntactic function) both express grammatical meanings through some forms" (p. 37). "In the past, I just regarded morphology as the form to express the meaning of a part of speech. This view is too narrow, and now I should say that the morphological change, combination capability and syntactic function of a word and so on are all the exterior signs for the meaning of a part of speech. The problem is that no matter from what perspective, Chinese notional words show their multiple types of meaning, including the part-of-speech meaning without displaying the fixed characteristics of a part of speech" (p. 38). "A word having multiple parts of speech means that it has no parts of speech" (p. 38). Gao Mingkai admitted that "Chinese has the category of a part of speech" and that a grammatical function may reflect the properties of a part of speech. But because a Chinese part of speech has multiple functions, "a word can be simultaneously used as noun, adjective and verb" (meaning that a notional word can occur at the position where subject, predicate or attributive can). Hence, every notional word has multiple parts of speech, and this is the same as saying that there is no part of speech.

Gao Mingkai's arguments can be summed up as follows:

1. A part of speech is, in essence, the type of grammatical meaning a word expresses.
2. The morphology and grammatical function of a word express its grammatical meaning in a certain form.
3. Both the morphology and the grammatical function of a word express the exterior form of a part of speech.
4. Both the morphological and the grammatical functions of Chinese notional words demonstrate multiple types of part-of-speech meaning without displaying the fixed characteristics of a part of speech.
5. A word having multiple parts of speech means that there is no part of speech.
6. Therefore, a Chinese notional word does not have its part of speech.

Zhu Dexi (1960) pointed out that "the classification of parts of speech according to morphology is just a method or a means, which is possible because it is still based on the syntactic function of a word. Morphology is merely the indication of a function". Although the classification of parts of speech according to syntactic constituents is done from the perspective of function, "because the criterion is chosen too carelessly and the method too simple, it not only fails to classify parts of speech but also reaches the conclusion that a word does not have its fixed part of speech. This method has the fundamental mistake that it assumes that there is a close correspondence between sentence constituent and part of speech . . . but as a matter of fact, the relations between a sentence constituent and a part of speech are complicated" (p. 42). The classification of parts of speech according to sentence constituents concludes that a word has no fixed parts of speech, there being no part of speech in essence. This is one of the two important pieces of evidence for Gao Mingkai's insistence that Chinese has no parts of speech. Zhu Dexi pointed out that a word occurring at the position of subject is not necessarily a noun. For example, the adverb 不 (not) in the sentence 哭是不好的 (crying is not good) can be added before 哭 (cry); this proves that 哭 (cry) is a verb (p. 43). Therefore, it is wrong to believe that Chinese has no parts of speech simply because a sentence constituent is not enough to classify parts of speech.

The discussions on parts of speech in the 1950s mainly centered on whether Chinese has parts of speech or not. Earlier, Gao Mingkai, Liu Zhengtan and Li Xingjian held that Chinese does not have parts of speech, whereas others held the basic conclusion that Chinese has parts of speech, which, however, should be classified according to the function of a word. This raises two critical questions: (1) What is the criterion for classification? Because a Chinese part of speech does not correspond with a sentence constituent, the question is how to choose the classification criterion; (2) What is the essence of a part of speech? Because these two questions have not been answered, there are underlying disagreements. Moreover, the affirmative part of Gao Mingkai's arguments (for example, Arguments 1 and 3) failed to be accepted; instead, it was rejected together with the mistaken part.

Zhu Dexi (1985a) maintained that Chinese has two characteristics: (1) a part of speech does not correspond with a syntax constituent; (2) the principles for constructing a sentence and a phrase are the same. Xu Tongqiang (1994a, b) held that the discussions on parts of speech in the 1950s did criticize the approach of looking at Chinese from the perspective of Indo-European languages (a Chinese notional word does not have parts of speech because it has no morphology). This, however, opened up a new road for the popularity and development of another Indo-European language perspective. Parts of speech in Indo-European languages correspond well with sentence constituents; hence, it is necessary to classify their parts of speech. Since Chinese parts of speech correspond with multiple sentence constituents,

Chinese has no parts of speech. One sentence construction of Indo-European languages is "subject + predicate"; hence, their parts of speech correspond with sentence constituents. One Chinese sentence construction is "topic + description", which cannot be analyzed as "subject + predicate"; hence, it is impossible to classify Chinese parts of speech. The classification of Chinese parts of speech looks at Chinese from the perspective of Indo-European languages.

As a word has multiple functions and corresponds with multiple sentence constituents, it is impossible to classify its part of speech. Such a viewpoint is essentially identical to that of Gao Mingkai (1960). Namely, he assumed that there is a strict correspondence between a sentence constituent and a part of speech. If there is no such correspondence, then there is no classification of parts of speech. Zhu Dexi (1960) criticized this viewpoint. Its root cause is the failure to understand the nature of a part of speech, which is viewed as the capability of a word to function as sentence constituents.

Lv Shuxiang's criticism of Gao Mingkai's morphological classification of parts of speech also applies to classification according to sentence constituents. If one thing or several things can be used to classify parts of speech, what does it matter if morphology cannot be used? We can see that the viewpoint that Chinese has no part of speech mainly appears in two forms. In the 1950s, morphology was seen as the sole criterion for classifying parts of speech, and since Chinese has no morphology, it has no parts of speech. After the 1960s, the correspondence of a sentence constituent with a part of speech was established. Thus, since Chinese parts of speech do not correspond with sentence constituents, there is no way to classify them.

3.1.2 The evidence that Chinese has parts of speech: selectional restriction of grammatical positions on words

Grammatical positions have selectional restriction on words, as shown by the following example:

(1)　　 这　 一　 本　 书
　　　　|a||　　 b　　 |
　　　　|　　 c　 ||d|
　　　　|e|　 |f|

The hierarchical analysis shows that the example has a total of six grammatical positions, the five positions of b, c, d, e, f can be substituted by the following words:

Position b: 纸 (paper), 鱼 (fish), 石头 (stone), 花生 (peanut), 苹果 (apple) . . .
Position c: 那 (that), 每 (each), 任何 (any), 某 (certain), 另 (another), 惟一 (only) . . .

Position d: 不少 (not a few), 一切 (all), 许多 (many), 俩 (both) . . .
Position e: 两 (two), 三 (three), 四 (four), 十 (ten), 半 (half), 几 (several) . . .
Position f: 张 (sheet), 条 (bar), 块 (piece), 粒 (grain) . . .

Such substitutions have restrictions. For example, words in Position b cannot substitute words in Position c, and words in Position c cannot substitute words in Position f, and vice versa. That is to say, when words are combined, they are arranged not randomly but in an orderly way. Such orderliness is shown by the selectional restriction of grammatical positions on words. Different grammatical positions allow different words to enter. This reveals that a word itself has different properties, which can be used to classify words into different parts of speech.

Gao Mingkai and Xu Tongqiang mainly held that it is difficult to classify Chinese words into nouns, verbs and adjectives. With the above method, we can do so:

	no/not ~	*very ~*	*very ~ <object>*	*subject/object*
Verb	+	−/+	−/+	−/+
Adjective	+	+	−	−/+
Noun	−	−	−	+

Gao Mingkai maintained that the syntactic function of a word cannot be used to classify parts of speech. He admitted that words have different functions in different sentences, but that a part of speech belongs to the category of morphology, whereas a syntactic function belongs to the category of syntax. A part of speech belongs to a type of a back-up unit rather than the type in use. Therefore, the syntactic function cannot be used to classify parts of speech. Since a word has different syntactic functions, we have to ask why it has such differences. The reason still lies in the fact that a word itself has different properties. Though a syntactic function is not a part of speech, it reflects differences in the latter. This can be compared to wood and steel. Though their function is not identical, they both can be used as a beam, but wood can be used to make fire, while steel cannot. In contrast, steel can be used to make artilleries, while wood cannot. Their differences in function still result from their differences in properties. If we cannot directly tell them apart, we can distinguish them by their functions. That is, we should distinguish between the nature of things and the means to distinguish them. To distinguish them, we tend to adopt the exterior form or function as the means rather than directly recognize their essential properties. For example, we recognize something as wood by its appearance (wood texture) or by the feeling that it is heavy.

The use of grammatical functions as the criteria for classifying parts of speech does not mean that every difference in grammatical function can distinguish parts of speech. We just choose some of the grammatical functions to serve as the classification criteria. We will discuss this in detail later.

Judging from the universal characteristics of languages in the world, classifying parts of speech, especially classifying words into nouns and verbs, is common. Some scholars believe that some languages, for example, Nootka, do not have the classification of nouns and verbs (see Schachter, 1985):

(2) a.   Mamu•k-ma   qu•?as-?i
          Work (present tense)   man   this
          This man is working.
     b.   Qu•?as-ma   mamu•k-?i (mamu•k: statement→reference)
          Man (present tense) work   this
          The one who is working is a man.

Tagalog:

(3) a.   Nagtatrabaho   ang   lalaki
          is working   (topic)   man
          Man is working.
     b.   Lalaki ang   nagtatrabaho (nagtatrabaho: statement → reference)
          Man   (topic) is working
          The one who is working is a man.

Actually, this is just the transfer reference of a verb. A noun serves as the predicate of a judgment sentence. This is not enough to explain that there is no classification of nouns and verbs, however. For example, when a verb has a transfer reference and serves as a subject or object, the definite determiner "?i" is required (similar to the transfer reference of an adjective in English). Hence, Example (4) in the following is invalid. Furthermore, the meaning of a transfer reference is produced only in a special context.

(4) * Qu•?as-ma mamu• k
       man (present tense) work
       One is working is a man.

3.2 Purpose for classifying parts of speech

The purpose for classifying parts of speech is actually concerned with the attitude toward language. Householder (1952) classified the then structural linguists into two schools: the Hocuspocus group and the God's Truth School. The attitude of the Hocuspocus group to language structure is that language is merely a pile of messy materials, and that a linguist's task is just to arrange and combine them together so as to work out a structure; hence, structure relies on man's arrangement to some extent.

The attitude of the God's Truth School to language structure is that the structure of a language is inherent and lies in its materials, and that the task of a linguist is to find out such a structure and describe it as clearly, economically and precisely as possible.

Z.S. Harris and J.R. Firth belong to the Hocuspocus group, and K. L. Pike belongs to the God's Truth School.

Today's argument on the purpose for classifying Chinese parts of speech and whether they are objective is similar to the attitude of the above two schools toward language.

A part of speech is based on the properties of a word, which exist objectively in language. To classify parts of speech, one should first determine the properties of a word in that language and how many properties a word contains, and then one can consider how to classify it into parts of speech according to its properties.

The classification has two types: natural classification and artificial classification. Classification according to the basic characteristics of an object is called natural classification, while artificial classification is opposite to natural classification. Artificial classification tends to serve a particular practical purpose, whereas natural classification mainly reveals natural laws but does not serve a practical purpose.

From the perspective of natural classification, parts of speech are summed up from syntactic structures rather than artificially determined in advance for the convenience of grammatical analysis. Judging from the processes of classifying parts of speech, syntactic rules exist first and then the classification. So, the convenience of grammatical analysis is not the purpose for, but the result of, classifying parts of speech. The purpose is to reveal the nature of a word itself and to build a general reference system. In other words, a language is not chaotic but well structured and has its natural order independent of a linguist. A word has its own grammatical positions in this natural order. Our views on language belong to the God's Truth School. We do not object to other scholars for their adopting the language views of the Hocuspocus group, but this book adopts those of the God's Truth School.

Therefore, from the perspective of natural classification, we should not consider how to make part-of-speech classification helpful for syntactic analysis; instead, we should do so as it should be done and, as a matter of fact, not take the convenience of syntactic analysis into consideration. For example, "the old" in English can serve as a subject; for the convenience of syntactic analysis, "old" can be classified into noun, as was done in the past. This is indeed convenient for syntactic analysis: noun + verb = sentence. But this analysis is not true to reality; in fact, the "old" here still has the properties of an adjective:

The (extremely) old need a great deal of attention.
The (very) best are yet to come.
He is acceptable to both (the) young and (the) old.
The number of jobless is rising.

From the perspective of natural classification, part-of-speech classification for the purpose of syntactic analysis may easily lead to wrong parts of speech, and the so-called convenience thus obtained may be false. For example, Li Jinxi's loaned parts of speech and his statement (1924) that the part of speech of a word is based on a sentence may be very convenient for syntactic analysis. A verb becomes a noun when it serves as a subject; a noun becomes an adjective when it serves as an attributive. Such treatment can simplify syntactic rules, yet this is convenient but not true to fact. At least a large number of verbs in the position of a subject still have the properties of verbs. Actually, this is not convenient at all because such treatment changes the question into judging whether a word is a noun or a verb. This is still as difficult as before.

Only when we deal with a word that belongs to several parts of speech simultaneously should we consider the convenience of grammatical analysis (see Chapter 7).

Classification not only discovers an objective natural order but also establishes a general reference system, which refers to such a system that expresses multiple relationships among things or phenomena. It has the characteristic that, though it may be established on the basis of one characteristic, it can explain many other relationships (Forey, 1983: 152–153). Biological classification is such a system (which reveals not only the evolutionary relationship of living things but also their habitus and physical characteristics). The classification for the Periodic Table of Elements also falls into such a system (which reveals both the chemical and physical properties of an element). The classification of parts of speech also belongs to such a general reference system. Of course, in specific applications, there are some changes in how elaborately detailed the classification is. The strategies for classifying conversional words and some minor parts of speech may be ignored, but the overall pattern should be kept.

Many people do not think about universality and believe that the purpose for classifying parts of speech is for the convenience of grammatical analysis. Therefore, they think that different types of grammar (grammar for experts, for computing and for foreigners to learn Chinese) should have different systems of parts of speech. In fact, behind these different systems, there exists a fixed and universal system, and the changed system is just the temporary adaptation of the universal system to a circumstance.

4 Essence and expressional functions of a part of speech

4.1 The paradoxes of distribution nature theory

4.1.1 Viewing distribution as the essence of a part of speech

The essence of a part of speech is concerned with what it is.

One view holds that a part of speech is concerned with distribution, and that its essence is distribution. This has been a common view since structural linguistics was born and is mainly explained in two ways: (1) directly explained with the distribution view; (2) explained with Saussure's syntagmatic and paradigmatic relations in addition to the distribution analysis according to US descriptive linguistics.

US descriptive linguistics links distribution with word classes. Bloomfield (1926) held that the position occupied by a form is its function, and that all the forms that share the same function make up a word class. The largest word class in a language is the part of speech in the language.

Saussure's *Course of General Linguistics* points out that language is a form but not an entity. It is so called because the value of a linguistic constituent is not decided by the constituent itself but by relations among constituents. There are two types of relations among linguistic constituents: syntagmatic relation and associative relation. The syntagmatic relation means that linguistic constituents combine one with another, for example, in French:

Dieu est bon (God is kind).
Re-lire (reread).

The associative relation means that the constituents that share common things cluster into classes through association in a human's memory. For example, the French word *enseignement* (education, noun) makes one associate *enseigner* (educate, verb) because they are cognates. *Changement* (change, noun, the suffix -*ment* is the same as -ment in *enseignement*), *education* (education, noun, synonymous). *Enseignement* has associative relations with these words.

Saussure's associative relation is not the relation in the sense of distribution; it mainly refers to a cognate relation, a similar word-formation relation, a synonymous relation and so on.

To avoid the notion that the term "associative relation" may have a psychological meaning, later scholars use the term "paradigmatic relation" (see Cheng Zenghou, 1988).

Furthermore, Chen Wangdao (1941, 1942, 1978) combined paradigmatic relation with distribution analysis: constituents make up larger combination units; the constituents located in the same grammatical positions in a combination unit form paradigmatic classes (in terms of words' paradigmatic relations, a paradigmatic class is a part of speech); however, combination selects members from a paradigmatic class. That is to say, a combination unit is a sequence of parts of speech. For example:

Combination relation

p	我	读	书 (I read books)
a	他	看	报 (He reads newspaper)
r	王同志	写	文章 (Comrade Wang writes articles)
a			
d	a	b	c
i			
g			
m			
a			
t			
i			
c	noun	+ verb + noun	

There are three possible scenarios of distribution in the idea that words having the same distribution form a part of speech:

1. Single-item distribution (for the convenience of explanation, distribution here refers to the grammatical position a constituent occupies, differing from the definition of Harris). The definition of a part of speech in terms of paradigmatic relation belongs to this scenario; that is to say, words having the same function belong to the same part of speech.
2. Overall distribution. It means that all the distributions are the same, which is basically the view held by Bloomfield.
3. Partial distribution. Words having in common partial distribution characteristics are clustered into one part of speech.

No matter in what sense the distribution is, the viewpoint that a part of speech is of distribution type cannot be upheld. The viewpoint that a part of speech is of a distribution type is not self-contained. In the following, we will prove this.

4.1.2 Paradoxes of the single-item distribution view

The explanation for this is threefold.

1. Words having the same single-item distribution do not necessarily belong to the same part of speech, for example:
    (1) Adverb-headword: 很大 (very big); 拳头大 (the fist is big)
        Subject-predicate: 今天晴 (today is fine); 今天晴天 (today is a fine day)
        Subject-predicate: 人好 (the person is good); 去好 (to go is good)
        Predicate-object: 喜欢吃 (like to eat); 喜欢酒 (like wine)
        For another example, words that can function as subject include the words that belong to different parts of speech, such as 电话 (telephone), 认真 (serious), 休息 (rest), 许多 (many), 慢性 (chronic) and 十 (ten).
2. Words falling into the category of the same part of speech do not necessarily have the same single-item distribution. For example, 年事 (person's age) and 现年 (current year) can only function as subjects; 剧毒 (high toxicity) and 泡影 (zilch) can only function as an object. They do not have the same single-item distribution, but all are nouns.
3. There are quite a huge number of grammatical positions. It is hard to tell clearly how many grammatical positions there are exactly; however, words that can enter into each and every grammatical position are quite different. If a single-item distribution represents one part of speech, then there may also be a huge number of parts of speech, many of whose members are conversional. The classification of words into their parts of speech according to single-item distribution makes a part of speech have one-to-one correspondence with a syntactic constituent; thus, nearly every word belongs to several parts of speech. Therefore, such a classification makes no sense.

Hence, the view that words having the same single-item distribution fall into the same part of speech is not valid.

4.1.3 Paradoxes of overall distribution

1. The more grammatical positions for classifying parts of speech there are, the larger numbers of parts of speech may exist. Even if the grammatical position for classifying parts of speech is a little different, the parts of

speech thus classified may be quite different. Therefore, the classification of words into their parts of speech according to overall distribution has almost no possibility of definite parts of speech.

2. Even if we can discover all the grammatical positions in a language to classify parts of speech, we may find that words whose distributions are completely identical barely exist. If we firmly believe that words having the same distributions belong to one part of speech, then nearly every word belongs to a part of speech, which is almost like saying that there is no part of speech.

To demonstrate this point of view, we select 60 words and examine their distributions to 36 grammatical positions, with the examination results given in Table 4.1-1 (see appendices). The results show that among the 60 words, only four pairs, such as 人 (person) – 桶 (barrel), 岁数 (age) – 举动 (action),慢性 (chronic) – 私人 (private) and 究竟 (on earth) – 亲自 (personally) have completely identical distributions. If parts of speech are classified according to overall distribution, then the 60 words should be classified into 56 parts of speech. Chen Xiaohe (1999) tried to classify parts of speech with the overall distribution of words having the capability to function as syntactic constituents, resulting in more than 1,000 parts of speech. Such a classification of parts of speech follows a rather strict distribution. The word classes thus classified belong to the "distribution classes of words" rather than "parts of speech". Obviously, a "part of speech" is a class in its specific sense, and not all "classifications of word classes" belong to a part of speech. The classification of parts of speech is based on categorization. That is to say, the classified parts of speech are different in their categories and patterns. The classification of words solely according to the same or different distribution and the classification of words into monosyllable/double-syllable words or simple/compound words do not constitute parts of speech. In fact, the way most scholars classify parts of speech is to select some of distribution characteristics, while neglecting some other distribution characteristics. This way of classifying parts of speech is in conflict with the view that a part of speech has the nature of distribution. If we accept that this is reasonable, we should negate it. Furthermore, what distributions should be selected for classifying parts of speech is not decided by distributions themselves but relies on other factors.

4.1.4 Paradoxes of the partial distribution view

Some people have held the first two distribution views, but there are only a few practitioners. Most scholars select partial distribution characteristics to classify parts of speech, while neglecting other distribution characteristics. If parts of speech are viewed as distribution classes, in theory, what problem does this view bring about?

1. If distribution is viewed as the nature of a part of speech and partial distribution characteristics can be selected among the distribution of words as the criteria for classifying parts of speech, then a certain class of words should have the distributions of internal universality and external exclusivity. But our examination results show that such distributions cannot be found actually.

    This phenomenon will be illustrated by the main grammatical functions of the following major parts of speech. First, let us look at the distribution that has no internal universality (for specific data on noun, verb and adjective, see the statistical results in Chapter 2.1 in Volume 2):

    (1) Nouns

    - * Subject: 作为 (action), 地步 (extent), 新生 (rebirth), 剧毒 (high toxicity), 来由 (cause), 泡影 (zilch), 一体 (oneness), 着落 (whereabouts), 国际 (internationality), 乐子 (fun), 鬼胎 (evil plot)
    - * Object: 年事 (person's age), 谈锋 (eloquence), 现年 (current year), 浑身 (whole body), 爱憎 (love and hatred), 常言 (proverb)
    - * Quantity ~: 私人 (privacy), 人类 (mankind), 总和 (sum), 航运 (navigation), 列强 (power), 内心 (heart), 手工 (handwork), 哥 (brother), 军事 (military affairs), 利弊 (advantages and disadvantages)
    - *Attributive ~: 私人 (privacy), 外界 (exteriors), 出手 (disposal), 现年 (current year), 敌我 (enemy and ourselves), 中外 (China and foreign), 国际 (international)
    - *Attributive: 把戏 (trick), 称号 (title), 大局 (overall situation), 法子 (method), 方针 (policy), 害处 (harm), 举动 (action), 巨响 (blare), 计策 (stratagem), 理由 (reason), 勾当 (deal), 胆子 (gut), 跟头 (fall), 差错 (error), 措施 (measure)

    (2) Verbs

    - * 不 (not) / 没 (not) ~: 致使 (cause), 看待 (regard), 注定 (doom), 查收 (check), 胆敢 (dare), 活像 (look exactly like), 有关 (relate to), 总计 (total), 连绵 (stretch), 出落 (grow), 有待 (await), 捉摸 (fathom), 地处 (locate), 肄业 (attend college)
    - *Predicate: 住 (able to, for example, 抓不住 (unable to grasp)), 着 (used for emphasis, for example, 打不着 (cannot beat)), 透顶 (thoroughly), 绝顶 (extremely)
    - *Adverbial: 备用 (standby), 参半 (half), 留念 (souvenir), 不息 (incessantly), 不等 (variously), 同上 (ibid.), 扑鼻 (assail nostrils)
    - *~ real object: 工作 (work), 休息 (rest), 飞跃 (leap), 搏斗 (fight), 劳动 (labor), 成长 (grow), 到来 (arrive), 倒退 (reverse), 着想 (consider), 发育 (growth), 浮动 (float), 交际 (social), 考试 (examination), 崩溃 (collapse), 相反 (opposite), 颤 (quivering), 颠倒 (reversed)

    (3) Adjectives

    - *Not ~: 荣幸 (honored), 异常 (abnormal), 微小 (trivial), 有趣 (interesting), 难免 (unavoidable), 无情 (ruthless), 不安 (uneasy), 不错 (alright)

- *very ~[1]: 平衡 (balanced), 相同 (same), 耐烦 (patient), 景气 (prosperous), 道德 (moral), 像话 (right), 起眼 (eye-catching), 要脸 (face-saving), 寻常 (ordinary)
- *Predicate: 个别 (individual), 巧合 (coincidental), 停当 (ready), 停妥 (orderly)
- *Complement: 荣幸 (honored), 异常 (abnormal), 辛勤 (diligent), 间接 (indirect), 静 (quiet), 固执 (stubborn), 抱歉 (sorry), 个别 (individual)
- *Attributive: 不错 (good), 高兴 (glad), 荣幸 (honored), 齐全 (complete), 停当 (ready), 糟糕 (bad), 一样 (same), 对 (right), 多 (numerous), 挤 (crowded), 久 (long time), 痒 (aching), 痛 (painful)

(4) State words

- *Predicate: 飞快 (fast), 崭新 (brand-new), 火热 (fervent)
- *Complement: 羞答答 (bashful), 皑皑 (snow-white), 好端端 (in perfectly good condition), 雄赳赳 (valiant), 指指点点 (gossiping-about), 磨磨蹭蹭 (dawdling), 旖旎 (graceful), 闪闪 (sparkling), 重重 (numerous)
- *Followed by de[2]: 皑皑 (snow-white), 闪闪 (glittering), 旖旎 (graceful), 优良 (excellent), 崭新 (brand-new), 金黄 (golden-yellow), 碧绿 (green)

(5) Distinctive words

- *Attributive: 亲爱 (dear), 心爱 (lovely)
- *Followed by ~ de (的): 公共 (public), 机要 (confidential), 日用 (daily), 聋哑 (deaf and dumb), 接力 (relaying), 集约 (intensive)

Distributions that genuinely have internal universality presumably include "~ 量 (quantity)" of a numeral, "数 (several) ~" of a measure word and an adverb's function as adverbial, but all of them have no external exclusivity.

Let us look at the distributions that have no external exclusivity in the following:[2]

(1) Subjects, objects: Nearly all the parts of speech of notional words, except adverbs, can function as subjects and objects; for example, nouns, verbs, adjectives, locatives, time words, place words and numerals can do so.
(2) Attributives: Nearly all of the parts of speech of notional words except adverbs and measure words can function as attributives; for example, nouns, verbs, adjectives, distinctive words and numerals can do so.
(3) Attributives ~: Nearly all of the parts of speech except distinctive words, adverbs and numerals can be modified by attributives; for example, nouns, time words, measure words, verbs and adjectives can do so.
(4) Predicates: Nearly all of the parts of speech except distinctive words, adverbs and numerals can function as predicates. Generally, verbs,

adjectives and state words can function as predicates. Under certain conditions, nouns, time words, numerals and adverbs can also function as predicates.

(5)   Adverbials: adverbs, adjectives, state words, numerals and measure words, time words, locatives and place words can function as adverbials.

(6)   Verbs and adjectives have the grammatical function that they can be placed after 不 (not).

(7)   Verbs and adjectives have the grammatical function that they can be placed after 很 (very) or 很不 (not at all).

(8)   Verbs, adjectives and state words can function as complements.

(9)   Verbs and adjectives can have their complements.

(10)   Verbs and adjectives can function as objects.

(11)   Verbs, adjectives, state words, nouns, time words and numerals can be modified by adverbials.

(12)   Link-verb predicates: verbs, adjectives and state words can be the immediate constituents of a link-verb predicate construction.

(13)   Verbs, adjectives, nouns and time words can be followed by le (了).

(14)   Verbs and adjectives can be followed by zhuo (着).

(15)   Verbs and adjectives can be followed by guo (过).

(16)   Nouns, verbs, adjectives and time words can be modified by numerals and measure word phrases.

(17)   Measure words and nouns can be modified by numerals.

(18)   Locatives, place words and time words can function as the objects of 在 (in), 到 (to), 往 (toward).

(19)   Numerals, adjectives and demonstratives have the grammatical function of being followed by measure words.

The general grammatical functions[3] that can be genuinely deemed to have external exclusivity presumably include only "suo (所) plus verb", "state word followed by de (的)" and the "possessive attributive plus numeral and measure word plus noun" of demonstratives, but all of them have no internal universality.

2.   Some words have quite different distributions but belong to the same part of speech. 年事 (person's age) and 现年 (current year), as cited above, can only function as subjects; 剧毒 (high toxicity) and 泡影 (zilch) can only function as objects. They have quite different distributions, but all are nouns. 活像 (look exactly like) and 企图 (attempt) can only appear at the central position of a predicate and cannot be modified by 不 (not); zhu (住) and zhuo (着) can only appear at the position of a complement but belong to verbs.

3.   Even if we can select some distribution characteristics to classify parts of speech, we find that we cannot actually use the distribution characteristics themselves to answer why we select these distribution characteristics instead of others as the criteria for classifying parts of speech. Different

parts of speech are obtained with the selection of different criteria for classifying them. For example, we classify into adverbs the words that can only function as adverbials, but why cannot we classify the words that can only function as complements into only-complement words and the words that can only function as objects into only-object words? In other words, if we have no classification of parts of speech in mind beforehand, if factors other than distribution characteristics are not considered, we cannot classify parts of speech purely according to distribution characteristics.

In the following, the distinctions between verb and adjective are taken as examples to show that they cannot be determined only by distribution.

Table 4.1 gives the distinctions between verb and adjective proposed by Zhu Dexi (1982b):

Theoretically speaking, there are, indeed, at least the following methods for classifying parts of speech of the language facts reflected by these two grammatical functions:

1. Classifying the language facts into two types according to whether they can take their real objects or not: Type A (transitive predicate words: 想 (think), 唱 (sing)) and Type B (intransitive predicate words: 醒 (wake), 大 (great)).
2. Classifying the language facts into two types according to whether they can be modified by 很 (very) or not: Type A (degree predicate words: 想 (think), 大 (big), Type B (non-degree predicate words: 唱 (sing), 醒 (wake)).
3. Give conjunctive relationship to words that can be modified by 很 (very) and take objects, and they are classified into four types: Type A (+ very ~ ∧ + ~ object: 想 (think)), Type B (- very ~ ∧ + ~ object: 唱 (sing)), Type C (* very ~ ∧ – ~ object: 醒 (wake), Type D (+ very ~ ∧ * ~ object: 大 (big)).
4. Give conjunctive or disjunctive relationship to words that can be modified by 很 (very) and take objects, and classify them into two types: Type

Table 4.1 Zhu Dexi's (1982b) criteria for distinguishing between verbs and adjectives

	Taking 很 (very)	Taking objects	Example
1	+	+	想 (think), 怕 (fear), 爱 (love), 喜欢(like), 关心 (concern), 相信 (believe)
2	—	+	唱 (sing), 看 (watch), 切 (cut), 有 (have), 讨论 (discuss), 分析 (analyze)
3	—	—	醒 (wake), 锈 (rust), 肿 (swell), 咳嗽(cough), 游行 (parade), 休息 (rest), 死(die)
4	+	—	大 (big), 红 (red), 远 (far), 累 (tired), 饱(full), 结实 (strong), 干净 (clean)

A (* very ~ ∨ + ~ object: 想 (think), 唱 (sing), 醒 (wake)), Type B (+ very ~ ∧ * ~ object: 大 (big)).

5. Give conjunctive or disjunctive relationship to words that can be modified by 很 (very) and take objects, and classify them into two types: Type A (+ very ~ ∨ * ~ object: 想 (think), 醒 (wake), 大 (big)), Type B (* very ~ ∧ + object: 唱 (sing)).

6. Give conjunctive or disjunctive relationship to words that can be modified by 很 (very) and take objects, and classify them into two types: Type A (+ very ~ ∨ + ~ object: 想 (think), 唱 (sing), 大 (big)), Type B (* very ~ ∧ * ~ object: 醒 (wake)).

7. Give conjunctive or disjunctive relationship to words that can be modified by 很 (very) and take objects, and classify them into two types: Type A (* very ~ ∨ * ~ object: 想 (think), 唱 (sing), 醒 (wake), 大 (big)), Type B (+ very ~ ∧ + ~ object: 想 (think)).

8. Give conjunctive or disjunctive relationship to words that can be modified by 很 (very) and take objects, and classify them into two types: Type A ((+ very ~ ∨ + ~ object ∨ (* very ~ ∧ * ~ object)): 想 (think), 醒 (wake)), Type B ((* very ~ ∧ + ~ object)∨(very ~ ∧ * ~ object)): 唱 (sing), 大 (big).

In addition, there are some other classification methods and criteria. Table 4.2 gives all the possible classifications:

The table shows that both "很 (very) ~" and "~ object" are not the grammatical characteristics of a verb or an adjective. Only when the two functions are given a conjunctive or disjunctive relationship can grammatical characteristics be obtained. For example, "*很 (very) ~ ∨ + ~ object" is the grammatical characteristic of a verb. "+ 很 (very) ~ ∧ * ~ object" is the grammatical characteristic of an adjective. But the problem is that, as shown

Table 4.2 The possible classifications obtained with the two criteria of "~ object" and "很 (very) ~"

	a	b	c	d		a	b	c	d
1	想 (think), 唱 (sing)	醒(wake), 大 (big)			8	想(think), 醒(wake)	唱(sing), 大(big)		
2	think, big	sing, wake			9	think sing	wake	big	
3	think	sing	wake	big	10	think wake	sing	big	
4	think, sing, wake	big			11	think big	sing	wake	
5	think, wake, big	sing			12	sing, wake	think	big	
6	think, sing, big	wake			13	sing, big	think	wake	
7	sing, wake, big	think			14	wake, big	think	sing	

in the above table, when the two functions are joined together with a conjunctive or disjunctive relationship, there can be numerous classifications. If only distribution is taken into account, it is hard to explain the reason why only Method Four instead of other methods should be selected. The reason why we select Method Four is that its syntactic function is in agreement with its semantic type. The parts of speech classified according to this syntactic criterion exactly exhibit the differences in semantic type: action and properties.

4.1.5 Paradoxes of the similarity theory

Because it is difficult to identify the distribution characteristics of a part of speech that have internal universality and external exclusivity, the view that distribution characteristics are its nature can be questioned. Scholars attempt to use the similarity theory to explain the distribution nature of a part of speech, thinking that it is collected according to the distribution similarity of words. According to whether or not words are collected with their prototype, there are the prototype theory of a part of speech and its overall similarity theory.

4.1.5.1 Paradoxes of the prototype theory

Shi Youwei (1994) held that Chinese parts of speech should be treated flexibly. Yuan Yulin (1995, 1998) used the prototype theory or the family similarity theory to deal with the relationship between distribution and a part of speech. He (1995, 1998, 2001) thought that a part of speech belongs to the prototype category, and that its typical members share some distribution characteristics that other parts of speech do not have. The distribution characteristics of atypical members are incomplete, but we can put them into one class according to their similarity with typical members. For example, 耐烦 (patience) and 景气 (prosperity) cannot be modified by 很 (very), but typical adjectives can not only be modified by 很 (very) but also be followed by 不很 (not very). The two words in the above example can also be followed by 不很 (not very). Therefore, according to the family similarity principle of distribution, we can assert that 耐烦 (patient) and 景气 (prosperous) belong to adjectives. For another example, words such as 极 (extremely) can be used as adverbials or complements. In the light of the typical adverb 太 (too), which can only be used as an adverbial, we can classify 极 (extremely) into an adverb. Then, in light of the atypical adverb 极 (extremely), we can classify into an adverb the word 透顶 (thoroughly), which can only be used as a complement.

This brings about the following problems:

1. According to the family similarity principles of distribution, we can place almost all notional words into one class. For example, typical adjectives can function as attributives; hence, we may think that nouns such as 相同 (sameness), 大型 (large-scale), 彩色 (color), 木头 (wood), 社会 (society)

that can function as attributives belong to atypical members of adjectives, thereby classifying them as adjectives. Typical adjectives can function as adverbials; hence, we may classify into adjectives words such as 亲自 (personal) and 全力 (all-out effort) that can function as adverbials. They may function as complements; hence, we may classify into adjectives words 雪白 (snow-white), 来 (come), 着 (zháo) that can function as complements. They can function as predicates; hence, we may classify into adjectives words such as 吃 (eat), 洗 (wash) and 休息 (rest). You may presumably say that 颜色 (color), 木头 (wood) and 雪白 (snow-white) cannot be modified by 很 (very); therefore, they are not adjectives. But the question is: how do you know that being preceded by 很 (very) is a necessary grammatical function of an adjective, whereas "functioning as an attributive is its sufficient grammatical function"? The family similarity principle itself cannot answer this question. Because of this, there is no way to operate in reality. For example, because typical adjectives can be preceded by 完全 (completely) ~, we may classify into adjectives not only words such as 相同 (same) and 相反 (opposite) that behave like this but also words such as 属实(verify), 腐烂 (perish), 静止 (standstill), 停顿 (pause) and 融化 (melt) that usually belong to verbs.

2. A word may be classified into Class A or B according to Distribution Characteristics x or y. Then, the family similarity principle works by relying on perception. For example, it is possible to classify into distinctive words, words such as 主要 (primary), 次要 (secondary), 新型 (new-type), 亲爱 (dear) and 基本 (basic) that can be used as attributives but not predicates. It is also possible to classify them into adjectives because they are typical adjectives and thus can be modified by 最 (the most). In other words, when a word has the distributions of either Class A or B words, the family similarity principle cannot be used to classify their parts of speech.

3. In reality, there is no way to implement this method.

Shi Youwei (1994) first determined the distribution characteristics of typical members of a part of speech and then determined which part of speech the atypical members belong to according to the correlation values (membership degree) of the distribution and the word-formation of atypical and typical members. For example, compared with 冷 (cold), a typical member of adjectives, the correlation value of 温 (warm) is only 1.5; its value of correlation with 彩色 (colorful), a typical member of distinctive words, is 6. Because 温 (warm) has a higher correlation value than a typical member of distinctive words, it is classified into distinctive words. But the fact that it can be preceded by 有点~了 (a bit ~) can contradict that it belongs to distinctive words; instead, it should be classified into adjectives. Hence, correlation values do not truly reflect the parts of speech of a word.

Lu Yingshun (1998) proposed a formula for calculating the similarity degree: S=N/M, where M refers to the number of standards of a certain part of speech, and N refers to the number of words that satisfy such standards. If S ≥ = 0.5, then words basically belong to the part of speech. He gave the five standards of a verb: (1) A verb can be modified by 不 (not) and can have the question form of "X or not X". (2) It can be followed by dynamic auxiliary words such as le (了) and qilai (起来) and so on to denote perfection, commencement and so on, or be followed by a zero label to denote a habitual action or attribute. (3) A good many verbs can be followed by an object. (4) A verb can occur after a noun to form a subject-predicate relation. (5) It can be followed by numeral and measure-word objects and go together with other constituents to form the predicate and complement constructions.

According to his calculation, 吃 (eat) satisfies all these standards, and S=1. 跑步 (run) satisfies Standards 1, 2 and 4, and S=0.6; thus, they can be classified into verbs. 课文 (text) satisfies no standards, and S=0. 春天 (spring) satisfies Standards 2 and 4, and S=0.4; thus, they cannot be classified into verbs.

The standard that S≥0.5 is too broad and includes ordinary adjectives. But Lu Yingshun thought that verbs and adjectives should belong to one part of speech. For the time being, we will not discuss this issue here. We should look at whether or not they have internal universality. Now we use this method to test the following words:

担待 (undertake) satisfies Standards 4 and 5 but does not satisfy 1, 2 and 3. S=0.4;
雷动 (thunderous) satisfies Standard 4 but does not satisfy Standards 1, 2, 3 and 5. S=0.2;
媲美 (rival) satisfies Standards 3 and 4 but does not satisfy Standards 1, 2 and 5. S=0.4.

All these words belong to verbs; if S ≥ 0.5 is followed, then we can only exclude them from verbs; hence, this method still does not work. Yuan Yulin (1995) thought that "because a part of speech is a prototype category, all the members of a part of speech often do not share the distribution characteristics that the members of another part of speech do not have. Therefore, there is no way to use the conjunction/disjunction relations among several distribution characteristics to strictly determine the part of speech of a word. We can only use the advantageous distribution probability of a certain class of words to broadly determine their parts of speech. But the broad determination is too fuzzy and not satisfactory". "We can use the distribution characteristics unique to typical members to determine their parts of speech comparatively strictly".

Let us look at whether or not we can use the prototype theory as the criterion for classifying parts of speech.

The strict definition of noun: a noun is a class of words whose members can be modified by numerals and measure words but not adverbs.

This definition is very strict indeed. Only 78% of nouns can be modified by numerals and measure words, and only a small number of nouns can be modified by ordinary adverbs (2%). If scope adverbs are also taken into account, then many more nouns can be modified by adverbs, for example: 光馒头就吃了三个 (Three pieces of steamed bread alone have been taken). Thus, we do not know which nouns are typical nouns.

The broad definition of a noun: a noun is a class of words that is often used as a typical subject (doer of an action) and a typical object (object of an action and resultant object), and generally cannot be modified by adverbs.

Yuan Yulin treated 野外 (out in the field) and 下面 (underneath) as nouns, but following the prototype theory, it is difficult to classify them into nouns. If nouns generally cannot be modified by adverbs, then how should nouns that can be modified by adverbs be handled? Should they be regarded as generally not being modified by adverbs or generally being able to be modified by adverbs? Should words such as 年事 (person's age) that can only be used as subjects, and words such as 地步 (extent) that can only be used as objects still be classified into nouns? Should words such as 私人 (private) that are not often used as subjects still be classified into nouns?

Adverbs are defined as words that can only be used mainly as adverbial.

Can 很 (very) and 极 (extremely) be considered to be used only as adverbials by and large? Yuan Yulin classified 透顶 (thoroughly) and 透 (thorough) into adverbs, but these two words really fall short of the criterion that they can only be used as adverbials by and large.

The broad definition of state words: a state word is often used as a predicate, a complement and an adverbial, and cannot be modified by adverbs such as 很 (very) and 不 (not) and so on. Only 86% of state words can be used as a predicate; only 50% of them can be used as a complement; only 15% of them can be used as an adverbial. It is not clear whether there are conjunctive or disjunctive relations among the three grammatical functions. If there is a conjunctive relation, then only 6% of words can be classified into state words; if there is a disjunctive relation, then adverbs are also classified into state words.

All in all, (1) we should not only look at the grammatical functions of a word but also their frequencies, but it is almost impossible to do such complicated calculations. (2) There are no clear criteria for judging "often". (3) Almost every part of speech has an imbalance among its grammatical functions; therefore, it is unsafe to classify parts of speech according to their major grammatical functions (see Chapter 2.4.7 in Volume 2).

4. The prototype theory does not give a method for determining the prototype of a part of speech. In fact, it is impossible to determine its prototype according to distribution itself.
5. The root problem is that the prototype theory argues in a logical circular way. The determination of the prototype of a part of speech can only be achieved under the condition that, first, categories are classified and their typical distribution characteristics are known. In other words, when you say that words such as 桌子 (desk), 石头 (stone), 人 (person) and 马 (horse) are typical members of nouns, you already know that a noun is

a part of speech and that a typical noun can be modified by a numeral and a measure word. If you do not know these facts, you cannot say so. Therefore, this actually causes circular arguments: on the one hand, the prototype of a part of speech and its distribution characteristics must be determined after categories are classified; on the other hand, the category classification depends on the determination of the prototype of a part of speech.

We do not prefer to classify parts of speech based on the prototype theory; this does not mean that we altogether deny their prototype nature. In our opinion, although parts of speech do not belong to the prototype category and the prototype theory is not operable, they do have a prototype nature in terms of apparent characteristics (rather than intrinsic characteristics). The prototype nature expresses itself mainly in the following four respects:

1. The prototype nature of lexical meaning. A part of speech has its prototype lexical meaning. For example, nouns denote things; verbs denote action; typical nouns denote three-dimensional material objects (see Taylor, 1989).
2. The interconnection among parts of speech, lexical meanings and syntactic constituents has a prototype nature. For example, the interconnection among actions, verbs and predicates is prototypical and unmarked, whereas the interconnection among actions, verbs and subjects is non-prototypical and marked (see Croft, 1991).
3. Humans' perception of parts of speech is prototypical. Namely, they rely on a prototype to identify them.
4. A certain class of words has a prototypical nature in terms of distribution.

But these are not of the intrinsic prototypical nature of parts of speech. What is similar to this phenomenon is sex. Sex is not a prototypical class. What determines sex is the XY sex chromosome or the XX sex chromosome. Male and female can be clearly classified according to whether there is a Y chromosome or not, but from the perspective of the apparent characteristics of sex, it has its prototype. These apparent characteristics include (taking human beings as an example) physiological characteristics, physical appearance characteristics, clothing characteristics, behavior characteristics, disposition characteristics, occupational characteristics and so on. Sometimes things of the same type are so different in apparent characteristics that it is difficult to establish the interconnection among them only according to these apparent characteristics. Only through their intrinsic characteristics can we establish their interconnection, for example, between coal and diamonds.

The prototype of a class expresses itself at different levels. We can neither regard the prototypical nature of apparent characteristics as that of intrinsic characteristics nor classify objects into a class solely according to the similarity of apparent characteristics. We cannot think that a part of speech belongs to a prototype category because it has a distributional prototype, just as we cannot think that sex belongs to a prototype category because it is prototypical in terms of clothing characteristics and disposition characteristics.

Because the prototype theory does not hold and is not operable, we do not use it; instead, we use the characteristic theory. Fundamentally speaking, the reason why the prototype theory does not hold is that distribution is not an intrinsic characteristic of a part of speech; its intrinsic characteristic is an expressional function. Distribution is but the apparent characteristics of a part of speech. Therefore, we cannot successfully classify parts of speech only according to distribution.

4.1.5.2 *The overall similarity clustering view*

To avoid a circular argument, we can use another method, which is not to determine the prototype of a category in advance but to cluster words into their classes solely according to their distributional overall similarity. Following the prototype theory, a part of speech is a class of words classified and clustered according to their distributional similarity. To verify the feasibility of the method, we carried out the clustering analysis of the distributional similarity degree of the 60 words listed in Table 4.1-1 (see appendices in Volume 2). Assuming $0 \leq S \leq =100$, the formula for calculating the distributional similarity degree (S) between two words is as follows:

$$S = 100 \times I/(P - I),$$

where I is the number of identical grammatical positions at which two words appear, and P is the sum of the numbers of grammatical positions. For example, there are 19 grammatical positions where 干净 (clean) may appear, and there are nine grammatical positions where 附近 (nearby) may appear. Five grammatical positions are shared by the two words, whose similarity degrees are:

$$S = 100 \times 5/(285)=22.$$

Table 4.1-2 (see appendices in Volume 2) gives the mutual distributional similarity degrees of the 60 words calculated according to Table 4.1-1. The sequencing of the mutual similarity degrees of the 60 words according to their size produces Table 4.1-3 (see appendices in Volume 2).

The tables show an interesting fact: the word that is the most similar to another word in terms of distribution does not necessarily belong to the same part of speech. For example, the ten words that have the highest degree of distributional similarity to the state word 花白 (grizzled) include 日常 (daily), 临时 (temporary), 野生 (wild), 慢性 (chronic, distinctive word), 私人 (private, noun), 众多 (multitude, numeral), 相同 (same, adjective), 注定 (doom, verb), 个别 (a few, numeral) and 钢笔 (fountain-pen, noun). However, the ten words that have the highest degree of distributional similarity to the verb 着想 (consider) include 荣幸 (honored, adjective), 酷热 (swelter, state word), 注定 (doom), 休息 (rest, verb), 野生 (wild, distinctive word), 相同 (same, adjective), 洗 (wash, verb), 花白 (grizzled, state word), 慢性 (chronic, distinctive word) and 亲爱 (dear, distinctive word).

Of course, to cluster individual words into their classes strictly according to their overall similarity, we need to do so with clustering analysis. Clustering analysis uses a mathematical technique to gather individual words of a close distance (large similarity degree) into clusters and further gather them into larger clusters and eventually into one large cluster. There are different methods for calculating the distance among individuals or clusters, thereby forming different clustering analysis methods. The most commonly used clustering analysis methods include the nearest neighbor linkage technique, the neighbor linkage technique and the average linkage technique. The nearest neighbor linkage technique treats the nearest distance (the largest similarity degree) among individuals in two clusters as the distance between them. For example, the similarity degrees among five individual words such as a, b, c, d, e respectively are:

The similarity degree between *a* and *b* is the largest (10), and we gather them first and foremost into one cluster (A). Among the remaining individuals, the similarity degree between *d* and *e* is the largest (9). We then gather them into one cluster (B). The similarity degree between the individual *a* in Cluster A and the individual *e* in Cluster B is 8, larger than the remaining similarity degrees. Therefore, Clusters A and B are gathered into the larger Cluster C. The similarity degree between the individuals *c* and *a* in Cluster C is 7. Thus Cluster C is gathered into the larger Cluster D. The above clustering operation can be expressed in a tree-hierarchy diagram (Figure 4.1):

The furthest neighbor linkage technique treats the longest distance (the smallest similarity degree) among clusters as the distance between them. Taking the scenario in Table 4.3 as an example, the clustering results with the furthest neighbor linkage technique are represented as Figure 4.2.

The average linkage technique treats the average distance among individuals in two clusters as the distance between two clusters. Taking the scenario in Table 4.3 as example, the clustering results with the furthest neighbor linkage technique are represented as Figure 4.3 (see p. 70):

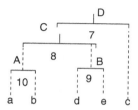

Figure 4.1 The nearest neighbor linkage hierarchy

Table 4.3 The similarity degrees among five individual words

a	b	C	d
b			10
c	7	4	
d	3	5	5
e	5	8	5	9

We carried out a clustering analysis of the distributional similarity degrees among the 60 words listed in Table 4.1-3 (see appendices in Volume 2). Because the furthest neighbor linkage technique is rather extreme, the book uses only the nearest neighbor linkage technique and the average linkage technique to perform the clustering analysis, whose results are shown in Figures 4.4 and 4.5.

As we can see, the results clustered with either the nearest neighbor linkage technique or the average linkage technique are quite different from the parts

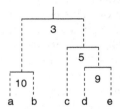

Figure 4.2 The furthest neighbor linkage hierarchy

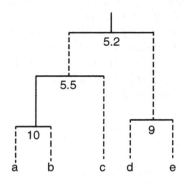

Figure 4.3 The average neighbor linkage hierarchy

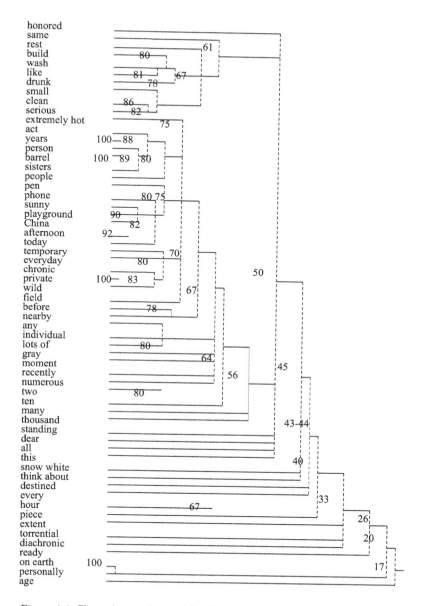

Figure 4.4 Clustering analysis of distributional similarity degrees of 60 words (nearest neighbor linkage technique)

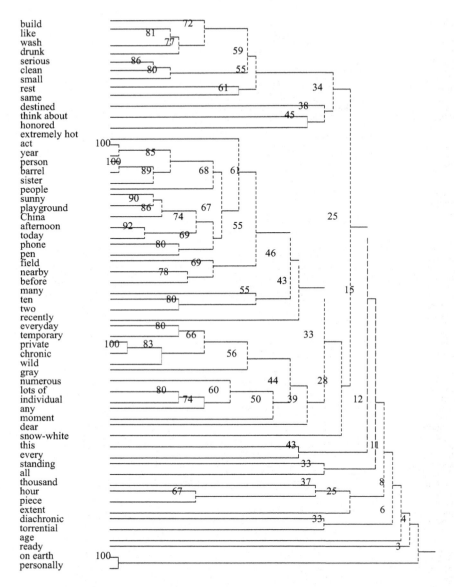

Figure 4.5 Clustering analysis of distributional similarity degrees of 60 words (average linkage technique)

of speech classified in the usual ways. For example, if the average linkage technique is used, the state word "grizzled" first and foremost clusters into one class the words that are usually classified into distinctive words. The verb 着想 (consider) gathers the adjective 荣幸 (honored) first and then the transitive verb 注定 (doom). The adjective 相同 (same) first gathers the verb 休息 (rest). The distinctive word 慢性 (chronic) first gathers the noun 私人 (private). Classifying parts of speech in this way is perhaps meaningful in the engineering sense but obviously has no linguistic meaning. These are not the parts of speech in a linguistic sense.

In 1986, when we had just begun the study of Chinese parts of speech, we held the distribution view and tried to classify them according to the overall distribution similarity degrees of words. But small-scale experiments indicated that parts of speech thus classified show no resemblance to those in a linguistic sense. Therefore, we abandoned our view of their distribution nature and explored their further level of distinction.

4.1.6 Brief summary

It is impossible for us to classify parts of speech solely according to the distribution of words. We actually neglect some of their distributional differences and select some others in order to do so. Which distributional characteristics are to be selected are not determined by distribution itself; some other factors must be taken into account. In fact, we are seeking valuable grammatical meanings of the parts of speech thus classified. In the following sections, we shall mention that we classify parts of speech by selecting those characteristics that can separate parts of speech in terms of their grammatical meanings. Hence, the nature of a part of speech is not of the distribution type.

The nature of classifying parts of speech according to distribution is to classify them according to the selectional restriction of the syntactic positions on words. This selectional restriction must have certain bases to be used as the conditions for selectional restriction; otherwise, the selection may be unrestricted. Then, what are the bases for the selectional restriction? If we think that parts of speech are of the distribution type and that the basis for selectional restriction is distribution, then we can only say that the reason why a word can appear at a certain grammatical position is that the word can appear at that position. This is actually a tautology. In other words, some words belong to a certain part of speech is because they have the same distribution. The reason why they have the same distribution is that they belong to the same part of speech. This becomes a circular argument. But in the view of conjuring structuralists, this is the final solution to the problem; they refuse to talk about meaning or justification. At this moment of linguistic development, we are already not satisfied with such a solution and still desire to understand the reason behind it. In our opinion, the reason why words have identical or different grammatical distributions is that they have identical or different expressional functions and semantic types, which are the intrinsic nature of a part of speech.

4.2 Bases of selectional restriction of a grammatical position on words

What is the intrinsic nature of part of speech? We discuss this question on the basis of a grammatical position's selectional restriction on words.

As mentioned before, a grammatical position has selectional restrictions on words that may enter into it. Here we explain that this selectional restriction requires bases. In the following, we shall cite examples of how a syntagmatic position selects words, to explain the basis for selectional restriction.

(1) Among words such as 送 (send), 买 (buy), 卖 (sell), 借 (borrow), 抢 (rob), 炒 (fry), 还 (return), 赔 (compensate), 偷 (steal), 沏 (infuse), 做 (make) and 织 (weave), some can enter Position I, and some can enter Position II, while others can enter Position III:

(2) Words such as 送 (send), 买 (buy), 卖 (sell), 借 (borrow), 还 (return) and 赔 (compensate) can have two objects, for example:

    I.   ~ + 给 (give) + A + B. For example, 送给他一本书 (give him a book): 送 (send), 卖 (sell), 借 (borrow), 还 (return), 赔 (compensate)

    II. 给 (give) + A + ~ + B. For example, 给他买一本书 (buy a book for him): 买 (buy), 借 (borrow), 偷 (steal), 抢 (rob), 炒 (fry), 做 (make), 沏 (infuse), 织 (weave)

    III. ~ + A + B. For example, 送他一本书 (send him a book): 送 (send), 卖 (sell), 借 (borrow), 还 (return), 赔 (compensate), 买 (buy), 偷 (steal), 抢 (rob)

According to the different positions in which they appear, we can classify them into the following three classes (see Zhu Dexi, 1979):

a. Send, sell, borrow, return, compensate (appearing at Positions I and III)
b. Buy, borrow, steal, rob (appearing at Positions II and III)
c. Fry, infuse, weave (appearing at Position II)

Although the parts of speech are classified according to distribution, they are scarcely regarded as a distributional type. What factors influence a word's appearance position? We may not hesitate to give the answer that it is the semantic meanings themselves: Class A has the "giving" meaning; Class B has the "obtaining" meaning; Class C has the "making" meaning. In other words, the selectional restriction of the above three positions is based on the semantic meanings of the words themselves; words of different semantic meanings enter into different positions. Therefore, speaking intrinsically, the three classes belong to semantic types.

As a matter of fact, there must be bases for the syntagmatic position's selectional restriction on words. Unless a syntagmatic position has no selectional restriction on words, then any words can enter into the position optionally. The above examples are based on the semantic meanings; similarly, the more abstract grammatical positions that exclude semantic meanings are also based on the selectional restriction on words. Let us consider the following English example:

(3)　(The) ~ are/is acceptable.

At the position given in Example (3), the following can appear: children, adults, students, teachers, young, old, smoking, teaching and son on. But the appearance of "grow, born, study, teach, smoke" is not allowed. Then what are their selectional bases? Apparently it is not their semantic meanings. We should not think that the basis for selectional restriction is a part of speech because this leads to a circular argument. Not all words that can appear at this position are nouns. "Young" and "old" can take adverbials of degree, for example: "The very young are acceptable". They can have comparative degrees and superlative degrees. "Smoking" is not a noun because it can take its object, for example: "Smoking cigarettes is acceptable". Analysis of the similarity and difference of the words that can or cannot appear at a certain position shows that the similarity of the words that can appear at Position 3 is that they have the function of reference, while those that cannot have the function of statement. The basis for the positional selectional restriction is expressional function.

Let us consider the following Chinese examples:

(4)　X de (的) ~　　　　(5) ~ 好治 (It is easy to treat ~)

The words that can appear at the position in Example (4) include 书 (book), 桌子 (desk), 愿望 (desire), 感觉 (perception), 出版 (publication), 研究 (study), 到来 (arrival), 依赖 (dependence), 美丽 (beauty), 开明 (enlightenment) and 邪恶 (evil), and all having referential meanings. Words that cannot appear at this position include 是 (be), 有 (have), 知道 (know), 觉得 (feel), 舍得 (willing to part with), 看见 (see) and 愿意 (willing), and all having statement meanings. Words that can appear at the position in Example (5) include 肠炎 (enteritis), 红眼病 (acute conjunctivitis), 感冒 (cold), 拉肚子 (diarrhea), 流鼻血 (nosebleed), 急性 (acute), 慢性 (chronic) and so on. What do these words have in common? They are all referential words. The basis of the two grammatical positions' selectional restriction on words can also be regarded as their expressional function.

In our opinion, the reason why words have different distributions is that they have different properties, which are, therefore, their expressional functions and semantic types.

4.3 Types and hierarchies of the expressional function

4.3.1 What is the expressional function?

In our opinion, the intrinsic nature of the large category of parts of speech such as substantive words, predicate words and modification words is the expressional function. Therefore, it is necessary to make a special effort to discuss it.

As mentioned before, a grammatical position has a selectional restriction on words, whose root basis is the expressional function of a word.

Zhu Dexi (1982b) was the first to propose the concepts of reference and statement, which we call the expressional function.

The main reason for proposing the expressional function is to describe the distinction between *a* and *b* in the following examples:

(6) a. 想打球 (want to play basketball) (object of statement) – want what
     b. 看打球 (watch playing basketball) (object of reference) – watch what

(7) a. 子贡贤于仲尼(《论语・子张》) (Zigong is more virtuous than Zhongni) (*Zizhang* in *Analects of Confucius*)
     b. 见贤思齐焉,见不贤而内自省焉(《论语・里仁》) (When we see a man of virtue and talent, we should think of equaling him; when we see a man of a contrary character, we should turn inward and examine ourselves.) (*Liren* in *Analects of Confucius*)

(8) a. 失所长则国家无功,守所短则民不乐生. (With a lack of the meritorious, the state will be powerless; if keeping the unmeritorious, the people will not enjoy their life.)
     b. 以无功御不乐生,不可行于齐民. (《韩非子・安危》) (Without power, it is not feasible for the Qi people to enjoy their life.) (*Chapter on Safety and Danger* in the book *Han Fei Zi*)

(9) a. 急性肠炎好治,慢性肠炎不好治. (Acute enteritis is easy to treat, but chronic enteritis is not easy to treat) (modification).
     b. 急性好治,慢性不好治. (The acute are easy to treat, but the chronic are not easy to treat.) (reference)

(10) a. 我们研究问题 (We study problems), (embodied as an assertion)
     b. 研究很成功 (The study is highly successful), (embodied as an object)

(11) a. 这个苹果大 (The apple is large)
     b. 有大有小 (Some are large; some are small)

(12) a. 一切财产 (all property)
     b. 放弃一切 (abandon all)

(13) a. I walk every day (embodied as an assertion)
     b. I take walk every day (embodied as an object)

Although the meaning of a word is identical on different occasions, it can be expressed by different patterns. For example, 研究 (study), 大 (large), 一切

(all) and "walk" in Examples (10) *a* and *b* through (13) have identical lexical meanings, their meaning expression patterns are different: *a* is expressed as a statement, while *b* is expressed as a reference. An expressional function refers to the pattern by which words express their semantic meanings.

The expressional function is different from a syntactic constituent. On the one hand, an identical expressional function can be used as different syntactic constituents, for example, 研究 (study) in Example 10 (b) and 一切 (all) in Example 12 (b) both have reference meanings, but the former is a subject, while the latter is an object. On the other hand, a different expressional function can be used as identical syntactic constituents, for example, 保持安静 (keep quiet) and 觉得安静 (feel quiet). The first 安静 (quiet) has a reference meaning, and the second has a statement meaning, but both are used as objects. A syntactic constituent starts from the relationship among immediate constituents, while an expressional function is based on a word's own properties. In other words, we should regard the expressional function as a word's own properties rather than the properties of its grammatical environment.

An expressional function has four basic types: a statement denotes assertion and can be modified by adverbials; a reference denotes object and can be modified by attributives. A modification modifies or restricts a statement or reference, which depends on whether a word modifies a statement or a reference; it can be further classified into a predicate modification and a substantive modification. An auxiliary has a regulatory effect.

4.3.2 *Types of expressional function*

4.3.2.1 *Statement and reference*

The two most fundamental expressional functions of a language are a statement and a reference. Zhu Dexi (1982b) distinguished between a statement and a reference, pointing out that a statement is used to answer the question "in what manner?" and that a reference is used to answer the question of "what?" An object and a subject both can be a statement or a reference. For example, Example (6) *a* is a statement, and *b* is a reference. He further pointed out that a reference means that there is a referent, and that a statement means that something is signified. Further explanation is as follows:

A statement denotes an assertion, points to another constituent and is generally used to answer the question of "in what manner".

A reference denotes an object, has an inward meaning and is generally used to answer the question "what?"

The distinction between de (的) and di (地) in a modifier position somewhat reflects the mental distinction between a reference and a statement.

A statement can be modified by an adverbial; a reference denotes an object and can be modified by an attributive.

There are exceptions for the above formal characteristics, for example:

(14) 公认他是好人 (It is generally recognized that he is a good person) – *recognize what; *recognize in what manner

(15) 彩色电视 (color television) – what television (but 彩色 (color) is not a reference)

(16) 悄悄对他说 (talk to him in whispers) – talk to him in what manner (but 悄悄 (in whispers) is not a statement)

The opposition between a statement and a reference is the most fundamental in language, but it still has not been completely settled how to use formal characteristics to distinguish between the two.

4.3.2.2 Modification

Some constituents are neither references nor statements. The following three scenarios show that the constituent at a modifier position should be regarded as the third type of expressional function – a modification.

1. When distinctive words, adverbs, numerals and measure words are used as modifiers, they are neither subjects nor objects. Only at the position of subject or object are they subjects or objects; only at the position of predicate are they statements. Compare the following:

    (17) a. 急性肠炎好治，慢性肠炎不好治 (Acute enteritis is easy to treat, but chronic enteritis is not easy to treat).

    b. 急性好治,慢性不好治 (The acute are easy to treat, but the chronic are not easy to treat).

    (18) a. 有男生,有女生 (There are schoolboys and schoolgirls).

    b. 有男有女 (There are men and women).

    (19) a. 许多题都不会 (I cannot answer many questions).

    b. 许多都不会 (Many I cannot answer).

    (20) a. 我不去 (I do not go).

    b. 我不 (I do not).

2. An adjective has different properties at a predicate position or a modifier position:

    (21) a. 衣服干净 (The clothes are clean). 衣服不/很干净 (The clothes are not/very clean).

    b. 干净衣服 (the clean clothes)   *不/很干净衣服 (the not/very clean clothes)

    (22) a. 学习认真 (study seriously)   学习不 / 很认真 (The study is not/very serious)

    b. 认真学习 (serious study)   *不/很认真学习 (study not/very seriously)

干净 (clean) and 认真 (serious) can be modified by adverbials at the predicate position but cannot be modified at the modifier position, indicating that their properties have changed.

A noun has different properties at the subject or object position, or at the modifier position:

(23) a. 买木头 (buy wood)   买十根木头 (buy ten pieces of wood)
      b. 木头房子 (wooden house)   *十根木头房子 (a house of ten pieces of wood)

木头 (wood) can be modified by numerals and measure words at the subject or object position, but cannot be modified at the modifier position, indicating that its properties have changed. But with de (的) or di (地) added, the original ungrammatical sentences are now grammatical:

(24) 不/很干净的衣服 (not/very clean clothes)
(25) 不/很认真地学习 (study not/very seriously)
(26) 十根木头的房子 (a house of ten pieces of wood)

Therefore, the constituent at a modifier position should be regarded as the third expressional function: a modification.

The characteristics of a modification are as follows: it modifies and restricts a statement or reference; its meaning is outward oriented, dependent by itself and dependent on a statement or a reference, and cannot be modified by attributives and adverbials.

There are two types of modifications: substantive modifications and predicate modifications. A substantive modification modifies a reference and functions as an attributive; a predicate modification modifies a statement and functions as an adverbial.

The direct use of 干净 (clean), 认真 (serious) and 木头 (wood) as attributives or adverbials has different properties from the above words followed by de (的)/di (地) to be used as attributives or adverbials. When they are directly used as attributives or adverbials, their expressional function is a modification, and thus they cannot be modified by other modifiers. But when they are followed by de (的)/di (地) and used as attributives or adverbials, they still function as statements or references, and still have the characteristics of a statement or a reference. Namely, they can be modified by other modifiers.

4.3.2.3 Auxiliary

Auxiliaries refer to the expressional functions of functional words such as prepositions, conjunctions, modal particles, auxiliary words and so on. They can be regarded as neither statements nor references nor modifications, and are added to functional words to play the following auxiliary roles:

1. Change the expressional function of a supplementary constituent. For example, de (的) denotes a modification; zhe (者) a reference; zhi (之) a modification.
2. Denote a certain supplementary meaning. For example, a modal particle denotes a mood; auxiliary words like le (了), zhuo (着) and guo (过) denote tense or aspect.
3. Play a conjunctive role like a conjunction.

In addition, the expressional function of an interjection is neither a statement, a reference, a modification nor an auxiliary. An interjection denotes a call, answer or exclamation. In fact, it is a constituent beyond the language system because it has a special phonological system without tone and is always used independently.

4.3.3 *The expressional patterns and performance mechanisms of a language*

References and statements form the basic building blocks of expressional patterns of a language. A modification cannot be used independently but modifies or restricts referential and statement constituents by being attached to them. An auxiliary word is attached to referential, statement or modification constituents to play a regulatory or transformational role (see Guo Rui, 1997). The relationships among expressional functions are shown in the following diagram:

reference————statement   (primary opposites)

| |

Substantive modification————predicate modification (secondary opposites)

Auxiliary constituents are attached to references, statements or modifications and are not shown in the diagram. The diagram indicates that a complete meaning can be expressed with the opposite of a reference and a statement. A modification does not change the primary opposition but restricts it. In other words, a modification is attached to a reference, and its combined form is still a reference, for example, 彩色电视 (color television). A modification is attached to a statement, and its combined form is still a statement, for example, 认真学习 (study seriously). Namely, a modification has no independence. An auxiliary word can be attached to any position of the two opposites and play a regulatory role.

We notice that the combination of a statement with a reference forms a larger unit whose expressional function is still a statement, for example, both 看+书 (read a book) and 他+看 (he reads) are still statements. Thus, we can say that a statement is more independent than a reference. Therefore, we can conclude that a statement is the most primary and important expressional function in a language. A modification depends on a statement or a reference; the combination of a statement with a modification still produces a statement on the whole. The combination of a reference with a modification still produces a reference on the whole. Therefore, the status of a modification is the lowest. Its independence, importance and size can be expressed with the following inequation:

Statement > reference > modification > auxiliary

4.3.4 *Hierarchies of expressional functions*

(27) a. 小王黄头发 (Little Wang has yellow hair).
      b. 小王也黄头发 (Little Wang has yellow hair, too).
      c. 小王一头黄头发 (Little Wang has a head of yellow hair).

In Example (27) *a*, 黄头发 (yellow hair) can be used to answer the question "what is it like?" and can be added with an adverbial, thus being a statement. However, it can also be added with an attributive, and in this regard, it should be considered as reference. This is contradictory. But if an adverbial and an attributive appear simultaneously, the adverbial is always preceded by the attributive. Namely, the adverbial is in the outer layer; the attributive is in the inner layer.

(28) a. 小王也一头黄头发 (Little Wang has a head of yellow hair, too).
      b. 小王一头也黄头发 (The head of Little Wang has yellow hair, too).

This indicates that the expressional function of 黄头发 (yellow hair) has two layers: the inner layer is a reference; the outer layer is a statement. For another example:

(29) a. 这本书的出版 (the book's publication)
      b. 这本书的及时出版 (The book's punctual publication)
      c. *及时这本书的出版 (*Punctual the book's publication)

In Example (29) *a*, 出版 (publication) is modified by an attributive and is thus a reference. But it can be added with an adverbial, which can only be followed by attributive *b* but not preceded by attributive *c*. Therefore, 出版 (publication) is a statement in its inner layer but a reference in its outer layer.[4]

In the above, we classified expressional functions into two combination layers. From the perspective of their own properties, we can classify them into intrinsic and external expressional functions. The intrinsic expressional function of a word is inherent; the external expressional function is the one ultimately realized by a word in its certain grammatical position. The expressional functions in the two layers are in agreement. 小王 (Little Wang) in Example 25 is a reference either in the inner layer or in the outer layer. Sometimes they are not in agreement, for example, 黄头发 (yellow hair) in Example (28) *a* and 出版 (publication) in Example (29) *a*. In this case, the external expressional function of a word works temporarily.

The distinction between a statement and a reference by using "what is it like?" and "what" is in the outer layer. Example (28) *a* can only answer the question "what is it like"? instead of "what"? Example (29) *a* can only answer the question "what"? instead of "what is it like"?

4.3.5 *Expressional functions and parts of speech*

In essence, expressional functions are the bases for distinguishing words in the large category of parts of speech such as substantive words, predicate words and modification words. Please look at the following examples (Lu Jianming, 1991a):

(30) 我们厂只做~,不做~ (Our factory only makes ~, does not make ~).

The words like 柜子 (cabinet), 桌子 (desk), 沙发 (sofa), 板式 (plate type) and 框式 (frame type) can appear at the two positions in Example (30), having the construction "make ~". Some of them are substantive words and others are non-substantive words like 板式 (plate type) and 框式 (frame type), but 做 (make) is usually regarded as a verb that can take only a substantive object. In fact, the so-called substantive object is a reference object.

Furthermore, 应该 (should) in Chinese can be followed by either 去 (go), 看 (see) or 三个人 (three persons), 星期一 (Monday), 阴天 (overcast) and others. It is regarded as a verb that can take a predicate object.

Words like 赏 (reward), 罚 (punish) and 诛 (kill) in classical Chinese are regarded as verbs that take substantive objects, but we can find examples such as 赏有功 (reward the meritorious), 罚有罪 (punish the guilty) and 诛不义 (kill the unrighteous). In fact, the so-called substantive object is a reference object.

In the above examples, the concepts of word properties such as the so-called substantive word and predicate word actually involve the expressional functions such as reference and statement. It is a pity that we did not realize this in the past. Here we can identify word properties with expressional functions. But how should we explain the contradictions that a verb functions as a substantive object (reference object) such as 有功 (meritorious) in the phrase 赏有功 (reward the meritorious), and that a substantive word functions as a predicate object (statement object) such as 阴天 (overcast) in the phrase 应该阴天 (should be overcast)? This has something to do with the hierarchies of parts of speech. Just like an expressional function is classified into two layers, so is a part of speech.

The intrinsic basis for the distinction among parts of speech such as a noun and a verb is actually the distinction between expressional functions such as reference and statement. The distributional and morphological distinctions between parts of speech are simply the extrinsic manifestations of distinctions in expressional function. Just like expressional functions have layers, so should parts of speech be classified into two levels. The parts of speech that correspond to intrinsic expressional function are called parts of speech at the lexical level; the parts of speech that correspond to extrinsic expressional function are called parts of speech at the syntactic level. The part of speech at the lexical level is a word's inherent one, which is that labeled in a dictionary, while that at the syntactic level results from the use of a word, which needs to be controlled by syntactic rules. The parts of speech at the two levels are generally the same, but are different in a few cases. The 出版 (publication) in Example (29) *a* is a verb at the lexical level but a noun at the syntactic level. Corresponding to the intrinsic levels of three expressional functions, the parts of speech of substantive words can also be classified into three: predicate word (statement), substantive word (reference) and modification word (modification). If parts of speech are not classified into levels, it may be difficult to describe Chinese sentence structures with categories such as NP and VP. For example, Example (10) *b* is represented as "VP+VP" and Example (27) *a* as "N+NP". Such representations hardly reveal their phrasal structures. How should we understand the difference in the two layers of expressional function? We believe that there exists a covert marker of expressional function transformation, as shown in the following analysis:

(31) 小王也一头黄头发 (Little Wang has a head of yellow hair, too).

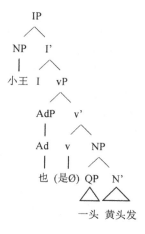

(32) 学习很重要 (Study is very important).[5]

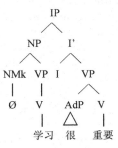

(33) 这本书的出版 (the publication of the book)

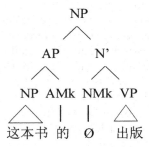

黄头发 (yellow hair) in Example (31) still has the properties of a noun because it can take its attributive 一头 (a head of). Because the functioning of a substantive phrase as a predicate denotes judgment and requires the appearance of the overt 是 (is), for example, 小王不是黄头发 (Little Wang is not of yellow hair.), it can be treated in the way that its syntax requires that it should have a covert link verb. Because the link verb 是 (is) is silent, it seems that the pronounced 一头黄头发 (a head of yellow hair) undertakes the function of 是一头黄头发 (is of a head of yellow hair), thus having the properties of a predicate word on the whole. In Example (32), the verb 学习 (study) does not turn into a noun because it can still take its object or adverbial, for example, 学习语法很重要 (studying grammar is very important); 认真学习很重要 (studying seriously is very important). We believe that the verb 学习 (study) in the position of subject takes the covert marker (NMk) of a substantive word, whose property of reference is created by the covert marker. In Example (33), AP denotes a substantive modification phrase; AMk denotes the substantive modification word de (的), namely the attributive marker de (的, meaning "of"). The attributive 这本书的 (of this book) modifies 出版 (publication), which has the covert marker of the properties of a noun. Therefore, the nature of the distinction between the parts of speech at the internal and external levels is the distinction between the language classes at the upper and lower levels: the upper level is NP; the lower level is the nominalization label and VP. Because the nominalization label is covert, the upper and lower levels have the same form.

It is difficult to do a comprehensive analysis of Chinese with formal grammar. One of the reasons for this is the difficulty in describing phrasal structural rules, which are caused by the multiple functions of Chinese parts of speech. It is perhaps feasible to solve the problem by classifying parts of speech into two levels and treating the difference in the two levels with a covert constituent.

The classification of parts of speech into two levels can better explain the contradictions in such examples as 诛无礼 (kill the impolite) and 敌大 (rival the large), in which verbs that should take substantive objects, however, take predicate objects. The two phrases come from: 得志於诸侯,而诛无礼,曹其首也 (successful because of dukes and princes, but kill the impolite and get them beheaded) (*The 23rd Year during the Xigong's Reign* in *The Book of Zuozhuan*); 小固不可以敌大 (the small cannot rival the large) (*Book One on Lianghuiwang* in *Mencius*). 无礼 (impolite) and 大 (large) are predicate words at the lexical level but substantive words at the syntactic level, meeting the requirements for the verbs 诛 (kill) and 敌 (rival) that take substantive objects. Therefore, the verbs that take substantive objects and predicate objects use the parts of speech at the syntactic level. Auxiliary verbs in modern Chinese are usually regarded as verbs that take predicate objects, but we also find that some auxiliary verbs can take substantive objects, for example, 应该阴天 (should be overcast). The contradiction that verbs that usually take predicate objects can take substantive objects can be solved only by classifying parts of speech into two levels. 阴天 (overcast) is a substantive word at the lexical level but a predicate word at the syntactic level; therefore, it is still a predicate object.

In general, English adjectives can play the role of the headword of a noun phrase. Similar to all noun phrases, these adjectives can function as subject, object and prepositional complement, but the difference is that they have no plural suffices and no changes in possessive case suffices (Quirk, Greenbaum, Leech & Svartvik, 1985). This can be explained at the level of word properties: adjectives have their noun properties at the syntactic level but are still adjectives at the lexical level, thereby being able to be modified by degree adverbs and having changes in degrees. However, the plural forms and possessive cases of English nouns have their noun properties at the lexical level, which cannot appear at the syntactic level.

4.4 Essence of a part of speech

At the hierarchy of large categories such as substantive words, predicate words and modification words, a part of speech is actually the classification of words into their categories that uses their expressional functions at the lexical level as an intrinsic basis. The difference in a word's part of speech comes before its distributional difference; the properties of its part of speech are inherent rather than temporarily resultant in use.

Hengeveld (1992) corresponded parts of speech with the four grammatical positions in a statement phrase and a reference phrase (see Chapter 3.1 in Volume 2 for detailed discussion). The four grammatical positions out of two core positions actually contain different specific grammatical positions respectively:

Reference phrase core: subject, object, attributive ~ (adjective ~, numeral and measure word ~, numeral ~)

Statement phrase core: predicate, ~ object, ~ complement, complement, adverbial ~

Modifier of a reference phrase: attributive

Modifier of a statement phrase: adverbial

In other words, grammatical positions such as "predicate, ~ object, ~ complement, complement, adverbial ~" have the same functions for classifying parts of speech. The presence of one of the functions indicates that a grammatical position has the properties of a predicate word. Why? Because these functions have the same expressional function – statement. Grammatical positions such as "subject, object, attributive ~" represent the properties of a substantive word; a modifier represents the properties of a modification word.

In practice, thousands upon thousands of possible classifications of parts of speech may be obtained purely according to distribution. The fundamental reason why we choose the part-of-speech system of predicate words, substantive words, predicate modification words and substantive modification words is that out of the thousands upon thousands of possible classification results, we merely choose the classification results that are in agreement with expressional functions. The fundamental reason why we should choose the part-of-speech system that is in agreement with expressional functions is that expressional functions such as statements, references, predicate modifications and substantive modifications reflect the basic working mechanisms of a human language, which, in other words, express meanings by forming sentences through combining statements with references. The vocabulary of a human language by and large differs in grammatical function and morphology in accordance with differences in its expressional functions. Just for these reasons, the vast majority of human languages distinguish among predicate words (verb), substantive words (noun), adverbs and adjectives (distinctive word) that are dependent on predicate words and substantive words. Therefore, the part-of-speech system that is in agreement with expressional functions can most effectively grasp the basic grammatical rules of a language.

The large category of part of speech (predicate words, substantive words, substantive modification words and predicate modification words) is, essentially, a type of expressional function, but whether a type is classified into different parts of speech or not depends on whether a lexical item differs in terms of expressional function or not. For example, in some languages, there is no difference between words that can enter the reference phrase core and words that can enter the reference phrase modifier and the statement phrase modifier; they basically belong to the same type of words. Then, in spite of differences in expressional functions such as a reference and a modification, there is no need to classify substantive words and modification words. Only when lexical items roughly differ in terms of expressional functions, and when the words that appear in different grammatical positions do not basically coincide is it necessary to classify them into different large categories.

Pattern 1: No need to classify parts of speech

Pattern 2: Need to classify parts of speech

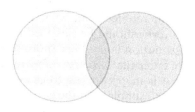

Pattern 3: Need to classify parts of speech, and treat the overlapping part as a conversional word

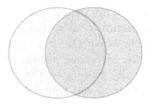

Pattern 4: Need to classify parts of speech, and treat the overlapping part as conversional word or not as a conversional word

The classification of predicate words, substantive words and modification words into such minor categories as nouns, verb, adjectives, distinctive words and adverbs is not decided by distribution entirely. The minor categories inside predicate words, substantive words and modification words (nouns, measure words, locatives, time words, place words, verbs, adjectives, state words, distinctive words, adverbs, numerals, measure words and demonstratives) are types that combine a semantic type with its syntactic function. A semantic type is the categorized semantic meaning, including entity, position, state, method, number, numeral and measure word, demonstrative and so on. Only when the semantic type is in agreement with its syntactic function is it necessary to classify words into their independent parts of speech. In other words, only when the difference in semantic type agrees with the difference in syntactic distribution is it necessary to classify words into their parts of speech.

For example, a unit word is different from an entity word in terms of semantic meaning, but in terms of syntactic distribution, the two are differentiated: a unit word can enter into the "numeral ~" environment, whereas an entity word cannot. Therefore, modern Chinese can have the different parts of speech of measure words and nouns. However, although the Chinese during the Pre-Qin dynasty (221–207 BC) differed in semantic types such as unit word and entity word, its syntactic distribution did not differ. Both types of words can enter the "numeral ~" environment, and as a result, there is no need to classify them into measure words and nouns.

Action words and attribute words within a predicate word differ in semantic type. Their syntactic distributions also differ: an attribute word can enter the 很 (very) ~ environment, but an action word generally cannot. Therefore, adjectives and verbs should be classified into two parts of speech, but this difference in distribution is not very thorough. Words such as 害怕 (fear) and 喜欢 (like) can enter the 很 (very) ~ environment but are closer to action words. Obviously it is inappropriate to classify them into adjectives. Accordingly, it is necessary to supplement the criterion "很 (very) ~, ~ object" and to take 害怕 (fear) and 喜欢 (like) away from adjectives and include them in verbs.

Attribute words and state words within the category of predicate words are different in semantic type; their syntactic functions are also different: state words cannot enter the 很 (very) ~ environment. Therefore, they should be classified into different parts of speech.

The difference in pure distribution cannot be taken as the reason for parts-of-speech classification. For example, 年事 (person's age) can only function as a subject; 地步 (extent) can only function as an object. They are different in distribution, but their semantic meanings belong to the same category (entity); therefore, there is no need to classify them into different parts of speech. 采取 (adopt) can take object, but 休息 (rest) cannot. They are different in distribution, but their semantic type is the same (behavior); therefore, they should be classified into verbs.

Neither is the pure identity of semantic type the reason for a word to be in the same part of speech. For example, 睡觉 (sleep), 打仗 (fight) and 开刀 (operate on) semantically denote action. 睡眠 (sleep), 战争 (war), 手术 (operate) also semantically denote action, but their distribution differ greatly. Therefore, they cannot be classified into the same part of speech. The former belong to verbs, while the latter belong to nouns. 分 (minute), 天 (day), 年 (year) 月 (month) and 钟头 (o'clock) are all units for measuring time, but their distribution is different. The former can enter the "number ~" environment, whereas the latter cannot. Therefore, the former should be classified into measure words, and the latter should be classified into nouns.

荣幸 (honored), 痛 (painful), 饱 (full) and 大型 (large-scale), 野生 (wild) and 急性 (acute) all denote attributes, but their distribution is greatly different. The former can function as predicates but cannot function as attributives; the latter can function as attributives but cannot function as predicates. More importantly, differences in predicates and attributives reflect those in the expressional functions such as statements and modifications. The two large categories of predicate words and modification words should be classified. Therefore, it is inadvisable to classify the two categories of words into adjectives. The classification of the former into adjectives and the latter into distinctive words has not only a distribution basis but also a semantic basis. Although adjectives and distinctive words have the semantic type of properties, a Chinese adjective (predicate word) is an attribute word that has the properties of degree and can be modified by a degree adverb, whereas a distinctive word is an attribute word that has no properties of degree (modification word) and cannot be modified by a degree adverb.

Therefore, the classification of words into different parts of speech requires both a distribution basis and a semantic basis. The difference in pure distribution and pure semantic meaning cannot be used as the basis for classifying parts of speech. Comparatively speaking, the difference in semantic type may be more important for classifying parts of speech. If there is a difference in semantic type but no difference in distribution, then the classification should be preferably based on semantic type. For example, 滂沱 (pour), 逶迤 (meander), 斑驳 (mottle), 旖旎 (graceful) and 交加 (mixed), 参半 (half-and-half), 洞开 (bright) and 参天 (towering) are predicate words, which, however, can only function as predicates so far as their predication function is concerned. But so far as their semantic type is concerned, the former denote state, whereas the latter denote action. Therefore, words like 滂沱 (pour) should be classified into state words, and those like 交加 (mixed) should be classified into verbs.

The study of Chinese grammar in earlier days tended to regard parts of speech as semantic types. Since the 1950s, the distribution theory has come into fashion in the Chinese grammar circle. During recent years, some scholars have picked up again the view that a part of speech belongs to a semantic type (Shi Dingxu, 2007, 2009; Lu Bingfu, 2010; Ren Ying, 2010). My view lies in between the two extreme views: a part of speech, in essence, is neither a pure distribution type nor a pure semantic type. Basically, the large categories of parts of speech (substantive words, predicate words, modification words) are classified according to the intrinsic expressional functions of a word. The basic categories of parts of speech (nouns, measure words, locatives, place words, time words, verbs, adjectives, state words, distinctive words, adverbs, numerals, measure words, demonstratives and others) are types that combine the semantic type of the word with its syntactic function. The reason why the semantic type is important for a part of speech is that it reflects language categorization, while the distinctions among parts of speech are exactly the categorization results. The expressional function is the meaning-expression pattern of a word, and the semantic type is the categorized meaning. The two belong to grammatical meaning; thus, we can say that grammatical meaning is the intrinsic basis for parts of speech.

Regarding the combination of expressional function, semantic type and distributional type rather than distribution as the nature of a part of speech can explain why parts of speech are comparable in terms of different times and languages. The view that distribution is the nature of a part of speech cannot explain why words distributing differently in different times and languages yet belong to the same part of speech. For example, the words 看 (see) in modern Chinese and 视 (watch) in classical Chinese distribute differently. The former can take a numeral and a measure-word object but cannot be modified by a numeral, such as 看三次 (see three times) but not *三看 (three sees), while the latter cannot take a numeral and a measure-word object and can be modified by a numeral, such as 三视 (watch three times) but not *视三 (watch three). But both are verbs. The English word 石头 (stone) can be modified by a numeral, for example, two stones, and can function as the object of a place preposition, for instance, on the stone, whereas the Chinese word 石头 (stone) does not have these functions. But both are nouns. The view that the nature of a part of speech is the combination of its expressional function, semantic type and syntactic function can produce a reasonable explanation: because they have the same expressional functions and semantic types.

A part of speech is a category. That is to say, different parts of speech must have qualitative distinctions, which are the basis for comparison among different languages.

We regard the basic category of parts of speech as the combination of the distribution with the semantic type. Just because of this, different parts of

Table 4.4 Semantic bases of parts of speech

Part of speech	Expressional function	Semantic type
Verb	Statement	Behavior and action
Adjective	Statement	Property or degree
State word	Statement	State description
Noun	Reference	Entity
Measure word	Reference	Measurement unit
Time word	Reference	Absolute time position
Place word	Reference	Absolute space position
Locative	Reference	Relative position
Numeral	Modification	Numerical value
Numeral and measure word	Modification	Quantity
Distinctive word	Modification	Property of non-degree
Demonstrative	Modification	Demonstration
Onomatopoeia	Modification	Sound imitation
Functional word	Supplementation	Supplementary meaning
Interjection word	Interjection	Independent interjection and echo

speech have different semantic bases, and we can use the lexical meaning to help judge them. But definition and explanation do not mean criteria; expressional functions or meanings can be used to give definitions and explain the nature of parts of speech, but cannot be used as criteria for classifying parts of speech simply because they cannot be directly observed. Therefore, we still should find directly observable criteria for classifying parts of speech, such as distribution and morphology.

In fact, it is not this book that originally created the view that distribution is not the essence of a part of speech. Many other scholars hold a similar viewpoint, which can even be regarded as returning to old ways. In the following, we present other views that hold that distribution is not the essence of a part of speech:

1. Discourse function is the nature of a part of speech. Hopper and Thompson (1984) pointed out that the aim of discourse is to report events that happen to a participant. There are two basic discourse functions: eliciting participants and reporting events, which are lexicalized exactly by nouns and verbs. Against a deeper background, Hopper and Thompson thought that discourse function is the root factor for restricting grammar, and that grammatical forms simply make it permanent. Speaking in the extreme, there is only discourse function and no grammar at all. From a historical genesis point of view, language forms lack categories in principle. Namely, there is no categorical opposition between parts of speech per se; rather, there are only different discourse requirements. It is considered that a large number of words have such requirements, and an opposition between a noun and a verb is thus formed.

Our viewpoint is different; we use the language expression pattern to observe the opposition between parts of speech in terms of category, holding that the opposition between parts of speech is fundamentally the different classification of labor of lexical forms in a language expression pattern. In other words, there exists first and foremost the opposition between expressional functions, which simply lexicalize parts of speech or make them permanent in a lexical form. A discourse function is quite exterior and based on an expressional function. Its motive tends to be grammatical and semantic features, which are fundamental. The discourse function is simply the manifestation of grammar and semantics. In other words, it must rely on a certain grammatical or semantic feature. For example, the basis of "eliciting participants" is reference, and that of "reporting events" is statement or assertion. The expressional function comes before discourse function and is therefore the nature of a part of speech.

2. Meaning is the nature of a part of speech. This view's different versions are briefly described below:

(1) Traditional grammar: nouns denote names of things; verbs denote actions; adjectives (attached to nouns) denote properties. This starts from a conceptual meaning, which obviously cannot give a clear explanation. For example, 手术 (operation on) denotes an action but it is a noun.

(2) The theory of four categories by Magnusson (1994) borrows Aristotle's theory of category to explain the nature of a part of speech. Aristotle classified solitary words into ten categories: material object: 人 (person) or 马 (horse), numeral and quantity, for example: 三尺长 (three feet long); property: 白的 (white), 懂语法的 (grammar-knowing)); relation: 一倍 (one time), 大于 (larger than); place: 在市场上 (in the market); time: 昨天 (yesterday), 去年 (last year); posture: 躺着 (lie down), 坐着 (sit); state: 穿鞋的 (show-wearing, 武装的 (armed)); activity: 切割 (cut), 烧灼 (burn); passive meaning: 被刺 (assassinated), 被烧灼 (get burned) (Aristotle, *Categories*). He mainly discussed the categories from two perspectives. One is the ontological perspective, which considers category as an existential class and holds that a material object can exist independently and be self-explained. Other categories are generally called attributes (Aristotle, *Posterior Analytics*) and cannot exist by themselves but exist in their subjects, thus being substantially concomitant (Aristotle, *Metaphysics*) and forming an opposition between substance and property. Magnusson extracted the four most important categories of substance, quantity, quality and relation to explain the essence of a part of speech: an adjective denotes attribute; a noun denotes substance and property instead of relation; a pronoun denotes substance instead of property; a preposition, adverb and conjunction denote relations; an article denotes quantity; a verb denotes substance, property and relation.

Fundamentally speaking, this is still a part of speech from the perspective of conceptual meaning.

(3) The universal and rational grammar thinks that a word denoting substance is a noun, and that a word denoting accident is an adjective. Both noun and adjective denote the object of thought. A verb denotes a way of thinking; in other words, it denotes the judgment of a thing and makes an assertion (see Antoine Arnaud, Claude Lancelot 1660). We agree with this viewpoint and think that the view that an expressional function is the nature of part of speech returns to the old view of universal and rational grammar in this regard. The universal and rational grammar simply did not say explicitly the expressional function, but the essential idea is the same. That is to say, both start from the perspective of a language expressional pattern or organization (the universal and rational grammar called this a form of thinking and held that speech is its expression) to explain the opposition between parts of speech. Of course, the universal and rational grammar only rather carelessly distinguishes between two types of functions: object of thinking (nouns, articles, participles, prepositions, adverbs) and way of thinking (verbs, conjunctions, interjections).

(4) Givón (1984) uses time stability to explain the meanings of a part of speech. Language tends to encode what is relatively stable in time as a noun and what is rapidly changing as a verb. The attribute meaning is intermediate in time stability; therefore, some languages encode it as a noun, and others encode it as a verb.

Some scholars argue that it is difficult to control time stability. For example, the time stability of "fire" and "flicker" is weak, but they are nouns, whereas that of "to tower" is strong, but it is a verb (see Whaley, 1996).

(5) Langacker (1987a, b) started from cognitive grammar to explain the meanings of a part of speech. Nouns denote things; verbs denote processes; adjectives/adverbs denote a temporal relation. Fundamentally speaking, this approach still uses conceptual meaning and is perhaps right, but its operation and falsifiability are too weak.

4.5 Nature of classifying parts of speech

The aim of part-of-speech classification is actually to deduce the intrinsic grammatical properties (expressional functions) of a word from observable extrinsic characteristics. Strictly speaking, the nature of part-of-speech classification is thus to discover and identify classes. The criteria for classification are not necessarily the intrinsic characteristics of a class. A form is not the nature of a part of speech, but we can use it as criteria for classifying parts of speech. Similarly, distribution also is not the nature of a part of speech, but we simply use it as criteria for classifying parts of speech. Of course, some of the extrinsic characteristics we use to classify parts of speech are closer to intrinsic characteristics; others are further away. For the purpose of classifying parts of speech, form is a relatively extrinsic characteristic, whereas distribution is a rather intrinsic characteristic. Generally speaking, intrinsic characteristics are more reliable than extrinsic characteristics but are not easily observable, whereas extrinsic characteristics are easily observable but not so reliable.

Then, can we classify parts of speech directly according to intrinsic characteristics instead of deducing them indirectly according to extrinsic characteristics? Theoretically yes. The key is that we can directly observe intrinsic characteristics. Whether they are observable or not sometimes depends on our analysis instrument. As progress in analysis instruments is made, what we cannot observe today will perhaps be observable in the future. The reason why today we do not use the intrinsic characteristics (expressional functions) of parts of speech as the criteria for classifying them is that the characteristics are not directly observable. If some day progress in analysis instruments is made and we can observe expressional functions, we may well use them as criteria for classifying parts of speech.

After the intrinsic characteristics for classifying parts of speech are well understood, we can answer the following question raised by Gao Mingkai: since the properties of parts of speech are static and inherent, why can they be classified according to grammatical functions (dynamic uses)? This simply deduces the inherent properties of a word according to its extrinsic form. The functions in use are not used as the nature of a part of speech.

Just because distribution is not the nature of a part of speech but simply its extrinsic characteristics, it is not the only criterion for classifying parts of speech.

This book suggests that the properties of a word exist before a linguist's classification of parts of speech and are part of a language's constituent structures. The part of speech based on the properties of a word is not of the distributional class; distribution is only their extrinsic manifestation. Parts of speech have no entire correspondence with distribution. It is impossible to classify parts of speech purely according to the similarity or difference in distribution even if the prototypal model is used. The root cause of the selectional restriction of a grammatical position on words is that words themselves have differences in their properties. To classify parts of speech, we use distribution to infer the differences in a word's own properties that cause different distributions. These properties are the nature of a part of speech.

Therefore, we entirely agree with Gao Mingkai's (1960) view that a word's morphological changes, combinational capability, syntactic functions and so on are all the extrinsic manifestations of its part-of-speech meaning. Our difference from him is that Gao Mingkai thought that Chinese notional words are versatile and that a word has no parts of speech. But we do not think so and believe that the selectional restriction of grammatical position on a word exists. Although the selectional restriction of the rather abstract grammatical position (syntactic constituent) on Chinese words is not as strict as that on Indo-European languages, the selectional restriction is quite strict at rather specific grammatical positions such as 很 (very) ~ or 不 (not) ~. Hence, we can use the rather specific distributional characteristics of a word to classify its part of speech. Moreover, at the position of a syntactic constituent, the dominant selection is very obvious. For example, more than 88% of subjects are held by substantive constituents; over 99% of predicates are held by predicate constituents.

4.6 Bases and criteria for classifying parts of speech

We accept Wen Lian's (1995) view that there should be a distinction between the basis for classifying parts of speech and the criteria for doing so. The basis for the classification refers to the intrinsic characteristics of a part of speech; the criteria refer to the conditions required to pinpoint which class a word belongs to. The basis may be what cannot be observed directly, but the criteria must be what can be observed. The two may be in conformity or not, but the criteria must be able to reflect the basis for classification. The basis is the intrinsic expressional function or grammatical meaning of a word, but because they cannot be observed directly, we use its observable morphology or grammatical function as the criteria. They can reflect the intrinsic expressional function or grammatical meaning.

The use of different things as the intrinsic basis for classifying parts of speech may produce very different results. The use of morphology as the intrinsic basis may produce Varro's classification. Not supported by expressional function or grammatical meaning, this kind of classification is similar to Linnaeus' bio-taxonomy. The use of distribution as the intrinsic basis may produce Chen Xiaohe's (1998) classification, which is also similar to Linnaeus' bio-taxonomy, and in which the classes do not reflect categories. But the use of expressional function as the intrinsic basis is different from the above-mentioned two kinds of classification because the difference in distribution, in our opinion, is only the extrinsic manifestation of expressional function. We should obtain different or similar expressional functions from different or similar distributions. In this way we do not classify parts of speech simply according to distribution but neglect some differences in distribution, for example, whether a word can be modified by 没 (no) or 不 (not). We also neglect some commonality in distribution (for example, nouns, verbs and adjectives all can function as subjects). Through analyzing distribution compatibility, we find the expressional functions that restrict distribution and connect certain distributions with certain expressional functions (see Chapter 6).

Therefore, classifying parts of speech is to identify the existing properties of a word and then do the classification according to certain classification strategies (see Chapter 7). The properties of a word exist first, and then criteria are identified.

4.7 Transformation of expressional function and part of speech

4.7.1 *What is the transformation of expressional function?*

Zhu Dexi (1983) pointed out that a statement can be transformed into a reference. "The addition of de (的) to the end of VP transforms the VP that originally indicates a statement into the 'VP de (的)' that indicates a reference". Although we do not agree that the function of de (的) is a reference, we agree that an expressional function can be transformed. Lu Jianming (1991) discussed the transfer reference in modern Chinese. We will further discuss the transformation of expressional functions as follows:

急性 (acute) and 慢性 (chronic) in Example (9) *b* in Chapter 4.3 can be regarded as the transformation of a modification into a reference; 黄头发 (yellow hair) in Example (27) *a* is the transformation of a reference into a statement; 出版 (publication) in Example (29) *a* is the transformation of a statement into a reference. Classical Chinese also has the transformation of expressional functions, for example, 贤 (virtuous), 不贤 (a person of no virtue and ability), 无功 (not meritorious) and 不乐生 (not enjoy life) are the transformations of a statement into a reference.

As a universal phenomenon, other languages also have the transformation of expressional functions, for example:

In English:

(34) The extremely old need a great deal of attention. (extremely old: a modification transformed into a reference)

(35) The number of jobless is rising. (jobless: a modification transformed into a reference)

(36) Mary's was the prettiest dress. (Mary's: a modification transformed into a reference)

(37) We'll meet at Bill's. (Bill's: a modification transformed into a reference)

In Spanish:

(38) a. Saludemos a los valientes combatientes.
       Salute first person to fixed reference.
     b. Siempre muestra gran respeto a los valientes. (valientes: modification→ reference)

In Hungarian:

(39) a. szép ház   b. A ház szép.
     c. A szép   kevés, a rossz sok. (szép, rossz: a modification or a statement → a reference)

In the Amis language:

(40) a. ta ajaj kuni a kuar.
   b. nilkaj tuni a taʔaajaj kaku.(taʔarajaj: a statement → a reference)

(41) a. maumah-aj ku tʃiwama
   b. ninukaj-aj tu ku maumah-aj a maəmin. (maumah-aj: statement → a reference)

In addition, verbs or adjectives in a good many languages in the Altaic language family also have transfer reference, for example, the Uiguric language, Dongxiang language, Yugur language, Bonan language, Hezhen language and so on. Adjectives in the Qiang, Monba, Yao and Bisu languages and verbs in Vietnamese also have transfer references.

4.7.2 Types of expressional function transformation

First, the expressional function transformation can be classified into lexical and syntactic ones.

The lexical transformation refers to the expressional function transformation through word formation, taking English for example, from "see" to "worth seeing", from "read" to "reader", from "work" as a verb to "worker", from "happy" to "happiness". These are marked. "Lead" from verb to noun; "define" from noun to verb, "water" from noun to verb, "cook" from verb to noun. These have no markers.

The lexical transformation occurs at the level of intrinsic expressional function. The marked lexical transformation actually derives a new word; the part of speech of the word with no-marker transformation at its lexical level changes, thus being actually a conversional word. The lexical transformation is beyond the detailed discussion in this book.

The syntactic transformation refers to the change in expressional function through syntactic means, also having no-marker and marked transformations. The no-marker transformation has no marker, but there is a temporary transformation of the expressional function of a word at a certain syntactic position, namely changing its part of speech at the syntactic level. The marked transformation refers to the change in the expressional function of a word by adding a functional word. Examples for the marked transformation are as follows:

(42) 小王黄头发 (Little Wang has yellow hair). (from reference to statement)
(43) 这本书的出版 (the publication of this book) (from statement to reference)
(44) 急性好治 (The acute are easy to treat). (from a modification to a reference)
(45) 夫尚贤使能，赏有功，罚有罪，非独一人为之也……
   (《荀子·强国》(If the virtuous are esteemed and the able are motivated, then the meritorious are rewarded and the guilty

are punished; these cannot be done by one person (*Empower the Country* in *Xunzi*)). (from statement → reference)

The no-marker syntactic transformation does so actually from intrinsic to extrinsic expressional functions, namely transforming parts of speech from lexical to syntactic levels. The transformation that involves various intrinsic expressional functions is not a grammatical one but a lexical one, for example, 研究 (study), 讨论 (discussion), 危险 (danger) and 困难 (difficulty) have the intrinsic expressional functions of statement and reference. Examples for the marked syntactic transformation are as follows:

(46) a. 他看书 (He reads a book).
      b. 看书的人 (the person who reads a book) (transformed from a statement to a modification with the marker de (的)
(47) a. 生产有计划 (The production has a plan).
      b. 有计划地生产 (produce in a planned way) (transformed from a statement to a modification with the marker di (地)

The word zhi (之) in classical Chinese can be regarded as a marker for a modification; zhe (者) is a marker for reference. The word "to", a marker for an English infinitive, can be regarded as a marker for reference; the possessive case "-'s" attached to a noun is a marker for a modification. The marked syntactic transformation can be analyzed as follows (in the diagram, Mk indicates transformation marker; AMk indicates the marker for distinctive word; AdMk indicates the marker for adverb; NMk indicates the marker for noun):

(48) 有计划地生产 (produce in a planned way)

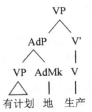

(49) 一箪食,一豆羹,得之则生,弗得则死,呼尔而与之,行道之人弗受. (If you get a basket of rice or a bowl of thick soup, you can live on; if not, you may die. If you are asked to give, do not give it to the person who preaches.) (*Volume 1 on Giving You Advice* in *Mencius*)

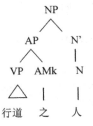

The no-marker syntactic transformation is caused by core constituent vacancy, including modification core constituent vacancy and marked core constituent vacancy, as analyzed previously. It is caused by different reasons. For example: 小王一头黄头发 (Little Wang has a head of yellow hair). 学习很重要 (Study is very important). 这本书的出版 (the publication of this book). The reasons are shown in Figure 4.6. The vacancy of Core Constituent X causes Constituent Y that collocates with Core Constituent X independently functions as the mother node XP of X and Y, thus changing Y's extrinsic expressional function and part of speech at the syntactic level. For another example, the VP modified by 不 (not) in the following Example (50) is actually vacant, and 不 (not), which was originally a modifier, now functions as a statement. 急性 (acute) in Example (51), which was originally a modifier, now functions as NP because the noun modified by 急性 (acute) is vacant. The modifier 干净的 (clean) in the sentence 衣服干净 (The clothes (are) clean), which originally formed a statement together with the link verb 是 (are), now independently functions as a statement because the link verb is vacant. In the following tree diagrams, Ø denotes a vacant constituent.

(50)　我不 (I do not).　　　　(51) 急性好治 (The acute is easy to treat).

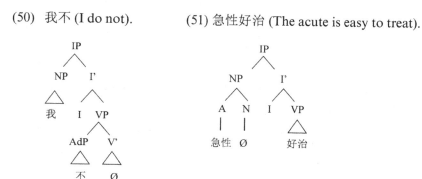

From this perspective, the no-marker syntactic transformation of expressional functions is caused by two types of constituent vacancy: (1) the vacancy of an expressional function transformation marker, for example, 学习很重要 (Study is very important); 这本书的出版 (the publication of this book); (2) the vacancy of a core constituent, for example, 小王一头黄头发 (Little Wang has a head of yellow hair); 我不 (I not). The expressional function transformation marker is also a core constituent; therefore, the no-marker transformation is actually caused by the core constituent vacancy.

Figure 4.6 The transformation caused by a vacant constituent

4.7.3 Reference and nominalization

Reference and nominalization happen at two levels respectively. The reference of an intrinsic expressional function corresponds to the nominalization at the lexical level, and the reference of an extrinsic expressional function corresponds to the nominalization at the syntactic level. The nominalization at the two levels must be distinguished; the one at the syntactic level cannot be identical with the one at the lexical level. The following examples show the nominalization at the syntactic level. The parts of speech at the lexical level do not change:

(52) 学习很重要 (Study is very important). (学习 (study) is a verb)
(53) 急性好治 (The acute are easy to treat). (急性 (acute) is a distinctive word)
(54) 有大有小 (Some are large; some are small). (大 (large) and 小 (small) are adjectives)
(55) 赏有功，罚有罪 (reward the meritorious; punish the guilty). (有功 (meritorious) and 有罪 (guilty) are verb phrases)
(56) 贤者以其昭昭使人昭昭 (The wise use their clarity to make others clear). (*With All Your Heart* in *Mencius*). Here 昭昭 (clear) is a state word.

4.7.4 Syntactic constructions of self-reference and transfer reference

Reference refers to the transformation from a non-referential into a referential constituent. It has the following three constructions (Y indicates a non-noun constituent; NMk indicates the marker for a noun):

Types A and B are referenced through a reference marker. The reference marker of Type A is overt; the reference marker of Type B is covert. Type C does not take a reference marker but has a covert noun headword. The three constructions have the following in common: a non-noun constituent functions as the mother node of a noun independently or together with a marker word.

Reference has self-reference and transfer reference. From the perspective of formal grammar, the difference between the designations such as self-reference and transfer reference lies in the referential relations between the mother nodes NP and Y. If the mother node NP refers to Y itself, then the self-reference is designated, for example, 学习很重要 (Study is very important), 这本书的出版 (the publication of this book). If the mother node NP does not refer to Y itself but refers to the same thing as another noun phrase at a certain node dominated by the mother node NP, then the transfer reference is designated. This noun phrase is usually vacant, for example, in Type C: 急性好治 (The acute are easy to treat), 看书的 (A person who reads books). Let us look at the following examples of Type C:

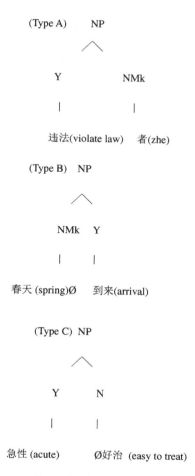

Figure 4.7 Syntactic constructions of reference

(57) <u>不备不虞</u>,不可以师. (《左传·隐公五年》) (If not prepared and not dangerous, then no fighting) (*The Fifth Year of the Yin Prince* in *Zuozhuan*)

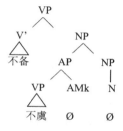

(58)   王亲受而劳之,所以惩不敬,<u>劝有功</u>也. (《左传 · 成公二年》) (The king himself receives and rewards him to punish those who are not respectful and to persuade the meritorious.) (*The Second Year of the Cheng Prince* in *Zuozhuan*)

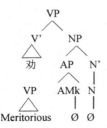

(59)   他有两个哥哥,<u>一个</u>高,一个矮 (He has two brothers; <u>one</u> is tall, and the other is short).

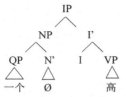

(60)   <u>看书的</u>比买书的多 (there are more <u>book readers</u> than buyers).

(61)   <u>The extremely old</u> need a great deal of attention.

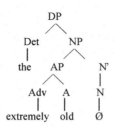

(62) <u>Mary's</u> was the prettiest dress.

We call the constituent referred to by the mother node NP a reference source and borrow the concept of "extraction" proposed by Zhu Dexi (1983). The process in which a reference constituent refers to a reference source is called extraction. Thus, we can say that self-reference extracts Y itself, and that transfer reference extracts an NP below the mother node NP. For example, the transfer reference of 急性 (acute) extracts the headword modified by 急性 (acute). 有功 (meritorious) is an extracted noun phrase modified by 有功 (meritorious).[6]

The above examples show that the transfer reference of a modification constituent in either Chinese or English usually extracts the modified vacant NP. The transfer reference of the predicate constituent in modern Chinese basically disappears.[7] In classical Chinese, under usual circumstances, the subject of a predicate constituent is extracted. For example (58), generally, the marker suo (所) should be added to the object to be extracted. For another example, 病而乞盟,所丧多矣 (《左传・僖公五年》) (When you are sick and ask for union, what you lose will be plentiful.) (*In the Fifth Year of Xigong Prince* in *Zuozhuan*). 寡人所好者,音也 (《韩非子・十过》) (What I like is music) (*Chapter on Ten Faults* in *Han Fei Zi*). There are seldom if ever objects of transfer reference without adding suo (所),[8] for example in (57). The predicate constituents in the Nootka (see example (2) in Chapter 3) and Tagalog (see example (3) in Chapter 3) languages also extract subjects.

4.7.5 *Functions of de (的) and di (地) in Chinese syntax*

The function of de[3] (的[3]) is actually related to the transformation of expressional functions and parts of speech at the syntactic level. It is a marker for a substantive modification word and can transform a predicate constituent or substantive constituent into a substantive modification constituent. The "X de (的)" that independently functions as a subject or an object is the no-marker transfer reference of a predicate modification constituent, namely the nominalization at the syntactic level. The function of di[1] (地) also transforms a predicate or substantive constituent into a predicate modification constituent.

看书的 (a person who reads a book) transforms a predicate constituent into a modification word. 木头 (wood) + de transforms a substantive constituent into a substantive modification constituent. 有计划地 (生产) (produce in a planned way) transforms a predicate constituent into a predicate modification word; 历史地 (看问题) ((look at an issue) historically) transforms a substantive word into a predicate modification word.

干净 (clean) in 干净的衣服 (clean clothes) is still a predicate word and equivalent to a clause. It still has the general characteristics of a predicate word: 不干净的衣服 (unclean clothes), 很干净的衣服 (very clean clothes). But 干净 (clean) in 干净的衣服 (clean clothes) is actually a modification word; therefore, it cannot be modified by 不 (not) and 很 (very): *不干净衣服 (* not clean clothes), *很干净衣服 (*very clean clothes).

It is crucially important to point out that de³ (的) and di (地) function as a transformation marker in Chinese syntax and cause constituents with different parts of speech to convert to each other. Therefore, the differences that a word can directly function as attributive and that only by adding de³ (的) can it do so reflect its different parts of speech. A word that can directly function as an attributive has a modifier property; that which can do so only by adding de³ (的) has no modifier property and is still a substantive constituent or a predicate constituent. Because of the special function of de³ (的) and di (地) in Chinese syntax, we strictly distinguish between the function a word has by adding de³ (的) and di (地) and the word's own function.

4.8 Correlations among part of speech, expressional function and syntactic constituent

Croft (1991) used typology to observe the universal parts of speech in the world languages. He links part of speech with semantic meaning and pragmatic function and believes that the three have correlations:

These are unmarked prototype correlations, whereas others are marked. For example, the noun "vehicle" used as reference is unmarked, but we can add a marker "'s" or use the derived adjective "vehicle's" to indicate a modification, or add the marker "be" to indicate a statement. The adjective "white" used as a modification is unmarked, becomes the noun "whiteness" by adding the marker "-ness" to indicate reference and becomes "be white" by adding the marker "be" to indicate a statement. The verb "destroy" used as a statement is

Table 4.5 Croft: Correlations among syntactic category, semantic type and pragmatic function

Syntactic category	Noun	Adjective	Verb
Semantic type	Object	Property	Action
Pragmatic function	Reference	Modification	Predication

Table 4.6 Croft: The unmarked or marked correlations in English

	Reference	*Modification*	*Statement*
Object	vehicle	Vehicle's, vehicular, of vehicle, in vehicle	be a/the vehicle
Property	white**ness**	white	be white
Action	Destruc**tion, to** destroy	Destroy**ing**, destroy**ed**	destroy

Note: Bold letters indicate marked constituents.

unmarked, but we add the marker *to* or *-tion* to indicate a reference and add the marker *-ing* or *-ed* to indicate a modification.

According to Croft's marker theory, the correlation among things, references and nouns, and that among actions, statements and verbs are all valid. But the correlation among attributives, modifications and adjectives is not universal. In Chinese and most of the Sino-Tibetan languages, an attributive mainly corresponds to a statement.[9] The correspondence between part of speech and semantic type is actually a matter of word formation but not a matter of syntax. Some markers such as "-ness" are also a matter of word formation but not a syntactic one. If we only take into account the syntactic matter, we can observe the correlation among part of speech, expressional function and syntactic constituent. The correlation among the three is as follows:

Part of speech	*Expressional function*	*Syntactic constituent*
Predicate word	Statement	Predication constituents (predicate, complement, object of real predicate-object verb)
Substantive word	Reference	Subject, objects of verbs with substantive object and quasi-predicate object, attributive
Modifier	Modification	Attributive, adverbial

The above is a prototypical correlation. Other correlations regarded as the multiple functions of a part of speech are non-prototypical: there is an expressional function transformation (marked or extrinsic expressional function transformation). For example, de (的)/di (地) is added in order for a statement or a reference to function as a modifier. To function as a predicate, a reference should be transformed into a statement; to function as a subject or object, a statement should be transformed into a reference; to function as a subject or object, a modification should also be transformed into a reference.

There is a loose correspondence between the position of a Chinese syntactic constituent and a part of speech, but at the combinatory positions of notional and functional words, there are rather strict requirements for parts of speech. For example, the positions followed by 不 (not) or 很 (very) permit the entry of only predicate constituents. That is the reason why we have to use specific distributions as the criteria for classifying parts of speech.

Notes

1 很 (very) represents an absolute degree adverb.
2 Because there are a great many grammatical functions, we discuss here only the greatly universal grammatical functions. As mentioned before, nearly all of the grammatical functions have no internal universality. For the convenience of the discussion, in the following, when we discuss the external exclusivity of a grammatical function, the grammatical function of a certain part of speech means that at least some of the words in the part of speech have a grammatical function.
3 A grammatical function has a distinction between general and concrete. For example, "combined with other constituents" is more general than "functioning as a syntactic constituent". "Functioning as a syntactic constituent" is more general than "functioning as a head word". "Functioning as a head word" is more general than "being modified by an adverbial". "Being modified by an adverbial" is more general than "being modified by 很 (very)".
4 See Xiao Guozheng (1991) for the inner and outer distinctions between references of predicate constituents at an object's position.
5 Chinese adjectives such as 大 (large), 红 (red) and 重要 (important) are predicate words and belong to VP syntactically, while English adjectives belong to AP (a modifier) syntactically. Chinese distinctive words belong to AP syntactically and are equivalent to English adjectives. Chinese adjectives that can directly function as attributives can be regarded as adjectives and distinctive words concurrently.
6 Lu Jianming (1991) discussed in some detail the transfer reference of a modifier.
7 大 (big) and 小 (small) in 那商店卖的盆儿有大有小 (some basins on sale in that store are big; others are small) are transfer references, but it seems that they should be analyzed into "NP→AP + Pro". Their constructions are the same as those for the transfer reference of a distinctive word, but different from the construction "NP → Pro + VP" for the transfer reference of an adjective in classical Chinese.
8 The object of a transfer reference without adding suo (所) usually has conditions: the predicate word takes a negative word or a modal verb 可 (can).
9 Shen Jiaxuan (1997) believed that the major function of a Chinese adjective is attributive. In the opinion of the author of this book, it is predication, and an adjective belongs to a predicate word; its direct function as an attributive is actually because some of adjectives concurrently have the property of a distinctive word.

5   Criteria for classifying parts of speech

5.1 Conditions for criteria for classifying parts of speech

Chapter 4.6 presented the idea that the bases for classifying parts of speech and the criteria are different. The two may be in agreement or not, but the criteria must be able to reflect the bases for classification.

Any factor that can be used as the criteria for classifying parts of speech must meet the following three conditions:

A. It can reflect the nature of a part of speech, namely the intrinsic expressional function. Different parts of speech show different expressional functions of a word. Therefore, only those factors that can reflect its intrinsic expressional functions can be used as the criteria for classifying parts of speech.

B. Observation. This means that the factor has an obvious extrinsic form or is itself a certain extrinsic form, thereby being definitely comprehensible. This is important because only through using observable things as the criteria for classifying parts of speech can discrepant classifications be avoided, thus making definite, reliable and operable classifications.

C. Comprehensiveness. This means that the factors used as the criteria for classifying parts of speech are applicable to all or most of the words. Only comprehensive factors can be used as the primary criteria for classifying parts of speech, whereas incomprehensive factors can at most be used as subsidiary criteria to supplement the primary criteria and can be used to classify the parts of speech of some other words when the primary criteria cannot be used to classify their parts of speech.

The previously mentioned classification criteria mainly include the following three: (1) the morphology of a word; (2) its meaning; (3) its grammatical function. In the present study, we use the grammatical function as classification criteria. Why? Our analysis is as follows:

5.2 A word's morphology, meaning and grammatical function

5.2.1 Whether the morphology can be used as classification criteria

Morphology means a word form and its changes. Morphology displays part-of-speech differences in two scenarios. First, the word form itself has systematic differences that reveal parts of speech. For example, Italian:

> Verbs: -are/-ire/-ere: benefiare, leggere, finire, amare
> Nouns: -o (masculine)/-a (feminine)/-e (neutral): beneficio, leggenda, fine, amore

Second, a word has its systematic changes that reveal differences in parts of speech. *On Latin Language*, written by W. T. Varro, a Roman who lived from 116 to 27 BC, classified words into four classes according to changes in word form:

> Noun: a word that has changes in case.
> Verb: a word that has changes in tense.
> Participle: a word that has changes in case and tense.
> Functional word: a word that has no changes in case and tense.

Only when the difference or change in word form that shows differences in parts of speech is systematic can it be sufficiently used to classify parts of speech. Intrinsically speaking, a part of speech is the class of intrinsic expressional functions, whereas a word form is not the nature of a part of speech but only the most extrinsic manifestation of a word's expressional function. Therefore, we should not think that a language has no parts of speech just because its words have no systematic differences or changes in word form. But the word form of a formal language often has a rather strict correspondence with the expressional function of a word. For example, in English, a word that has changes in plural form can function as a subject or object, and has a reference meaning. A word that has changes in tense and aspect can function as a predicate and has a statement meaning. Therefore, we can assume that the form of a word can indirectly reflect its expressional function and meet the first condition of the criteria for classifying parts of speech. The reason why we can use a word form to classify the parts of speech of a language that is rich in form is that there is a rather strict correspondence between its word form and the expressional function of its words. In other words, the form of a word can be regarded as a symbol of its intrinsic expressional function.

A word form, of course, is observable and also meets the second condition for classifying parts of speech.

But Chinese lacks word form symbols and morphological changes in their strict sense; its word form is incomprehensive. Only grammatical function can be used to classify the parts of speech of the vast majority of words that have no morphological change. Thus, the Chinese word form can at most only be used as the reference criteria for classifying parts of speech. For example, words such as 轻松 (relaxed), 凉快 (nice and cool) and 暖和 (warm) can only be classified into adjectives according to their grammatical functions, but they have their ABAB reduplication forms. If we regard the ABAB reduplication forms as a kind of morphological change of verbs, then we can use this as the basis to regard 轻松 (relaxed), 凉快 (nice and cool) and 暖和 (warm) as conversional words between adjective and verb. Nevertheless, as mentioned in Chapter 2.2, strictly speaking, Chinese has no genuine morphological reduplication but only word formation reduplication and syntactic reduplication. The ABAB reduplication form is a syntactic phenomenon and should be looked upon as a grammatical function.

5.2.2 Can word meaning be used as the criteria for classifying parts of speech?

Ma Jianzhong (1898) and Wang Li (*China's Modern Grammar*, 1943, *China's Grammatical Theory*, 1944) both used meaning as the criteria for classifying parts of speech.

There are two types of meanings: one is lexical meaning, and the other is grammatical meaning or category meaning. These two aspects must be taken into account when discussing whether meaning can be used as criteria for classifying parts of speech.

We begin with the above-mentioned three conditions for classifying parts of speech to examine whether the lexical meaning of a word can be used as criteria for classifying its parts of speech. First, the lexical meaning cannot reflect the expressional function of a word. For example, the following words in their groups have the same or about the same lexical meanings, but their expressional functions are quite different:

a)	不 (not) ~	很 (very) ~	complement	predicate	adverbial
突然 (sudden)	+	+	+	+	+
忽然 (unexpectedly)	—	—	—	—	+

b)	不 (not) ~	很 (very) ~	complement	predicate
白 (white)	+	+	+	+
白雪 (snow-white)	—	—	+	—
白色 (white color)	-	-	-	-

c)	没 (not yet) ~	很 (very) ~
胜利 (victory)	+	—
成功 (successful)	+	+

d)	subject	在 (in) ~	三天 (three days) ~	春节 (spring festival) ~
以前 (ago)	+	+	+	+
过去 (past)	+	+	—	—

Second, lexical meaning is not observable; it can only be perceived but cannot be definitely grasped. Therefore, although lexical meaning meets the third condition for the criteria, it cannot be used as the criteria for classifying parts of speech because it does not meet the first and second conditions. Can we use the grammatical meaning (or category meaning) of a word to classify its parts of speech? Wang Li (1943) took the category meaning as a criterion for classifying parts of speech; he was against using a word form or a grammatical function to classify them. "When we say that parts of speech can be indicated in a dictionary, we mean that a word itself can be grouped into a class, and that there is no need to wait for it to come into a sentence to decide its parts of speech. If a word is classified into classes according to its function in a sentence, then word properties are obtained" (p. 19). "Words can be classified into two major classes: any word itself that can indicate a concept is called a notional word; any word itself that cannot indicate a concept but is the tool for constructing a language is called a functional word. The classification of a notional word into parts of speech should be based on the type of its concept; the classification of a functional word into its parts of speech should be based on its function in a sentence". The following are Wang Li's criteria for classifying some notional words into their parts of speech (pp. 21–29):

Noun: all names of objects are called nouns.
Numeral: all words that indicate the numbers of objects are called numerals.
Adjective: all words that indicate the properties of objects are called adjectives.
Verb: all words that indicate actions or events are called action words or verbs.
Adverb: all words that can only indicate degree, scope, time, possibility, negation and so on but cannot separately indicate objects, truths or facts are called adverbs.

In Wang Li's opinion, because Chinese has no word forms, its classification into parts of speech is easier than Western languages. Although Western languages have word forms, they are incomplete, so the classification into parts of speech still relies on a grammatical function, which, however, does not completely correspond to a part of speech, ultimately relying on concepts to classify parts of speech. For example, in French, "Je suis fort (I am strong)" and "Je suis roi (I am a king)", "fort" and "roi" have no morphological difference, and we can only make conceptual distinctions that "fort" is an adjective and that "roi" is a noun. But Chinese has no part-of-speech label at all, and this happens to let us classify parts of speech purely according to concept, not being restricted by any form. As a result, it is easier to classify Chinese parts of speech than those of Western languages (p. 28).

The category meaning of a word has an approximate correspondence with its expressional function. For example, we say that objects correspond to reference, and that actions correspond to statement, but category meaning is not directly observable and cannot directly and definitely be grasped. Furthermore, it is extremely complicated: What do we mean by action, object or property? Where are their boundaries? How many types of category meaning in all are there? These can create inexhaustible controversies that may never be solved (Zhu Dexi, 1985a). Therefore, the category meaning does not meet the second condition for the criteria of classifying parts of speech. The statement that it is easy to classify Chinese parts of speech as Wang Li put it is a false appearance. The category meaning also does not completely correspond to an expressional function. For example, an action can correspond to a reference, such as "walk" in "to have a walk". Attribute can correspond to either a modification or a statement. Therefore, the category meaning does not meet the first condition for the criteria of classifying parts of speech.

In our opinion, the grammatical meaning of a word is not the experiential meaning such as an object, action or properties but the expressional function based on the relations among the internal constituents of a language, such as a reference, statement and modification. As mentioned before, because the expressional function is not directly observable, it also cannot be directly used as the criteria for classifying parts of speech.

A good many scholars recognize that the main basis for classifying parts of speech is the grammatical function of a word; however, they also emphasize that grammatical meaning is an important reference criterion. Some books say that equal attention should be paid to both function and meaning (Zhu Dexi, 1985a). But the reality is often that when the uses of a grammatical function as the criterion for classifying parts of speech are smooth, this is done. Once this is troublesome, or the parts of speech classified according to a grammatical function do not agree with the human intuition of the meaning, the grammatical function is just abandoned, and instead a grammatical meaning is used. Sometimes a grammatical function and sometimes an indefinite grammatical meaning are used as the criteria, thus causing chaos for the classification. For example, in the past, a good many scholars maintained that words that express properties are adjectives, and then they classified into adjectives the words such as 高等 (high-class) and 大型 (large-scale). Indeed, the differences in the grammatical function between 高等 (high-class) and 大型 (large-scale) and typical adjectives such as 高级 (advanced) and 大 (large) lie in the fact that 高级 (advanced) and 大 (large) can be modified by 不 (not) or 很 (very), and can function as predicates, while 高等 (high-class) and 大型 (large-scale) do not have these functions. But because they are deemed to indicate the same grammatical meaning, scholars would rather call words such as 高等 (high-class) and 大型 (large-scale) non-predicate adjectives than eliminate them from adjectives, consequently making adjectives become a mélange where the grammatical functions of their members have large discrepancies. In the last analysis, only the use of a grammatical function can help classify parts of speech.

5.2.3 *Classifying parts of speech according to a grammatical function*

The following three methods are used:

I.   Classifying parts of speech according to a syntactic constituent. With the one-to-one correspondence between a syntactic constituent and a part of speech, we use the implemented functions as the criteria for classifying parts of speech. This is inconsistent with Chinese facts, easily leading to the conclusion that words have no definite parts of speech or even that Chinese has no parts of speech at all, as Li Jinxi (1994) held.

II. Classifying parts of speech according to distribution in its narrow sense, namely using the combinatory environment of a word in relation to another word or phrase as the criteria for classifying parts of speech. For example:

   Numeral~[measure word: 个 (piece), 支 (count), 斤 (jin)]

   Numeral and measure word~[noun: 苹果 (apple), 山 (mountain), 纸 (paper)]

   The so-called identification word or test slot and the generalized word form (Fang Guangdao, 1939) use this method. English grammar commonly uses this method to classify parts of speech. The following are the criteria that J. M. Y Simpson (1979) used to classify English parts of speech:
   1. ~ hat is on the table.[Det.: a, the, that ...]
   2. (Det.) ~ is/are good. [Noun: man, oats, John...]
   3. (Det.) Noun ~ (Det.) Noun.[Verb: is, sings, smokes...]
   4. (Det.) ~ noun.[adj.: big, green, brackish...]
   5. Det. noun is ~ adj.[adv.: too, very, badly...]
   6. ~ Verb (Det.) noun.[pron.: I, you, he...]
   7. Noun Verb Pron. ~ (υ ≠adv.)[particle: ~ (up, over, out...)]
   8. Det. noun verb ~ Det. noun (~ ≠Adv.) [prep.: into, under, up...]

   The problem of this method is that only when the part of speech that enters into a certain position is the sole one can distribution effectively classify parts of speech. This method is problematic even in English. For example, it is hard to distinguish between noun and pronoun, and also between noun and adjective.

   In Chinese, because one grammatical position is commonly occupied by various parts of speech, a word combined with another word in different parts of speech often has more than one grammatical relation. Therefore, the use of this method for classifying parts of speech must attach some conditions, but too many conditions make the criteria complicated and not easy to control.

III. Classifying parts of speech according to syntactic constituent and distribution in its narrow sense. This has the following two aspects: (1) the capability of a word functioning as syntactic constituents; (2) the capability of one word to be combined with another.

The two capabilities combined make up for the shortcomings of the classi-fication with distribution in its narrow sense, which is a rather effective way to classify Chinese parts of speech.

This book uses the third method. The first method has the problem that it is difficult to determine syntactic constituents, and hence only the second method is used if possible. Only when the second method cannot effectively classify parts of speech, or when the criteria are too complicated, is the first method used to classify them. Both the first and the second methods use grammatical function and distribution. In the following, we shall explain the unity of the two.

Why can grammatical function be used to classify parts of speech? Previously, we mentioned that a grammatical position has selectional restric-tion on parts of speech. The criteria for the selectional restriction to select words are the words' own grammatical attributes. In other words, because the grammatical attributes are different, the grammatical positions a word can occupy are also different. The selectional restriction of grammatical position on words, namely distribution, can thus be used to classify parts of speech.

A word is capable of occupying grammatical positions (namely grammat-ical function reflects its intrinsic expressional function). The parts of speech classified according to the grammatical functions of a word are indeed gram-matical, thereby meeting the first condition of the classification criteria.

Grammatical functions also meet the second condition of the classification criteria. It has two aspects: (1) the capability of functioning as a syntactic con-stituent such as a subject, object, predicate or attributive; (2) the capability of being combined with other words or phrases, for example, being modified by 很 (very) or numerals and measure words, taking locatives and so on. The two aspects are observable.

Grammatical function also meets the third condition of the classification criteria. Every word has its own grammatical functions, which are therefore applicable to the classification of every word's parts of speech as a criterion. Therefore, grammatical function meets all the conditions and thus can be used as criteria for classifying parts of speech.

5.2.4 Brief summary

Theoretically speaking, a word's grammatical function, grammatical meaning or intrinsic expressional function all can be used as criteria for classifying parts of speech.

The form of a word is highly observable and can reflect its expressional function, but the Chinese word form is not comprehensive and can only be used as supplementary criteria.

A word has its lexical meaning and category meaning. The lexical meaning is comprehensive but does not reflect the word's expressional functions and is not observable, therefore being unable to be used as classification criteria. The category meaning is comprehensive but not observable and cannot fully reflect a word's intrinsic expressional function, while the expressional function itself also is not directly observable, thus being unable to be used as classification criteria.

Grammatical function can reflect a word's expressional function and is observable and comprehensive, thus being able to be used as classification criteria.

5.3 What is grammatical function?

The classification of parts of speech according to distribution can be traced back to the distribution analysis proposed by US descriptive linguistics. Bloomfield (1926) said,

29. [Definition]Every methodical unit in a construction is a position.
30. [Assumption]Every position in a construction can only be filled in by a certain form.
32. [Def.]The position a form occupies is its function.
33. [Def.]All the forms that have the same functions compose a form class.
37. [Def.]The form class of a word is the part of speech.
38. [Def.] The largest word class in a language is its part of speech.

Harris (1946) said, every class of morphemes has its special sentence positions and can be filled by any members of the class and only by those members. For example:

N: Appearing before the plural form -*s* or its variant or after "the" or adjective: hotel, butter, two.

V: Appearing before the past tense "-ed" or its variant; before "-ing", after an N plus "should, will, might": go, take, do.

Adjective: Appearing between "the" and N, but never appearing before "–s": young, pretty, happy.

Adverb: appearing between "the" and adjective, but not between "the" and a noun: rather, very, now, not.

Fries (1952) said that in a single free mode of discourse, English words that occupy the same positions must belong to the same part of speech.

What is distribution? Harris said that "the distribution of an element is the total of all environments in which it occurs, i.e. the sum of all the (different) positions (or occurrences) of an element relative to the occurrence of other elements" (Harris, 1951: 15–16).

What is the environment or position? Harris said that the environment or position of an element in a discourse is made up of its adjacent elements. The so-called "adjacency" refers to the position before or after the element or the position in which nonlinear elements such as intonation, stress and others appear simultaneously. (Harris, 1951: 15) If intonation is considered, it includes a simultaneous statement intonation.

The definitions of Bloomfield and Harris show that the position concept of US structural linguistics is based on a superficial and sequential position relationship among elements: before, after or simultaneously, not on the grammatical relationship between hierarchy and element. Yet this concept of distribution is too superficial. The root cause for the use of grammatical position to classify the parts of speech of an element is its selectional restriction on words, which is not decided by the superficial and sequential positional relationship, but by hierarchies and grammatical relationships. For example:

(1) 给我书 / 给我哥 (Give me a book/give to my brother)

The consideration of only a superficial and sequential positional relationship may lead to the view that 书 (book) and 哥 (brother) have the same grammatical positions. But actually the hierarchical structures of the two constituents are different, thereby occupying different grammatical positions. The position that the whole phrase 我哥 (my brother) occupies is equivalent to that occupied by 我 (me) in 给我书 (Give me a book).

(2) 这三个苹果 / 这三个好吃 (The three apples/the three are delicious)

Here, no consideration of a grammatical relationship may lead to the view that 苹果 (apples) and 好吃 (delicious) appear in the same grammatical position, but because their grammatical relationship is different, the two actually occupy different grammatical positions.

(3) 学习文件 (study documents)

In terms of only a sequential positional relationship, 学习 (study) in the phrase represents only one distribution, but actually it represents two types of distribution:[1] one type is equivalent to 学习 (study) in the phrase 学习汉语 (studying Chinese); another is equivalent to 学习 (study) in the phrase 学习时间 (study time).

Therefore, in our opinion, the position that is used to define distribution contains hierarchies and grammatical relations, and is thus called the grammatical position. Two factors stipulate the distribution of constituents:

1. The grammatical relations among immediate constituents and the grammatical roles of the immediate constituents thus stipulated.

    The grammatical relations include both quite abstract relations such as subject-predicate, predicate-object, attribute-headword and predicate-complement and quite specific relations, for example: 许多书 (many books), 新书 (new book), 一个 (one). In terms of their general relations, the distribution of 许多 (many), 新 (new) and 一 (one) is the same in these phrases, but in terms of their specific relations, they are different. This is also similar to 桌子腿 (desk leg) and 桌子上 (on the desk).

2. The larger environment in which the entire construction made up of two immediate constituents can exist.

For example, both 大型 (large-scale) and 大量 (massive) can appear in "~ noun", but "大型 (large-scale) + noun" can also appear in "numeral and measure word ~", while "大量 (massive) + noun" cannot. Therefore, the specific grammatical positions in which 大型 (large-scale) and 大量 (massive) appear are different.

The above analysis produces the following three important definitions:

Definition 1: In a syntactic structure, the position in which the immediate constituents that have certain grammatical relations exist is a grammatical position, which contains information on hierarchy and grammatical relation.

Definition 2: The grammatical position occupied by a word is its distribution.

Definition 3: The capability of a word to occupy a certain grammatical position is the word's grammatical function.

A word's distribution or function is often expressed as the position (or test slot) whose environment is a syntactic constituent, identification word or part of speech, for example: ~ object, 很 (very) ~, numeral ~. It is sometimes expressed as a syntactic constituent but is equivalent to the position that is expressed as the environment consisting of syntactic constituents. For example, a predicate is equivalent to a "subject ~".

The reason why we do not mention the sequential relational positions 之前 (before) and 之后 (after) is that the essence of a grammatical position is a grammatical relational position, namely the position decided by grammatical relations, while the sequential position does not matter. For example, because Latin has case markers, the sequential positions of a subject, object and predicate verb are fairly flexible:

(4) Puer amat puellam.
    A teenager loves a teenager girl.
    Puer puellam amamat.
    A teenager a teenager girl loves
    Amat puer puellam
    Love a teenager a teenager girl.
    Amat puellam puer.
    Love a teenager girl a teenager.
    Puellam puer amat.
    A teenager girl a teenager loves.
    Puellam amat puer.
    A teenager girl loves a teenager.

Where *puer* is the subject case (the original form: *puer*); *puellam* is the object case (the original form: *puella*); *amat* is the third person singular (the original form: *amere*). There are no changes in grammatical relations in the above different sentences, and so they should be deemed as occupying the same grammatical positions respectively.

Russian is similar to this (Shi Anshi & Zhan Renfeng, 1988: 110–111):

(5)　9 a u o 6 m o m a . I love my mother.

　　5 1 M a w M O U　K o . I mother love.

　　J h o 6 s m S I m a . Love my mother.

　　J L o 6 a i i o　m a T h　5 1 . Love mother I.

　　M a w 9 m o 6 m. Mother I love.

　　M a w m o 6 m o 5　I . Mother loves me.

Because of the case markers: M a T b (object case, J H O J J O M (the third person singular), all the different sequences mean the same: "I love mother". q j u o 6 . n t o . There are no changes in grammatical relations in the above different sentences, and so they should be deemed as occupying the same grammatical positions respectively.

Thus, we can understand why some English words appear before or after a sequential position but are classified into adverbs:

(6)　a. He always loses his pencils. b. He loved her deeply.

Although "always" and "deeply" occupy different sequential positions, their grammatical relational positions are the same: both form the adverbial-headword relation with their immediate constituents and occupy the positions in which they function as modifiers.

Then, why do we often express a word's distribution as a sequential position? This is because under usual circumstances, a sequential position reflects the only grammatical relation (relation and role). For example, 很 (very) ~ usually reflects the adverbial-headword relation. The positions stipulated by an identification word do not have grammatical relations superficially but actually contain them. Simply there is no mention of them because under usual circumstances grammatical relations are unique. For example, the sentence "Det. ~ is/are good" always has the subject-predicate relation. Zhu Dexi (1982a) said that "syntax can be discussed to a certain degree when the part of speech and hierarchy in Indo-European languages are grasped because they can control structural relations to a certain degree". In his opinion, that is one of the reasons why American structuralism does not stress grammatical relations. Therefore, syntactic constituents and grammatical positions stipulated by the environment consisting of an identification word and a part of speech can be unified by the capability of a word to occupy grammatical positions.

Two points need to be clarified:

A. Previously we said that distribution is determined by two aspects. But not all distributional differences reflect differences in parts of speech. Some distributional differences reflect differences in parts of speech, for example, 很突然/*很忽然 (very sudden/*very unexpectedness), but others do not, for example, 九个人/*九个人们 (nine persons/*nine folk). Some distributional differences only reflect the differences in subclasses, for example, 一个+名/*一下+名 (one + noun/*once + noun). What relation on earth do distribution and parts of speech have? How should distribution be used to classify parts of speech? We shall discuss these in Chapter 6.

B. Although distribution in its narrow sense and the capability to function as syntactic constituents can be unified, the two are somewhat different. In the following we shall discuss how different they are.

5.4 Generalization level of a grammatical function

5.4.1 Specific function and general function

Previously, we mentioned the factors that decide grammatical positions and excluded specific semantic differences. For example:

(7) a. 一～苹果(个) (a piece of apple)   b. 一～树(棵) (a stem of tree)

This kind of positional difference is purely caused by semantic factors, not by differences in grammatical relations. Therefore, the difference in grammatical positions does not tell the grammatical distributional difference of 一个 (a piece of) and 一颗 (a stem of). In other words, a grammatical position is actually a rather abstract position in which abstract words are combined. The degree of abstraction may be high or low. Comparatively speaking, the position that takes specific words or a class of words as its environment is a rather specific position, for example:

(8) numeral + measure word   measure word + noun
     九 (nine)   个 (piece)   一切 (all)   人 (persons)
     adjective + noun   demonstrative + noun
     坏 (bad)   人 (person)   这 (this)   人 (person)

The reason why we say that these four examples represent four pairs of grammatical position is not that the parts of speech or specific words that work as environmental constituents are different. The root cause is still that their grammatical relations are different and rather specific: the relations between number and measurement unit, between quantity and object, between attributive and object and between demonstrative word and its object. When these constituents co-occur, they more obviously occupy different grammatical positions.

(9) 这九个坏人 (these nine bad persons)　　这一切坏人 (all these bad persons)
*这个九坏人 (*this piece nine bad persons)　*这坏一切人 (*this bad all persons)
*人坏九这个 (*persons bad nine this piece)　*人坏一切该 (*persons bad all these)

If these attributives have strict substitution relations, then they cannot co-occur in the same noun phrase. But actually they can co-occur and hence are not real substitutions. Different attributives do not necessarily occupy the same grammatical position.

Because it is not easy or very trivial to express the grammatical relations in a specific grammatical position, we just directly use the environment consisting of specific words or parts of speech instead of using concrete syntactic relations. Clearly, this actually contains specific grammatical relations.

If we generalize these grammatical positions and abandon the differences in specific grammatical relations, only considering the more abstract grammatical relations such as subject-predicate, predicate-object and modifier-modified, then these grammatical positions can be generalized as two more abstract grammatical positions such as "attributive and headword".

Thus, we call the grammatical position based on concrete syntactic relations the specific grammatical position, and the grammatical position based on abstract syntactic relations the abstract grammatical position. The capability to occupy concrete syntactic positions is called specific distribution, and the capability to occupy abstract syntactic positions is called generalized distribution. This is the difference between the distribution in its narrow sense and the capability to occupy syntactic constituents: different degrees of abstraction.

Now, we can sum up the conclusion that a grammatical function includes two respects:

(1) The capability to combine one word or phrase with another (specific distribution).
(2) The capability to function as syntactic constituents (generalized distribution).

5.4.2 Whether we can classify parts of speech only on the basis of generalized or specific distribution

Can we classify parts of speech only on the basis of generalized distribution? This question is raised by Li Jinxi and Lu Zhiwei. Although Li Jinxi (1924) defined parts of speech from the perspective of meaning, he identified this term according to sentence constituents. "There is no way to tell differences among Chinese parts of speech from words themselves or their forms; which part of speech a word belongs to is set only by its position or function in a sentence". "Parts of speech are mostly differentiated from sentence constituents". He classified syntactic constituents into subjects, predicates, objects, complements, attributives (supplements of an adjective) and adverbials (supplements of an adverb) and established correspondence between parts of speech of notional words and their syntactic constituents:

Subject, object – noun, pronoun
Predicate – verb
Attributive – adjective
Adverbial – adverb

But because Chinese parts of speech have no simple correspondence with syntactic constituents, Li Jinxi proposed that "the part of speech of a word relies on sentence": "The nine Chinese parts of speech vary as the position or function of a word varies in a sentence, and there is no strict difference". For example:

铁桥 (iron bridge): 铁 (iron) changes from a noun into an adjective
律师的辩护 (a lawyer's defense): 辩护 (defense) changes from a verb
    into a noun
飞鸟 (flying bird): 飞 (flying) changes from a verb into an adjective

As a result, words have no definite parts of speech. Then he reached the conclusion that "no part of speech without a sentence". This actually means that there is no part of speech because a part of speech is the class of words themselves, implying that words have no parts of speech of their own.

Lu Zhiwei (1938) proposed the following two types of structural relationship:

(1) Supplementation: 红花 (red flower), 大海 (high sea), 好人 (good person)
     (supplement word + person or thing supplemented)
(2) Approximation: 吃饭 (have meal), 在家 (stay home), 指着他 (point to
     him) (approximator + person or thing approximated)

The two types of structural relationship stipulate the three kinds of basic parts of speech:

Noun: occupying the positions of the person or thing supplemented or
    approximated
Verb: occupying the position of an approximator
Adjective: occupying the position of a supplementer

The distribution proposed by Lu Zhiwei for classifying parts of speech is roughly equivalent to such generalizations as subjects, objects, predicates and attributives. Therefore, it is not substantially different from the classification method by Li Jinxi. If the Lu method is strictly implemented, then words still have no definite parts of speech, but it is not strictly implemented:

布鞋 (cloth shoe), 狗 (dog), 尾巴 (tail): It seems that 布 (cloth) becomes an adjective, but with the phrase 织布 (weave cloth), 布 (cloth) should be determined as a noun, which is used at the supplementation position, but still is a noun.

风大 (wind big), 墨臭 (ink odor): It seems that 大 (big) and 臭 (odor) become verbs. But with the phrases 大风 (big wind), 臭墨 (odorous ink), 大 (big) and 臭 (odor) are still adjectives.

死鱼 (dead fish), 断桥 (broken bridge): 死 (dead) and 断 (broken) are still verbs. (The examples cited by Lu Zhiweu are 飞船 (flying ship), 包车 (chartered vehicle), which are multisyllable words; if they could be broken down, they would still be "verb + noun". These two examples are imitated by the author according to Lu's statement.)

In Lu Zhiwei's mind, a part of speech does not change; therefore, once a word is identified as an adjective, it will be an adjective at any position. The initial identification is based on the four positions of two types of relations. But if it can occupy two positions, which position should be used? For example, we can well say that because there is the phrase 风大 (wind big), 大 (big) in the phrase 大风 (big wind) is also a verb. Lu does not explain this, but as we can see, he reverts to determining parts of speech according to meaning. In other words, although distribution is superficially used as the criteria, the classification is carried out not strictly according to the uniform distribution criteria but as needed according to the meaning of a word. The distribution criterion becomes only nominal.

Hence, Chinese parts of speech should not be classified according to generalized distribution.

Can we classify parts of speech only according to specific distribution?

Hu Mingyang (1996a) thought that "it seems that the simple classification of parts of speech with identification words or identification formats is objective and scientific, but actually it tends to fall into a circular argument because the initial criteria are subjectively selected and not proved". But in fact the classification of parts of speech with identification words is reasonable, merely not proved with a specific method. In the next chapter, we shall mention that the classification of parts of speech according to specific grammatical functions (including the specific functions stipulated by identification words) is demonstrable. That is to say, the great compatibility of some grammatical functions reflects the properties of the same part of speech and their equivalence. A series of equivalent functions represents the distinctive functions of a part of speech, and the criteria for classifying parts of speech (including the functions stipulated by identification words) are selected from the equivalent functions.

In contrast with the views of Hu Mingyang (1996a), Chen Baoya (1999) proposed that, due to the complicated correspondence between a part of speech and a syntactic constituent, the classification of parts of speech with syntactic constituents as criteria cannot resolve the criteria's external exclusivity. It is difficult to decide grammatical relations. Therefore, parts of speech should be classified only according to specific distribution (identification words). This method brings about the following problems:

1. It still cannot completely resolve the criteria's external exclusivity; there is scarcely any distribution in its narrow sense for only one class of words. For example:

   Verbs and adjectives have the grammatical function that they can be placed after 不 (not).

   Verbs and adjectives have the grammatical function that they can be placed after 很 (very) or 最不 (least).

   Verbs, adjectives, nouns and time words can be followed by ~了 (le).

   Verbs and adjectives can be followed by 着 (zhao).

   Verbs and adjectives can be followed by 过 (guo).

   Nouns, verbs, adjectives and time words can be modified by numeral and measure words.

   Measure words and nouns can be modified by numerals.

   Locatives, place words and nouns can function as the objects of 在 (in), 到 (to), 往 (toward).

2. The criteria's internal universality is poorer (see Chapter 2.3.4.1).

   Consequently, plentiful disjunctive criteria have to be employed, making them too complicated and not operational. For example, it is difficult to use specific distribution to classify words into distinctive words, adverbs and nouns, not to mention verbs and adjectives.

3. Parts of speech are not systematic. We shall discuss the relationship between systematicity and the criteria for classifying parts of speech in Chapter 1.2 in Volume 2.

   Therefore, only the combination of specific distribution with generalized distribution can effectively classify Chinese parts of speech. But sometimes it is really difficult for generalized distribution to decide grammatical relations; therefore, our method is to use specific distribution as much as possible, and only when specific distribution does not work or is too complicated do we use generalized distribution.

4. In fact, an identification word and syntactic constituent jointly indicate the grammatical position occupation capability. The identification word contains grammatical relations but clearly does not mention them. For example, the "numeral and measure word ~" is used to identify a noun, but 好 (good), 坏了 (bad) and other predicate words may also appear in this position and must be eliminated according to different grammatical relations. In other words, an identification word only has a specific function, and its difference from a syntactic constituent lies only in the generalization level.

5.5 Why can grammatical function be used to classify parts of speech?

Every position in a construction can only be filled in by a certain form (Bloomfield, 1926). Words are combined not randomly but in a certain order. This orderliness indicates that a syntactic position has selectional restrictions on words, and different syntactic positions allow different words to enter.

There must be bases for a syntagmatic position's selectional restriction on words. Unless the syntagmatic position has no selectional restriction on words, then any words can enter into the position optionally. There are bases for a grammatical position's selectional restriction on words. For example, the word that may appear in "不 (not) ~" indicates a statement; the word that can appear in "< quantity > ~" usually is a constituent with a reference meaning; the word that may appear in "在 (in) ~" is usually a locative word; the word that may appear in "numeral ~" is usually a measurement unit. The main basis of the grammatical position's selectional restriction on words is the grammatical meaning of a word. Therefore, the parts of speech classified according to distribution, in essence, have their grammatical meanings. The type of grammatical meaning of a word is its part of speech. We can use the grammatical position's selectional restriction on a word (namely the parts of speech reflected by a word's distribution) to classify its parts of speech.

The classification of parts of speech is essentially to infer the part of speech of a word according to its distributional characteristics. The reason why some words may appear in the same grammatical position is that they have the same grammatical meaning; the reason why some words cannot appear in the same grammatical position may be that they do not have the same grammatical meaning. In other words, the grammatical meaning of a word is the main intrinsic cause for constraining its distribution and basically determines its grammatical distribution. This is also the reason why although distribution is not the nature of a part of speech, words that belong to the same part of speech have a roughly similar distribution. Like a word form, distribution is only the extrinsic exhibition of the grammatical meaning of a word. That is to say, there is a "reflection-exhibition" relationship between the distribution of a word and its grammatical meaning: distribution reflects grammatical meaning, which in turn exhibits distribution. Therefore, although we think that the intrinsic basis of difference in parts of speech is the expressional function of a word or its grammatical meaning, and that a part of speech is not essentially of a distributional type, a word's distribution can be used as formal criteria for classifying its parts of speech because it reflects grammatical meaning.

5.6 How effective for classifying parts of speech is distribution?

Although a word's distribution can reflect its parts of speech, the relationship between distribution and a part of speech is complicated and displays the following:

I.   Only the part of speech of a word decides its distribution; its lexical meaning, pragmatic factors, word formation method, rhythmical characteristics and so on may also influence its distribution. This is illustrated as follows:

    1.   The lexical meaning of a word influences distribution. For example, 认识 (recognize) does not take 过 (guo) because the process of recognition does not end; 完成 (finish) and 毕业 (graduate) cannot take 着 (zhuo) because their actions do not continue (see Guo Rui, 1993); 切记 (caution) does not take 了 (le), 着 (zhuo) and 过 (guo) because its lexical meaning is imperative, while the predicate verb in an imperative sentence in general cannot take tense or aspect elements.

    2.   Pragmatic factors influence a word's distribution. For example, 耐烦 (patience), 像话 (proper), 好意思 (have the cheek), 要脸 (have a sense of shame) and 起眼 (attraction) cannot be modified by 很 (very). Words like 耐烦 (patience) indicate base quantity, namely the minimal quantity in a sense, which only appears in a negative sentence (see Shi Yuzhi, 1992) but cannot appear after the affirmative 很 (very). They can be modified again by 很 (very) only after being negated by 不 (not), for example, 很不耐烦 (very impatient), 很不像话 (very improper). This is decided by the pragmatic principle of sufficient-quantity expression. Namely human language usually requires that a quantity should be sufficiently expressed. But words like 耐烦 (patience) express a minimal quantity and a lower limit in a certain sense; its use as affirmative expression cannot meet this principle. The negation of a lower limit is the negation of a whole sense domain, meeting the sufficient-quantity principle. Therefore, the minimal quantity is commonly used to express a complete negation.

    3.   Word formation factors influence a word's distribution. A good many compound words in modern Chinese are formed by combining phrases; syntactic rules that restrict phrases still act on the word-form morphemes to a certain degree, thus influencing the function of a word.

The first prominent example in this respect is that when the first root of a verb or adjective is 不 (not), 无 (without) or 有 (have), the verb or adjective cannot be modified by 不 (not), for instance:

> (10) 不顾 (disregard), 不容 (not allow), 不如 (inferior, verb); 不安 (uneasy), 不幸 (unfortunate), 不利 (disadvantageous, adjective)

At a syntactic level, verbs such as 有 (have), 无 (without) and 没有 (have no) cannot be modified by 不 (not) and 没有 (have not); this kind of restriction also remains at the morphological level.[2]

> (11) 有喜 (expect), 有助 (conduce), 有请 (please, verb); 有趣 (interesting), 有名 (famous), 有害 (harmful, adjective)
> (12) 无关 (not matter), 无意 (not intend), 无视 (disregard, verb); 无情 (ruthless), 无聊 (dull), 无知 (ignorant, adjective)

Table 5.1 Word formation methods and the capability of verbs to take objects (double-syllable verbs)

Condition	VO case	Non-VO case
taking real object	194	4709
proportion	7.2%	75.4%
not taking real object	2495	1534
proportion	92.8%	24.6%
total	2689	6243
Z^1/prominent level	−92.331	++

Note: 1. Z refers to the standard score of normal distribution, see Chapter 2.2 in Volume 2 for details.

The second example is that a verb in the VO case usually cannot take a real object. At the syntactic level, except for verbs that can take double objects such as 给 (give), 送 (send) and 借 (lend), an ordinary verb that has taken a real object cannot take another real object. This kind of restriction still basically remains at the morphological level. The following verbs in their VO case cannot take real objects: 办公 (work), 闭幕 (close), 毕业 (graduate), 打仗 (fight), 发言 (speak), 见面 (meet), 就业 (employ), 失效 (fail), 破产 (bankrupt), 缺席 (absent), 上班 (go to work), 照相 (take photo). But this is just a tendency. Some verbs in their VO case can take real objects, for example, 进口 (import), 出土 (unearth), 担心 (concern) and 加工 (process). But statistical analysis shows that there is a significant difference in the capability of verbs in their VO and non-VO cases to take real objects (see Table 5.1).

(5) Rhythmical factors influence a word's distribution. This is a tendency;
(6) for example, verbs that function as attributives are usually polysyllabic ones (Table 5.2); the capability of a monosyllable adjective to function as a complement is much greater than that of a double-syllabic adjective.

II. Some grammatical positions reflect the same properties of a part of speech, and the distributional difference thus caused cannot reflect the difference in its properties. For example, "很 (very) ~" and "极 (extremely) ~" have the same requirements for words to enter into grammatical positions, but the difference in the two functions of the two words does not reflect different properties of their parts of speech.

III. It is possible that some grammatical positions allow several parts of speech to enter. For example, a noun, a verb, an adjective or a distinctive word can appear at the subject position, for example: 去是应该的 (Going is obligatory), 骄傲使人落后 (Being proud makes one lag behind), 急性好治 (The acute are easy to treat). Either a verb, an adjective, a state word or a noun can appear at the predicate position, for example: 今天阴天 (Today is overcast).

Table 5.2 The number of syllables and the capability of a verb to function as an attributive

Condition	Monosyllable	Double-syllable
as attributive	9	3147
proportion	1.0%	35.2%
not as attributive	872	5785
proportion	99.0%	64.8%
total	881	8932
Z^1/prominent level	−56.224	++

Note: 1. See Chapter 6.

Therefore, the difference in a part of speech is not simply manifested in the difference in distribution. "All the forms that have the same function compose a form class". The viewpoint of Bloomfield (1926) is not valid. It is impossible to classify parts of speech purely according to the similarity with a word's distribution (see Chapter 4).

In other words, the properties of a part of speech cannot be inferred entirely according to word distribution. Not all differences in grammatical function reflect differences in the properties of a part of speech. Thus, it is not difficult to understand why we shall give so many disjunctive classification criteria in the coming chapters. Even so, the classification of parts of speech entirely according to grammatical function may still be problematic. For example, distinctive words like 男 (male), 女 (female), 急性 (acute) and 慢性 (chronic) may function as subjects or objects and be classified into nouns by altogether using grammatical functions. For another example, the use of our criteria may classify most adjectives and verbs, but it is still hard to classify a few other adjectives and verbs. For example, 温 (warm) and 紫 (purple) may function as predicates and be modified by adverbs of an absolute degree but cannot take real objects, are not distinctive words and thus should be classified into adjectives. If 有点 (somewhat) is regarded as an absolute-degree adverb like 很 (very), then 温 (warm) and 紫 (purple) may be classified into adjectives, but intransitive verbs like 感冒 (catch cold), 咳嗽 (cough), 下雨 (rain), 哆嗦 (shiver) and 发慌 (panic) can also be modified by 有点 (somewhat); the use of this criterion may classify these verbs into adjectives. If 有点 (somewhat) is excluded from absolute-degree adverbs, then 温 (warm) and 紫 (purple) can only be classified into verbs.

In addition, some predicate words can only function as predicates, and it is difficult to determine whether they are verbs or state words, for example: 奇缺 (rare), 洞开 (bright), 参半 (half), 无双 (unrivaled), 交加 (occur simultaneously), 斑驳 (mottled), 依然 (still, classical Chinese).

Because there are limitations to the use of grammatical function as the criterion, we need other approaches to overcome this difficulty. First, we need to limit grammatical functions, namely excluding special uses. Second, we need to recognize exceptions. That is to say, the criteria of grammatical function cannot be used to classify all words. Before effective criteria are identified, 温 (warm) and 紫 (purple) can only be regarded as exceptions.

The limitations of distribution criteria are mainly caused by three factors: (1) there is no one-to-one correspondence between a part of speech and distribution; (2) the temporary transformation of expressional functions; for example, the functioning of a distinctive word as subject or object is the result of reference (transfer reference); (3) the difference in distribution caused by factors other than grammatical factors. The fundamental reason why distribution criteria have limitations is that parts of speech, in essence, are not of the distribution type.

But after all, the properties of a word's part of speech are the major factors that condition its distribution, whereas its grammatical meaning is not directly observable. Distribution is still the fundamental basis for classifying parts of speech. We should not only rely on word distribution to infer the properties of a part of speech but also use some means to eliminate the factors that influence the non-grammatical meanings of word distribution and the interference caused by incomplete correspondence between properties and grammatical positions. The correspondence between a part of speech and word distribution should be sought from the complicated relationship between properties of a part of speech and word distribution, thereby reasonably and justifiably classifying parts of speech according to distribution.

Notes

1 The distribution as Harris meant it refers to the total number of positions in which an element appears. For the convenience of description in this book, it calls a position in which the element appears a distribution of the element.
2 不无 (not without) is an exception.

6 How to classify parts of speech according to distribution

6.1 Other scholars' studies

After many years' discussion, scholars have reached the consensus that Chinese part-of-speech classification should be based on the distribution of words and proposed their specific classification criteria. But fundamentally they first have parts of speech in mind and then look for criteria, failing to prove them effectively. For example, why should we follow the criteria that a word that functions only as an attributive is a distinctive word. And that a word that functions only as an adverbial is an adverb, instead of classifying them into adjectives? Why don't we classify into an independent class words that can only function as subjects and classify into another independent class words that can only function as objects? Why do we classify them into nouns instead? We do not know the reason for using these distributional characteristics to have these parts of speech instead of using some other distributional characteristics to have other parts of speech. In the following, we will preliminarily prove our system of parts of speech and explain the reasons why these distributional characteristics should be used to classify parts of speech.

How should distributional characteristics be used to classify parts of speech? The common way is to choose some distributional characteristics to do the classification without explaining why these distributional characteristics are chosen. Some scholars have attempted to demonstrate their point of view:

6.1.1 Identification of classification criteria from grammatical characteristics

Lv Shuxiang (1979) said that the ideal classification criteria should have internal universality and external exclusivity. Zhu Dexi (1985a) thought that classification criteria should come from grammatical characteristics and gave an inequation that describes the relationship between classification criteria and grammatical characteristics: $U>V>W$, in which U denotes all the grammatical properties of a certain class of words; V denotes all the grammatical characteristics that only this class of words has but other classes do not have and meanwhile all the members of the class have; and W denotes the criteria for classifying parts of speech.

But in reality, U is not available.

Table 6.1 Quoted from Zhu Dexi's *Handouts on Grammar*, p. 55

	很 *(very)* ~	~ *object*	*Example*
A	+	+	想 (think), 怕 (fear), 喜欢 (like)
B	—	+	唱 (sing), 看 (watch), 讨论 (discuss)
C	—	—	醒 (wake), 锈 (rust), 休息 (rest)
D	+	—	大 (big), 好 (good), 干净 (clean)

To identify a grammatical function that has external exclusivity, we can endow some grammatical functions with conjunctive relations and regard them as a whole. For example, if the grammatical functions "很 (very) ~" and "~ ⟨object⟩ " are endowed with a conjunctive relation, then words can be classified into four groups:

In other words, although the individual "很 (very) ~" and "~ ⟨object⟩ " in Groups A, B, C and D have no externally exclusive grammatical functions, if the two are regarded as a whole, then [+very ~, + ~ ⟨object⟩] in Group A, [- very ~, + ~ ⟨object⟩] in Group B, [- very ~, – ~ ⟨object⟩] in Group C and[+ very ~, – ~ ⟨object⟩]in Group D all have external exclusivity.

However, as mentioned previously, the vast majority of grammatical functions do not have internal universality. The endowment of some grammatical functions with a conjunctive relation can help identify externally exclusive grammatical functions, but their internal universality is even poorer. Therefore, Groups A, B and C must be combined with one part of speech, namely a verb. This actually creates a self-contradiction: none of the three criteria for classifying into verbs are grammatical characteristics. If we strictly follow the principle that classification criteria must be identified from grammatical characteristics, then only three independent parts of speech are available. We actually endow some grammatical functions with a disjunctive relation and collectively classify words into one part of speech. For example, according to Table 6.1, the criteria for verbs are: ~[1] ⟨object⟩ (| * ~ ⟨object⟩ ∧ * very ~). Put another way, the predicate words that can take objects or can neither take objects nor be modified by 很 (very) are verbs. But on what basis do we combine Groups A, B and C with one part of speech?

The most fundamental issue is that the identification of classification criteria from grammatical characteristics may actually fall into a circular argument: only after parts of speech have already been classified can it be decided what grammatical characteristics exist; however, the classification itself depends on grammatical characteristics.

6.1.2 The use of major functions as classification criteria

Wang Li (1960: 13) said that "the determination whether a word is a noun or not depends on whether it often functions as subject or object. The determination whether a word is a verb or not depends on whether it often functions as a descriptor (the predicate headword in a declarative sentence). The determination whether a word is an adjective or not depends on whether it often functions as an attributive". After that, Chen Wangdao (1978: 48) also proposed that "the part-of-speech classification should be based on major functions". At first, the determination of parts of speech based on major functions meant that the determination should be based on the major functions (or regular function, advantageous distribution) of a word, but later the determination was changed to the determination of part-of-speech classification criteria based on major functions of a part of speech, for example, Mo Pengling and Shan Qing (1985).

This has the two problems:

(1) The overall functional frequency of a part of speech may differ greatly from the functional frequency of some words in the part of speech. Namely, the functions are out of balance. This is reflected in two respects: first, there is a great difference in functional frequency among the minor classes of words of the same major class; second, there may also be a great difference in functional frequency among various members of a class. Because of this unbalanced function, classifying parts of speech according to major functions certainly brings about chaos in the classification.

(2) The most fundamental problem is that the use of major functions to classify parts of speech has the logical fault of a circular argument: on the one hand, first parts of speech are classified and then their major functions are determined; on the other hand, the classification must be based on major functions. The classification of parts of speech according to the major functions of a word actually means that parts of speech have already been classified, thus leaving the classification not demonstrated.[2]

6.1.3 Classification based on the prototype theory

Please refer to Chapter 4 for the discussion on part-of-speech classification based on the prototype theory.

6.1.4 Classifying parts of speech purely according to general distribution

Please refer to Chapter 4 for the discussion on part-of-speech classification according to general distribution.

The common problem with these methods is a circular argument: on the one hand, first parts of speech are classified and then grammatical characteristics, major functions and typical members are determined; on the other hand, the classification must depend on the determination of the latter. Therefore, these methods are not effective.

In our opinion, the fundamental reasons why the previously mentioned methods are not successful are that parts of speech are treated as a distribution type, and that their classification totally depends on distributional similarity. In fact, the relationship between distribution and a part of speech is complicated. The difference in a part of speech is not simply manifested in the difference in distribution. A part of speech is essentially of a type that combines expressional function with a semantic type and grammatical function rather than a distributional type. Therefore, our methods should be changed from classifying the parts of speech of a word according to its distributional similarity to deducing them from its distribution. As mentioned previously, the grammatical meaning (namely the expressional function and the semantic type) of a word is the fundamental cause for constraining its distribution and basically determines its grammatical distribution. Like a word form, distribution is only the extrinsic exhibition of the grammatical meaning of a word. It reflects the grammatical meaning of a word, which is represented as distribution. Therefore, the basic task of classifying parts of speech is to determine the correspondence between grammatical function and a part of speech. Against this theoretical background, we will demonstrate the Chinese part-of-speech classification as follows:

6.2 Functional compatibility and selection of classification criteria

6.2.1 Grammatical function's values for classification

The reason why part-of-speech classification should be based on distributional characteristics is that the difference among some grammatical functions indicates the difference in parts of speech. For example, Word A has the function of "不 (not) ~" but does not have the function of " ⟨attributive⟩ ~", while the opposite is true for Word B. We can then deduce that Word A is a predicate word but that Word B is a notional word. Such a pair of grammatical functions can be called a heterovalent function. But the difference in some functions does not indicate the difference in parts of speech. For example, Word C has only the function of ⟨subject⟩ , and Word D has only the function of ⟨object⟩ , but both words are nouns. Such a function can be called equivalent function, namely reflecting several grammatical functions of the same part of speech. Because equivalent function cannot be used to distinguish one part of speech from another, it can be used as disjunctive criteria to classify the same part of speech. For example, the disjunctive criterion ⟨subject⟩ | ⟨object⟩ | ⟨attributive⟩ ~ can be used as the criterion for classifying notional words. The presence of an equivalent function shows that not all differences in distribution reflect differences in parts of speech.

Equivalent functions are transferable and form a cluster of functions, which are actually the distinctive functions of a part of speech and from which classification criteria are selected. A distinctive function can reflect the properties of the part of speech of a certain class of words. For example, the equivalent function clusters "不 (not) ~", ⟨predicate⟩ , ~ ⟨object⟩ and ~ ⟨complement⟩ reflect the properties of a verb; ⟨subject⟩ ~, ⟨object⟩ ~ and ⟨attributive⟩ ~ reflect the properties of a noun; and "很 (very) ~", "很不 (quite not) ~" and * very ~ ⟨object⟩ reflect the properties of an adjective. Different parts of speech have different distinctive functions. For example, ⟨subject⟩ is not the distinctive function of a verb or adjective. Strictly speaking, a distinctive function reflects the nature (expressional function or semantic type) of a certain class of words. For example, the properties of a noun are reference; then ⟨subject⟩ ~, ⟨object⟩ ~ and ⟨attributive⟩ ~ reflect the properties of reference. The property of a verb is a statement; then 不 (not) ~, ⟨predicate⟩ ~ and ~ ⟨object⟩ reflect the properties of a statement. The nature of an adjective is the statement of degree property, which is reflected by "很 (very) ~", "~ degree complement" and "more than X ~".

In other words, different functions have different values for classifying different parts of speech: some have distinctive values; others do not have distinctive values. Therefore, we cannot treat equally all the functions of a part of speech and only select those distinctive functions to classify parts of speech. This is the reason why we select only some distributional characteristics as the criteria for classifying parts of speech. Based on the selectional restriction of the grammatical position on words, the fundamental reason why words have their different distributions is that they themselves have differences in grammatical meaning. Therefore, the essence of a part of speech is the category of the expressional function or the semantic type of a word; distribution is only the extrinsic manifestation of the expressional function or semantic type. But some differences in distributional characteristics are distinctive, whereas others are not distinctive. Therefore, it is impossible to classify parts of speech purely according to words' distributional similarity. We select only some distributional characteristics, namely distinctive distributional characteristics, as the criteria for classifying parts of speech. In fact, the distinctive distributional characteristics refer to the grammatical functions that reflect the expressional function and semantic type of a word.

Theoretically speaking, the identification of all the functions of a language and the determination of their equivalence gather grammatical functions into clusters of equivalent functions. In this way the identification of distinctive functions of all parts of speech is, in effect, the classification of all the words into different parts of speech. Therefore, the determination of equivalent functions is the key to identifying classification criteria and determining how many parts of speech a language has.

6.2.2 The compatibility of grammatical functions and the determination of equivalent function

6.2.2.1 What information can the compatibility of functions provide?

Now that classification criteria must be selected from distinctive functions, the determination of equivalent functions becomes the key to classifying parts of speech. How should we determine equivalent function? We can use the compatibility of functions to determine their values so as to classify parts of speech, thereby identifying the functions that distinguish one part of speech from another and selecting among them the criteria for classifying parts of speech.

The compatibility of functions refers to the property that the same batch of words shares two or more grammatical functions. For example, words that can function as subjects can also function as objects, and vice versa. Words that can enter "很 (very) ~" can also enter "~ 极了 (extremely)" and "~ 得很 (nicely)"; words that can enter "~ 极了 (extremely)" and "~ 得很 (nicely)" can also enter "很 (very) ~". But the compatibility of some other functions is extremely small, for instance, "不 (not) ~", "numeral ~", " ⟨numeral and measure word⟩ ~" and ⟨adverbial⟩ . What does the large compatibility between two functions mean? What does the extremely small compatibility between two functions mean? As mentioned before, the fundamental basis for the selectional restriction of grammatical position on words is its grammatical meaning. Therefore, functions that have a rather big compatibility often reflect the same selectional restriction of two different grammatical positions on words and also the common properties of parts of speech, thus their functions being equivalent. Functions that have a rather small or no compatibility reflect different properties of a part of speech and are generally heterovalent functions. Hence, we can use the compatibility of functions to determine whether a grammatical function is equivalent or heterovalent.

6.2.2.2 Compatibility calculation and compatibility among major functions of Chinese

The size of compatibility among functions is different. The use of functional compatibility to determine the values for parts-of-speech classification should calculate the compatibility (c) between two functions. The formulae for calculating compatible degrees are given as follows: assuming $C \leq 1$, the unidirectional compatible degree of Function x relative to Function Y (c_{x-y}), the unidirectional compatible degree of Function Y relative to Function x (c_{y-x}) and the total compatible degree between Functions X and Y (c_{x*y}):

(1) C_{x-y}=xy number of overlapping words/number of x words
(2) C_{y-x}=xy number of overlapping words/number of Y words
(3) C_{x*y}=xy number of overlapping words/(number of x words + number of Y words – xy numbers of overlapping words)

For example:

In Figure 6.1, 100 words have Function X and 40 words have Function Y, among which 80 words have only Function X, 20 words have only Function Y and 20 words have concurrently X and Y functions. The compatible degrees are as follows:

Cx-y=20/100=0.2
Cy-x=20/40=0.5

The total compatible degree is not significant. As Figure 6.2 shows, Cx*y=20/(100+20-20)=20/100=0.2. Although the total compatible degree can reflect the compatible degree of X in relation to Y, it cannot reflect the compatible degree of Y in relation to x: Cy-x=20/20=1.

We use the above-mentioned method to calculate the compatible degrees among the major functions of Chinese notional words (see Table 6.2).

6.2.2.3 Methods for determining equivalent functions

Equivalent functions can be fundamentally determined by distributional compatible degrees. Although the distribution of a word is mainly decided by its part of speech, it may also be influenced by other factors such as semantic and pragmatic meanings, rhyme and word formation methods. Moreover, some grammatical positions may allow several parts of speech to enter; some words may have several parts of speech. Therefore, we cannot totally rely on functional compatible degrees to determine a function's values for classifying parts of speech; other factors must be considered and the interference on functional compatibility caused by them must be eliminated.

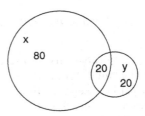

Figure 6.1 Example 1

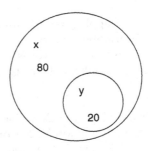

Figure 6.2 Example 2

We use the following rules to decide the equivalent relations among grammatical functions.

Rule 1: if the unidirectional compatible degree of two functions is less than 0.5 (c<0.5), then we can infer that they reflect different parts of speech and belong to heterovalent functions.[3] If a word has concurrently two functions, then it may be deemed to have concurrently two parts of speech. But if it is found and properly reasoned that a word meets the conditions for a certain function, then the word cannot be deemed to have several parts of speech; instead, it is because its grammatical position allows several parts of speech to enter. If any unidirectional compatible degree of two functions is larger than 0.5 (c>0.5), then it must be tested with Rules 2 through 4.

For example, the unidirectional compatible degree of 不 (not) ~ & ⟨attribute⟩ , 不 (not) ~ & ⟨adverbial⟩ , 很 (very) ~ & ⟨attributive⟩ , 很 (very) ~ & ⟨adverbial⟩ , 不 (not) ~ & ⟨noun⟩ ~ ⟨attributive and headword⟩ , ⟨attributive⟩ & ⟨adverbial⟩ respectively is less than 0.5 and can be deemed to have a heterovalent function. The ⟨numeral and measure word⟩ ~ & ⟨adverbial⟩ has a unidirectional compatible degree of less than 0.1, but can use as an adverbial a word that can be modified by numerals and measure words. For the word, conditions can be found and properly reasoned. There are mainly three kinds of conditions: (1) metaphors such as 拳头大 (as big as fist) and 碗口粗 (as wide as bowl rim);[4] (2) methods and tools such as 电话采访 (telephone interview), 公款请客 (meal treatment with public money) and 掌声鼓励 (encourage with applause); (3) places such as 操场去 (go to sports ground), 学校见 (see you at school) and 主场迎战对手 (play with an opponent head-on at home ground). The function whose conditions can be found and properly reasoned is a syntactic function but not a lexical one. Therefore, these words or phrases should not be considered as adverbs. In other words, the adverbial position also allows some nouns to enter.

Rule 2: if a word having one of the functions and a word not having the function exhibit great difference at other grammatical positions, then the functional compatibility is because the grammatical position allows several parts of speech to enter and because a word has several parts of speech. They should not be deemed to have equivalent functions. If the difference is small at other grammatical positions, then they are equivalent functions.

For example, the unidirectional compatible degrees of 不 (not) ~ | no ~ & ⟨subject⟩ | ⟨object⟩ are 0.58 and 0.2 respectively. But at the positions of ⟨numeral and measure word⟩ ~, predicate and complement, they exhibit great differences: the words that can enter 不 (not) ~ usually can also enter ⟨predicate⟩ and ~ ⟨complement⟩ but cannot enter ⟨numeral and measure word⟩ ~. But most of the words that can enter 不 (not) ~ can enter ⟨numeral and measure word⟩ ~ but cannot enter ⟨predicate⟩ and ~ ⟨complement⟩ . Therefore, we can conclude that compatibility is because the position ⟨subject⟩ | ⟨object⟩ allows several parts of speech to enter. Furthermore, the unidirectional compatible degree of ⟨predicate⟩ &

Table 6.2 Compatible degrees of the main grammatical functions of Chinese notional words

Grammatical function	Number of words			Compatibility				Cx * y	grade	Equal value
	x	y	x & y	Cx-y	grade	Cy-x	grade			
Not ~& no ~	11020	10790	9918	0.90	++	0.92	++	0.83	+	+
Not~& predicate	11020	13261	11000	1.00	++	0.83	+	0.83	+	+
No ~& predicate	10790	13261	10754	1.00	-+	0.81	+	0.81	+	+
Not: no ~ &predicate	11809	13261	11788	1.00	++	0.89	+	0.89	+	+
Not|no ~& bound complement	11809	506	497	0.04	--	0.98	++	0.04	--	-
Not|no ~& group complement	11809	6484	6090	0.52	+	0.94	++	0.50	+	+
Not|no ~& bound complement	11809	6820	6748	0.57	+	0.99	++	0.57	+	+
Not|no ~& ~ real object	11809	6163	5783	0.49	-	0.94	++	0.47	-	-
Not|no ~& ~ semi- object	11809	7467	6755	0.57	+	0.90	++	0.54	+	+
Not|no ~& ~zhuo, le, guo	11809	10459	10240	0.87	+	0.98	++	0.85	-	+
Not|no ~ & adverbial~	11809	13345	11837	1.00	++	0.89	+	0.89	+	+
Not|no ~ & very ~	11809	2552	2509	0.21	-	0.98	++	0.21	-	+
Not|no ~ & attributive	11809	23544	3764	0.32	-	0.16	-	0.12	-	-
Not|no ~ & adverbial	11809	1592	462	0.04	--	0.29	-	0.04	+|-	-
Subject & object	31394	33989	30351	0.97	++	0.89	+	0.87	+	+
Not|no ~& subject|object	11809	34796	6842	0.58	+	0.20	-	0.17	-	-?
Predicate & subject|object	13261	34796	7481	0.56	+	0.22	-	0.18	-	-?

Grammatical function	Number of words		x & y	Compatibility						Equal value
	x	y		Cx-y	grade	Cy-x	grade	Cx * y	grade	
Not|no ~ & noun (attributive)~	11790	14298	630	0.05	--	0.04	--	0.02	--	--
Predicate & adverbial~	13261	13477	13122	0.99	++	0.87	++	0.96	++	+
Predicate & bound complement	1573	506	53	0.03	--	0.10	-	0.03	--	-
Very ~&~ 得很 (nicely)	2552	1607	1607	0.63	-	1.00	++	0.63	-	+
Very ~&~ 极了 (extremely)	2552	2012	2012	0.79	+	1.00	++	0.79	+	+
Very ~& 很不 (very not) ~	2552	1008	985	0.39	-	0.98	++	0.38	-	+
Very ~ & bound complement	2552	506	192	0.08	--	0.38	-	0.07	--	+?
Very ~& group complement	2552	6494	1558	0.61	+	0.24	-	0.21	-	+
Very ~& attributive	2552	23544	709	0.28	-	0.03	--	0.03	--	-
Very ~& adverbial	2552	1592	273	0.11	-	0.17	--	0.07	--	-
Very ~&~ zhuo, le, guo	2552	10459	1888	0.74	+	0.18	--	0.17	--	+
Very ~& predicate	2552	13261	2533	0.99	++	0.19	--	0.19	--	+
Very ~&~ real object	2552	6163	203	0.08	--	0.03	--	0.02	--	+?
attributive & adverbial	23544	1592	296	0.01	--	0.19	--	0.01	--	-
adverbial & group complement	1550	6494	240	0.15	-	0.04	--	0.03	--	-
number ~& attributive	24314	23544	17731	0.73	+	0.75	+	0.59	+	-?
number ~ & adverbial	24314	1592	112	0.00	--	0.07	--	0.00	--	-

(continued)

Table 6.2 (Cont.)

Grammatical function	Number of words			Compatibility						Equal value
	x	y	x & y	Cx-y	grade	Cy-x	grade	Cx * y	grade	
subject| object & number ~	34796	24314	22887	0.66	+	0.94	++	0.63	+	+
subject| object & attributive	34796	23544	22105	0.64	+	0.94	++	0.61	+	–?
subject| object & adverbial	34796	1592	504	0.01	––	0.32	–	0.01	––	–
subject| object & attributive ~	34796	33706	30881	0.89	+	0.92	++	0.82	+	+
subject| object & noun (attributive) ~	34796	14538	14124	0.41	–	0.97	++	0.40	–	+
subject| object & adverbial ~	34796	13472	3272	0.09	––	0.24	–	0.07	–	–

Notes: 1. The number of words that have the ※ function is calculated from the statistical sampling proportion. 2. The critical value of compatible degrees: high compatible degree: (+)c>=0.5, including extremely high compatible degree (++): c>=0.9; low compatible degree (-):c<0.5, including extremely low compatible degree (–): c<0.1. 3. The "x & y" denotes the number of words that have Functions X and Y. 4. In the "equivalent" column, "+" denotes equivalence; "-" denotes degree (-): c<0.1 3. The "x & y" denotes the number of words that have Functions X and Y. 4. In the "equivalent" column, "+" denotes equivalence; "-" denotes unequivalence; "-?" indicates that the compatible degree is higher than 0.5, but according to relevant rules, 4j should be unequivalent; "+?" indicates that the compatible degree is less than 0.5 but should be applied according to relevant rules.

〈subject or object〉 is at most 0.56. Words that can function as predicates can also enter 不 (not) ~ but usually cannot enter 〈numeral and measure word〉 ~, while those that cannot function as predicates usually can enter 〈numeral and measure word〉 ~ but cannot enter 不 (not) ~. The compatible degree of the two functions is because the position 〈subject or object〉 allows several parts of speech to enter. The functions are not equivalent.

Rule 3: if a large portion of words having Functions X and Y have one function that can form the construction consisting of a modifier and the word it modifies, then the compatibility of X and Y, by inference, is because some words have several parts of speech. There is no way to determine whether the words have equivalent functions. For example, 〈numeral and measure word〉 ~ & 〈attributive〉, 〈subject or object〉 & 〈attributive〉 (桌子 (desk), 节目 (program) – 木头 (wood), 电视 (television)). These pairs of functions have the highest compatible degrees of 0.75 and 0.94 but can form the immediate constituents 木头桌子 (wooden desk) and 电视节目 (television program). Thus, it can be inferred that the words 木头 (wood) and 电视 (television) have several parts of speech, but it cannot be inferred that the two functions are equivalent.

The reason why we put forward this rule is that we find that the same word forms in the positions of the modifier and headword construction have very different syntactic expressions, for example:

(4) a. 也干净 (also clean), 也不干净 (also not clean), 也很干净 (also very clean)
    b. 干净衣服 (clean clothes), *不干净衣服 (* not clean clothes), *很干净衣服 (* very clean clothes)
(5) a. 都认真 (all serious), 都不认真 (all not serious), 都很认真 (all very serious)
    b. 认真学习 (serious study) *(不认真）学习 (*(not seriously) study), 很认真学习 (very serious study)
(6) a. 我的木头 (my wood), 我的十根木头 (my ten pieces of wood)
    b. 木头房子 (wooden house), *+根木头房子 (*house of ten pieces of wood)

木头 (wood) can be modified by numerals and measure phrases at the head-word position. This is the same as in the subject or object position, but it cannot be modified by numerals and measure phrases at the attributive position, indicating that its part of speech has changed (see Lv Shuxiang [1979], Zhang Bojiang [1994] and Guo Rui [1997a]). In terms of grammatical meaning, 干净 (clean) and 认真 (serious) are statements in the head-word position, which is the same as in the predicate position. But they are modifiers in attributive or adverbial positions. Just like in the subject or object position, 木头 (wood) is a reference in the head-word position, but is a modifier in the attributive position (see Chapter 4). The two functions are highly compatible but do not reflect the same part of speech. The fundamental reason for this is that the two parts of speech do not highly differ from each other in the lexicon (see Chapter 4).

Rule 4: If the number of words x and y significantly decreases as their frequency decreases, then by inference, the correlation between Functions X and Y is because some words have several parts of speech.

The reason why we put forward this rule is that we find that the times of appearance of one of the functions decrease significantly as the word frequency decreases, whereas another function has no significant or negative correlation with word frequency. As Table 6.3 shows, there is a positive correlation between the compatible degree between 很 (very) ~ and 〈attributive〉 and word frequency because the number of words that have 〈attributive〉 decreases significantly as their frequency decreases, whereas 很 (very) ~ does not decrease as the word frequency decreases but increases, presenting a negative correlation. In contrast, the compatible degrees between 很 (very) ~ and 不 (not) ~ and between 很 (very) ~ and ~ zhuo (着), le (了), guo (过) do not have a positive correlation with word frequency. Meanwhile, we find that there is a prominent positive correlation between a conversional word and word frequency (see Table 6.4). We can say that the number of parts of speech of a word has a positive correlation with word frequency,[6] and thus are justified in thinking that the compatibility of two functions is because some words have several parts of speech (concurrent parts of speech or a conversional word).

Rule 5: An equivalent function is transferable; if Function X is equivalent to Function Y, and Function Y is equivalent to Function Z, then Function X is also equivalent to Function Z, thus forming an equivalent function cluster. Although the compatibility degree among some functions is less than 0.5, because they are equivalent to a certain identical function, the two functions are transferable and thus equivalent. For example, the compatible degrees of the two pairs of functions of 很 (very) ~ & 〈complement〉 and 很 (very) ~ & ~ 〈real object〉 are less than 0.5, but 很 (very) ~ is equivalent to 不 (not) | 没 (no) ~, but the latter is equivalent to 〈complement〉 and ~ 〈real object〉. According to transferability, 很 (very) ~ is also equivalent to 〈complement〉 and ~ 〈real object〉.

Rule 6: The generalization levels of grammatical function and parts of speech represented by the grammatical function are consistent. The functions whose generalization level is low in the equivalent cluster can determine the equivalent functions at the same generalization level and represent different subclasses. If the unidirectional compatible degree between the function whose generalization level is high in an equivalent function cluster and the function whose generalization level is low is greatly disparate, as shown in Figure 6.2, then the function whose generalization level is low may represent a subclass. Reference should be made to other characteristics such as reduplication form and whether to classify subclasses or not.

As mentioned previously, the generalization level of a function such as a syntactic constituent is higher than that of the function of a specific word or a part of speech; the generalization level of the part of speech represented by the former is also higher than that of the latter. For example, 〈subject〉 | 〈object〉 | 〈attributive〉 ~, whose equivalent function has a high

Table 6.3 The correlation between compatible degree and word frequency, and that between function and word frequency[5]

Frequency level	Level 1		Level 2		Level 3		Level 4		Level 5		Total		Correlational coefficient	Markedness
Number of words	512		512		512		512		512		2560			
Medium word frequency	3113		535		167		48		4					
	Number of words	Compatibility	Number of words	Compatibility	Number of words	Compatibility	Number of words	Compatibility	Number of words	Compatibility	Number of words	Compatibility		
很(very) ~ & attributive	282	0.55	169	0.33	126	0.25	85	0.17	45	0.09	707	0.28	0.925	+
很(very) ~ & 不(not) ~	459	0.90	474	0.93	487	0.95	484	0.95	482	0.94	2386	0.93	-0.946	+
很(very) ~ & 着(zhuo), 了(le), 过(guo)	399	0.78	397	0.78	404	0.79	360	0.70	307	0.60	1867	0.73	0.444	-

	Level 1		Level 2		Level 3		Level 4		Level 5		Total		Correlational coefficient	Markedness
	Number of words	proportion	Number of words	proportion	Number of words	proportion	Number of words	proportion	Number of words	proportion	Number of words	Proportion		
很(very) ~	498	97%	506	99%	508	99%	510	100%	504	98%	2526	99%	-0.873	-
Attributive	292	57%	172	34%	126	25%	86	17%	46	9%	722	28%	0.931	+

Table 6.4 The correlation between number of conversional words and word frequency[7]

Frequency level	Level 1		Level 2		Level 3		Level 4		Level 5		total		Correlation coefficient	Markedness
Number of words	7622		7622		7622		7622		7622		38110			
Medium frequency	2901		401		114		33		6					
Conversional word	Number	Proportion	Number	Proportion	Number	Proportion	Number	Proportion	Number	Proportion	Number	Proportion		
	1308	17%	417	5.%	229	3.0%	136	1.8%	95	1.2%	2185	5.7%	0.996	++

generalization level, represents a notional word, but the compatible degrees between 〈numeral〉 ~, whose generalization level is low, and "在 (in) ~" are 0.01 and 0. They belong to heterovalent functions at the low generalization level and represent two subclasses. For another example, the unidirectional compatible degrees of 很 (very) ~ and 〈predicate〉 are 0.99 and 0.19 respectively, being greatly disparate. 很 (very) ~ has a function whose generalization level is low and thus represents a subclass.

6.3 Classification criteria for Chinese notional words

6.3.1 *Criteria for classifying major parts of speech of Chinese notional words*

According to the above-mentioned rules, we determine the equivalence of Chinese grammatical functions and form the following equivalent function clusters:

> Equivalent Function Cluster 1: 不 (not) ~, 没 (no) ~, ~ zhuo (着), le (了), guo (过), 〈predicate〉, 〈complement〉, ~ 〈complement〉, ~ 〈real object〉, ~ 〈quasi-object〉, 〈adverbial〉 ~, very~, 很不 (quite not)~, ~极了 (extremely), ~ 得很 (nicely)
> Equivalent Function Cluster 2: 〈subject〉, 〈object〉, 〈attribute〉 ~, 〈numeral and measure word〉 ~
> Equivalent Function Cluster 3: 〈modifier〉 [8]
> Equivalent Function Cluster 1 represents predicate words; Equivalent Function Cluster Two represents notional words; Equivalent Function Cluster 3 represents modifiers.

But an equivalent function cluster is not the criterion for classifying parts of speech because some grammatical positions may allow several parts of speech to enter. Therefore, although it has internal universality, it has no external exclusivity. This can be demonstrated by the co-occurrence[9] of unequivalent functions such as 不 (not) ~ and 〈subject〉 ; for instance, 不去是应该的 (not going is obligatory). Then, how can we decide which position allows several parts of speech to enter? This can be decided by the hierarchy of co-occurring functions: the functions at the outer hierarchy do so. Under this circumstance, the classification of parts of speech should give first priority to inner-layer functions, for example, 不 // 去/是应该的 (not // going/ is obligatory). A decision can be made that the 〈subject〉 function in the outer layer allows several parts of speech to enter. According to "不 (not) ~", 去 (going) should be a predicate word. For another example, 〈predicate〉 and 〈attributive〉 ~ are not equivalent but can co-occur in the following: 小王/黄 // 头发 (Little Wang/ yellow//hair). Its predicate function is at the outer layer. Therefore, we can assume that the predicate position allows several parts of speech to enter. According to its inner-layer function 〈attributive〉 ~, 头发 (hair) should be a notional word. For another instance, ⟨attributive⟩ ~ and ⟨adverbial⟩ ~ are not equivalent but can co-occur in the following examples:

(7) a. 这本书的 / 及时 // 出版 (The punctual // publication/of the book)
   b. *及时 / 这本书的 // 出版 (*The punctual/publication // of the book)
(8) a. (小王) 也/黄 // 头发 ((Little Wang) also/yellow // hair)
   b. *(小王) 黄/也 // 头发 (*(Little Wang) yellow/also // hair)

These two examples indicate that both ⟨attributive⟩ ~ and ⟨adverbial⟩ ~ allow several parts of speech to enter. According to its inner-layer function ⟨adverbial⟩ ~, 出版 (publish) should be a predicate word; according to its inner-layer function ⟨attributive⟩ ~, 头发 (hair) should be a notional word (see Chapter 4).

That is to say, an equivalent function cluster only shows that the functions in the same function cluster cannot distinguish one part of speech from another. The classification criteria must be selected from the equivalent function cluster and restrict the positions that allow several parts of speech to enter, thus having external exclusivity. For example, only words that can function as subjects or objects can be modified by attributives, and words whose functions in Equivalent Function Cluster 1 are used as inner-layer functions, are classified into notional words. In addition, classification criteria are also related to classification strategies. This issue will be discussed in Chapter 7. Here we assume that it has been solved. After considering the above-mentioned issues, we can formulate the following criteria for classifying all the major parts of speech of notional words:[10]

Predicate words: 不 (not) ~ | 没 (no) ~ | 很 (very) ~ | 很不 (very not) ~ | ~ ⟨object⟩ ⟨complement⟩ | ⟨complement⟩ | ⟨predicate⟩ ∧ * ⟨subject⟩ | ⟨object⟩

Substantive words: ⟨subject⟩ | ⟨real object⟩ | ⟨attributive⟩ ~ ∧ * ⟨predicate word⟩

Modifiers: ⟨modifier⟩ ∧ (* ⟨predicate word⟩ | ⟨substantive word⟩)

Substantive modification words: ⟨attributive⟩ ∧(* ⟨predicate word⟩ | ⟨substantive word⟩)

Predicate modification words: ⟨adverbial⟩ ∧(* ⟨predicate word⟩ | ⟨substantive word⟩)

6.3.2 Classification of basic classes

Rule 6 says that the generalization levels of grammatical function and parts of speech represented by the grammatical function are consistent. Therefore, predicate words, substantive words and modification words determined with the functions in the above-mentioned same equivalent function cluster can be further classified into such basic classes as nouns and verbs according to the equivalent function cluster whose generalization level is low. We also infer the classification values of a function according to the compatible degree among functions and relevant rules. In the following, we first look at the compatible degrees among the major functions of a modifier (see Table 6.5).

We must first make clear that we define grammatical functions by using the concepts of parts of speech such as ⟨numeral⟩ ~, ~ ⟨locative⟩ . Then do we fall into a circular argument? Yes. The circular argument can be resolved by listing all or some members of a class. For example, numerals and locatives belong to a closed class[11] and all their members can be listed. Some typical members of measure words can be listed, for instance, 个 (piece), 斤 (jin), 项 (item) and so on. According to the fixed-point theory, Bai Shuo (1995) demonstrated that the use of not yet defined parts of speech to classify parts of speech, in theory, does not involve a logically circular argument.

The present book holds that the use of parts of speech as an environment does not involve a logically circular argument: As mentioned before, a grammatical position refers to the position in which immediate constituents that have certain grammatical relations exist in a syntactic structure. Fundamentally speaking, the grammatical position that uses parts of speech as an environment is still decided by grammatical relations. For example, X ⟨locality⟩ refers to a construction consisting of a modifier and the word it modifies; the construction has its relative positional relations in a reference system. ⟨numeral⟩ X refers to the construction consisting of a modifier and the word it modifies; the construction has its numerical measurement unit relations. Therefore, the use of parts of speech to define the environment, in essence, is to use the specific grammatical relations represented by a part-of-speech combination, but grammatical relations are independent of parts of speech. Therefore, there is no circular argument.

Among modifiers, the compatible degrees of more specific functions ⟨attributive⟩ and ⟨adverbial⟩ than ⟨modifier⟩ are 0.01 and 0.19 respectively, thus leading us to conclude that they are not equivalent and form two equivalent function clusters:

Equivalent Function Cluster 3.1: ⟨attributive⟩
Equivalent Function Cluster 3.2: ⟨adverbial⟩

Consequently, we can classify modifiers into determiners and adverbs:

Determiner: ⟨attributive⟩ ∧(* ⟨predicate word⟩ | ⟨substantive word⟩)
Adverb: ⟨adverbial⟩ ∧* (⟨predicate word⟩ | ⟨substantive word⟩)
{马上(immediately), 亲自 (personally), 特意 (specially), 也 (also)}

Among determiners, the compatible degrees among the functions ~ ⟨quantity⟩ , for example, 三个 (three pieces), ~ X de (的) ⟨noun⟩ ,[12] for example,

Table 6.5 The compatible degrees among specific grammatical functions of modification words

Grammatical function	Number of words			Compatibility						Equal value
x & y	x	y	x & y	Cx-y	grade	Cy-x	grade	Cx * y	grade	grade
~ measure word & ~ x de (的) noun[1]	54	64	6	0.11	–	0.09	–	0.05	–	–
~ measure word & ~ numeral, measure word, noun	54	11	5	0.09	–	0.45	–	0.08	–	–
~ measure word&numeral, measure word ~ noun	54	449	0	0.00	–	0.00	–	0.00	–	–
~ numeral, measure word, noun & ~ x de (的) noun	11	64	3	0.27	–	0.05	–	0.04	–	–
~ numeral, measure word, noun & numeral, measure word ~ noun	11	449	0	0.00	–	0.00	–	0.00	–	–
~ x de (的) noun & numeral, measure word ~ noun	64	449	0	0.00	–	0.00	–	0.00	–	–
~ measure word & quasi-object	54	31	5	0.09	–	0.16	–	0.06	–	–
quasi-object & ~ numeral, measure word, noun	31	11	0	0.00	–	0.00	–	0.00	–	–
quasi-object & numeral, measure word ~ noun	31	449	0	0.00	–	0.00	–	0.00	–	–
quasi-object & ~ x de (的) noun	31	64	13	0.42	–	0.20	–	0.16	–	–

所有迟到的学生 (all the late students), ~ ⟨numeral and measure word plus noun⟩ , for example, 这三个学生 (these three students), ⟨numeral and measure word⟩ ~ ⟨noun⟩ , for example, 三台黑白电视 (three sets of black-and-white television) are very low. We basically conclude that the functions are not equivalent. Hence, we further classify determiners into four parts of speech:

Numeral:　~　⟨quantity⟩ ∧　*(not　~|~ ⟨numeral+　measure words+noun⟩ {一 (one), 几 (several), 半 (half), 十 (ten)}

Demonstrative:　~ ⟨numeral+measure word+noun⟩ ∧ (* ⟨predicate word⟩ | ⟨substantive word⟩){每 (each), 任何 (any), 其他 (other), 这 (this)}

Numeral and measure word: ~ X de (的) ⟨noun⟩ ∧ * ~ ⟨numeral + measure word + noun⟩ {许多 (many), 一切 (all), 俩 (both)}

Distinctive word:　⟨numeral and measure word⟩ ~　⟨noun⟩ ∧ *(⟨predicate word⟩ | ⟨substantive word⟩){高等　(high-class), 公共 (public), 野生 (wild), 日常 (routine)}

The criteria of the latter half for the four types of determiner use the negative values of conjunctive criteria in order to eliminate other parts of speech that may have the functions of the former half. Among criteria for numerals, adjectives and demonstratives may also occur in the position of ~ ⟨measure word⟩ . For example, 大块 (big piece), 每台 (each set) and (* not ~|~ ⟨numeral + measure word + noun⟩) need to be used to eliminate adjectives and demonstratives. Among criteria for demonstratives, predicate words and notional words may also occur in the position of ~ ⟨numeral+ measure word + noun⟩ , for instance, 雪白 (snow-white) and 一双鞋 (a pair of shoes), and therefore should be eliminated together. Moreover, classical Chinese demonstratives such as 本 (this) and 该 (these) cannot appear in the above-mentioned positions and are different from the function of a colloquial modern Chinese demonstrative, thus requiring other classification criteria. For detailed discussion, see Chapter 1.5.10 in Volume 2. Among criteria for numerals and measure words, a demonstrative may also occur in the position of ~ X de (的) ⟨noun⟩ . We use *~ ⟨numeral+measure word+noun⟩ to eliminate them. Among criteria for distinctive words, notional words and predicate words may also occur in the position of ⟨numeral and measure word⟩ ~ ⟨noun⟩ . We use * ⟨predicate word⟩ | ⟨notional word⟩ to eliminate them.

In terms of grammatical meaning, numerals and measure words indicate quantity and actually have the same integral function as a phrase formed by "numeral + measure word". Compare: 许多迟到的学生 (many late students) – 十个迟到的学生 (ten late students); 来了三个 (three came) – 来了许多 (many came). This is the reason why we classify them into numerals and measure words.

Actually, two types of modifiers can function as adverbials. One type always functions as an adverbial before a modified constituent and is classified into adverbs; another type is usually placed after a modified constituent and is called by Zhu Dexi (1982b) a quasi-object. For example, 高一点 (a little higher), 等候片刻 (wait for a while) and 沉思许久 (meditate for a long time). But in a negative expression, it is generally placed in front. For example, 一点也不高 (not high at all), 片刻不得安宁 (cannot be peaceful for a moment) and 许久未来 (for a long time not come). In our opinion, a quasi-object in its strict sense is actually a type of modifier and is identical to an adverbial placed in front in terms of its grammatical relations. Or we can call this a "rear adverbial" (see Guo Rui 1997a). Phrases such as 许久 (for a long time) and 片刻 (for a moment) actually indicate quantity in terms of their grammatical meanings, and their grammatical functions are the same as other phrases that indicate quantity. Compare: 等了三天/等了许久 (wait for three days / wait for a long time), 高两厘米/高一点 (two centimeters high / a little higher). Moreover, some words can actually appear both in ~ X de (的) ⟨noun⟩ and in the position of a quasi-object, for instance, 一些 (some), 许多 (many), 不少 (a good many), 片刻 (for a moment) and 一点 (a bit). Therefore, we can also classify into numerals and measure words the words that appear in the position of quasi-object. In this way, the properties of numerals and measure words are not completely consistent. Some of them have only the properties of substantive modification words such as 一切 (all), 少许 (a little) and 俩 (both); some have only the properties of predicate modification words (adverbs) such as 许久 (for a long time), 良久 (very long time) and 不久 (soon); some have the properties of both substantive modification words and predicate modification words such as 一些 (some), 许多 (many), 片刻 (for a moment) and 丝毫 (the slightest). The criteria for numerals and measure words can be amended as - X de (的) ⟨noun⟩ | ⟨quasi-object⟩ ∧ * ~ ⟨numeral + measure word + noun⟩ .

Can the rest of adverbs be classified into smaller subclasses? Quite a number of scholars have noticed that an adverb may have a virtual or a real meaning. For instance, the meanings of 也 (also), 还 (still) and 究竟 (on earth) are rather virtual, and those of 特意 (specially), 飞速 (rapidly) and 亲自 (personally) are rather real. But it is difficult to classify them into even smaller types. Zhang Yisheng (1995a) classified them into adverbs or adverbial words; Chen Yi (1989) classified them from adverbs into preattached words, but his criteria lack internal universality and cannot effectively classify the two types of words.

Among substantive words, the compatible degrees of ⟨quantity⟩ ~ and ~ ⟨locality⟩ are very high (see Table 6.6). We posit that they are equivalent functions according to the rules proposed in Chapter 6.2.2.3. The compatible degrees of "在 (in) [⟨notional words⟩]~"[13] and ⟨quantity⟩ ~, "在 (in)[⟨notional words⟩]~" and ~ ⟨locality⟩] are also more than 0.5. But the number of these two pairs of functionally overlapping words has a prominently positive correlation with word frequency (see Table 6.7). "在 (in)[⟨notional words]⟩ ~" decreases prominently as their word frequency decreases, but ⟨numeral and measure word⟩ ~ and ~ ⟨locality⟩ have no

Table 6.6 The compatible degrees among specific grammatical functions of substantive words

Grammatical function	Number of words			Compatibility						Equal value
x & y	x	y	x & y	Cx-y	grade	Cy-x	grade	Cx * y	grade	
<numeral> ~ & 在 (in) [notional word] ~	509	1313	6	0.01	--	0.00	--	0.00	--	--
<numeral> >~& <numeral, measure word > ~	509	21423	207	0.41	--	0.01	--	0.01	--	--
<numeral> ~ & ~ <locative>	509	22683	250	0.49	--	0.01	--	0.01	--	--
在 (in) [notional word] ~ & <numeral, measure word> ~	1313	21423	871	0.66	+	0.04	--	0.04	--	--?
在(in) [notional word] ~ & ~ <locative>	1313	22683	1018	0.78	+	0.04	--	0.04	--	--?
<numeral, measure word> ~ & ~ <locative>	21423	22683	19553	0.91	++	0.86	+	0.80	+	+

Table 6.7 The correlation between word frequency and compatible degree (substantive word)

Frequency level	Level 1		Level 2		Level 3		Level 4		Level 5		Total		Correlation coefficient	Markedness
Number of words	5541		5542		5542		5542		5542		27709			
Medium frequency	1094		142		34		6		0					
	Number	Pro-portion	Number	pro-portion	Number	Pro-portion	Number	Pro-portion	Number	Pro-portion	Number	Pro-portion		
在 (in) [notional word] ~ & <quantifier>	450	8.1%	164	3.0%	81	1.5%	36	0.6%	155	2.8%	886	3.2%	0.959	++
在 (in) [notional word] ~ & ~ <dialect>	554	10.0%	221	4.0%	110	2.0%	50	0.9%	160	2.9%	1095	4.0%	0.970	++
在 (in) [notional word]	558	10.6%	225	4.1%	111	2.0%	51	0.9%	162	2.9%	1137	4.1%	0.974	++
<quantifier> ~	4289	77.4%	4232	76.4%	4126	76.4%	4279	77.2%	4387	79.2%	21423	77.3%	-0.037	-
~<locational word>	4766	86.0%	4616	83.3%	4711	85.0%	4711	85.0%	4655	84.0%	23459	84.7%	0.652	-

prominent correlation with word frequency. According to Rule 4, we think that the compatibility is because the words that can enter "在 (in)[⟨notional words⟩]~" have several parts of speech. We cannot assert that these two pairs of words have equivalent functions.

Thus, there are three equivalent function clusters among substantive words:

Equivalent Function Cluster 2.1: ⟨numeral⟩ ~ (it may also take a numeral as the environment)

Equivalent function cluster 2.2: in[notional word]~ equivalent function cluster

Equivalent Function Cluster 2.3: ⟨numeral and measure word⟩ ~, ~ ⟨locational word⟩

Hence, we classify measure words, locational words and nouns. The criteria are as follows:

Measure word: (一 (one)│几 (several) ~ ∧ * ⟨subject⟩ {个 (piece), 次 (times), 年 (year), 斤 (jin)}

Locational word: 在 (in) [⟨notional word⟩]~ ∧ * ~ 里 (inside)│以南 (to the south)

Noun: ⟨subject⟩ │ ⟨real object⟩ │ ⟨attribute⟩ ~│~ 里 (inside)│以南 (to the south) ∧ (* ⟨predicate word >│ ⟨measure word⟩ │ ⟨locational word⟩){桌子 (desk), 面积 (area), 地步 (extent)}

Criteria for measure words: some nouns can enter 一 (one)│几 (several) ~, for example, 这一地区 (this one region) and 几兄弟 (several brothers) can be eliminated with * ⟨subject⟩ . Among criteria for locational words, some nouns can also enter 在 (in)[⟨notional word⟩]~, for instance, 在教室 (in a classroom), 在北京 (in Beijing) and 在操场 (at the sports ground). But these words can also enter ~ ⟨locality⟩ . We think that they have concurrently the properties of nouns and locational words. Here we do not treat them as conversional words with the homomorphic strategy but classify them into nouns with * ~ 里 (inside) │ 以南 (to the south) in order to eliminate this portion of nouns. The criteria for classifying nouns include the functions of ⟨subject⟩ , ⟨real object⟩ and ⟨attributive⟩ ~, whose generalization level is rather high, because ⟨numeral and measure word⟩ ~ and ~ ⟨locality⟩ have no internal universality. A noun is actually the residual class of substantive words and so can be classified by eliminating measure words and locational words from substantive words.

Locational words can also be classified into locatives, place words and time words; the classification can still be demonstrated with the previously presented method. But due to space limitations here, the demonstration is omitted and only classification criteria are listed as follows:

Locative: 在 (in) (〈substantive word〉 ~) ∧ * ~ 里 (inside) | 以南 (to the south) {周围 (ambient), 以前 (before), 附近 (nearby)}

Time word: 在 (in) ~ ∧ 等到 (until) ~ | ~ 以来 (since) | ~ 的时候 (time when){刚才 (just), 去年 (yesteryear), 最近 (recently)}

Place word: 在 (in) ~ ∧ (* ~ 里 (inside) | 以南 (to the south) | time word〉){原地 (in place), 一旁 (aside), 民间 (folk)}

Among predicate words, the compatible degrees of 很 (very) ~ and 〈predicate〉 are 0.99 and 0.19 respectively, being greatly disparate. Their generalization level is diverse. According to Rule 6, 很 (very) ~ may represent a subclass. The survey of other syntactic and morphological characteristics shows that most reduplicated forms of double-syllable or monosyllable predicative words that can enter 很 (very) ~ are AABB or AA (not neutral tone) forms. Therefore, we think that 很 (very) ~, ~ 得很 (nicely), ~ 极了 (extremely) and 很不 (quite not) ~, whose degrees of compatibility with 很 (very) ~ is extremely high, represent a subclass of predicate words that differs from other predicate words. The compatible degrees of 很 (very) ~ and 〈real object〉 are as low as 0.08 and 0.03 respectively. Most reduplicated forms of predicate words that can enter ~ 〈real object〉 are also ABAB or AA (neutral tone) forms. Although the two functions are equivalent (很 (very) ~ and 不 (not) ~ are equivalent; 不 (not) ~ and ~ 〈real object〉 are equivalent) according to the transferability of equivalent functions, they are not equivalent at a rather low generalization level. As for the co-occurrence of 很 (very) ~ and ~ 〈real object〉 , for example, 很喜欢他 (like him very much), because ~ 〈real object〉 is in the inner layer, they should be classified into verbs according to the principle of "~ 〈real object〉 priority". The criteria for classifying adjectives are as follows:

Adjective: 很 (very)[不 (not)] ~ ∧ (*很 (very) ~ 〈object〉){红 (red), 大 (big), 干净 (clean), 认真 (serious)}

Quite a large number of adjectives that can enter 很 (very) ~ can enter ~ 〈real object〉 . There are two scenarios: (1) the real object that denotes degree comparison appears only in ~ 〈real object〉 (comparative object) + 〈quasi-object〉 , for instance, 高他一头 (a head higher than him), 大他一岁 (one year older than him). Their degree just fits the degree of an adjective. (2) The real object denotes a certain change on a part of a whole; the subject and object have a relationship between part and whole, for instance: (脸) 红了半边 ((face) gets red on its half side), (手上) 黑了一块 ((hand) gets black a part), (你我)都白了头发 ((you and I) both have white hair). At a rather low generalization level, 很 (very) ~ and ~ 〈real object〉 are not equivalent. But this phenomenon has its conditions and can be properly reasoned by analogy. According to Rule 1, it should be regarded as a syntactic phenomenon and still functions as adjective, which does not change into a verb.

Furthermore, it is difficult to classify verbs and state words primarily because a state word belongs to a narrow type of function and does not have its special type, whereas a verb has a great individual difference and can hardly be separated from a state word with equivalent functions. Nevertheless, with the double-syllable predicate word excluded from adjectives, although most of its reduplicated forms are ABAB, its grammatical meanings and phonetic forms are different. The latter half parts of reduplicated forms of 调整 (adjust), 请示 (ask), 商量 (consult), 研究 (study) are pronounced in a neutral tone, and their grammatical meanings denote a small quantity, whereas the reduplicated forms such as 雪白 (snow-white), 通红 (red through), 矮胖 (stocky) and 干瘦 (skinny) are not pronounced in a neutral tone, and their grammatical meanings denote a deeper degree. Most of the former can enter 不 (not) ~, 没 (no) ~, ~ 〈object〉 , ~ 〈complement〉 and ~ zhuo (着) | guo (过), whereas the latter cannot. Thus we classify the two types of predicate words as follows:

Verb: 不 (not) ~ | 没 (no) ~ | ~ 〈object〉 | ~ 〈complem ent〉 | 〈bound complement〉 | (~ zhuo (着) | guo (过) | (〈predicate〉 | 〈adverbial〉 ~) ∧ * 〈subject〉 ∧ (* 很 (very)[不 (not)] ~ | (很 (very) ~ 〈object〉){吃 (eat), 看 (see), 研究 (study), 应该 (should)}
State word: 〈compound complement〉 | (〈predicate〉 ∧ (* 〈subject〉 | 〈object〉) ∧ (* 〈verb | adjective〉){通红 (red through), 花白 (gray), 酷热 (sweltering hot)}

Most state words are the quantitative forms of adjectives. On these grounds, a good many people think that they should be classified into adjectives. The change from adjective into its corresponding quantitative form is a form of word formation rather than a structural form, not being a syntactic phenomenon at all. Furthermore, a state word has prominently different syntactic characteristics from an adjective; in particular it no longer has fundamental functions of an adjective such as 很 (very) [不 (not)]~. Therefore, they should be separated into another type of words.

The above discussion shows that the compatible degree of at least one of the major functions determined as equivalent reaches the extremely high critical value ($c >= 0.9$), while the compatible degree among the functions that cannot be determined as equivalent generally cannot reach this critical value. Put another way, all the functions whose compatible degree is more than 0.9 are equivalent, with the only exception being 〈subject or object〉 & 〈attributive〉 . This shows the role of a compatible degree played in determining an equivalent function.

Equivalent function clusters plus other part-of-speech exclusive restrictions are the criteria for classifying parts of speech. The classification criteria are both disjunctive and conjunctive. Disjunctive criteria refer to classification criteria that play no distinctive role within the same equivalent function cluster. Conjunctive criteria refer to functions that are used to exclude other parts of speech.

We have discussed 13 out of 15 notional words, excluding pronouns and onomatopoeia. A pronoun is actually a type of word classified from the perspective of discourse function and is not, strictly speaking, at the same level as other parts of speech. From the perspective of a part of speech in its usual sense, it should be classified into notional words, predicate words, modifiers and other even smaller basic classes. Let us stop the discussion here. Onomatopoeia is a special part of speech whose status in a part-of-speech system we do not know sufficiently. We are not clear how to demonstrate it with the methods presented in this book.

6.4 Brief summary

What we did in the above is actually to determine the correspondence between grammatical function and part of speech. The determination of what grammatical function corresponds to what part of speech largely accomplishes the part-of-speech classification task.

The above analysis shows that the pairs between 不 (not) ~ and ⟨attributive⟩ , 不 (not) ~ and ⟨noun⟩ ~, 很 (very) ~ and ⟨attributive⟩ , 很 (very) ~ and ⟨adverbial⟩ , and ⟨subject or object⟩ and ⟨attributive⟩ are heterovalent functions and represent different parts of speech. Therefore, words such as 研究 (study) and 调查 (investigate) that can be modified by 不 (not), directly modified by nouns and function as attributives actually have the properties of verbs, nouns and distinctive words. Words such as 干净 (clean) and 新 (new) that can be modified by 很 (very) and directly function as attributives actually have concurrently the properties of adjectives and distinctive words. Words such as 迅速 (rapidly) and 妥善 (appropriately) that can be modified by 很 (very) and directly function as adverbials actually have concurrently the properties of adjectives and adverbs. Words such as 木头 (wood) and 质量 (quality) that can function as subjects or objects and directly function as attributives actually have concurrently the properties of nouns and distinctive words. We do not just treat them as conversional words according to the priority homomorphic strategy (see Chapter 7). Moreover, because ⟨predicate⟩ and ⟨complement⟩ are equivalent functions, there is no need to classify the so-called "only complement word" that can only function as a complement. Because words in different grammatical positions may belong to different parts of speech, the statement by Li Jinxi (1924) that "the part of speech of a word relies on a sentence" is reasonable to a certain extent. It is a pity that he did not establish the method for determining what grammatical position expresses different parts of speech and what grammatical position expresses identical ones. The statement goes to extremes in saying that "words have no definite parts of speech", and that "there is no part of speech without a sentence".

A part of speech is essentially the large category of expressional functions of a word and the basic type that combines its semantic type with its grammatical function rather than its distributional type. Therefore, it is impossible to classify parts of speech simply according to distributional similarity. But distribution is the extrinsic manifestation of the properties of a part of speech and can be inferred by determining the correspondence between distribution and a part of speech. The correspondence between distribution and a part of speech can be determined according to the compatibility with grammatical functions and relevant rules, thus identifying the criteria for classifying parts of speech of all words. However, after all, distribution is not the essence of a part of speech; many factors influence the distribution of a word, and there is a limitation to using distributional characteristics as criteria for classifying parts of speech. For example, there are two kinds of words that can only function as predicates. The first kind includes 交加 (occur simultaneously), 倍增 (multiply), 参半 (half) and 奇缺 (rare), and usually belongs to verbs; the second kind includes 旖旎 (graceful), 婆娑 (dancing), 皑皑 (snow-white) and 卓然 (outstanding), and generally belongs to state words. But it is difficult to classify them functionally. This notwithstanding, the use of distributional characteristics of a word as the basis can still classify the vast majority of words into their corresponding parts of speech, and it is difficult to determine the parts of speech of only a minority of words.

In the previous discussion, we demonstrated the internal classification of the parts of speech of Chinese notional words. We may also demonstrate the external classification, for example, from the typological perspective. For discussions on this, see McCawley (1992) and Guo Rui (2001).

Notes

1 ~ denotes the position in which a subject appears; | denotes disjunctive relation; ∧ denotes a conjunctive relation; * means that a certain function does not exist; the word inside ⟨⟩ is a part of speech or syntactic constituent.
2 See Chapter 2.4 in Volume 2 for detailed discussion.
3 According to the above-mentioned assumption, only functions that have extremely high compatible degrees belong to equivalent functions. To be safe, here we use the criterion that a heterovalent function should have a compatible degree of less than 0.5.
4 Of course, the use of what substantive word as a vehicle of metaphor is related to the typicalness of the substance and the social mentality and culture.
5 See Chapter 2 in Volume 2 for the correlation between word frequency and grammatical function
6 Many scholars have noticed a positive correlation between changes in language form and in meaning and word frequency. This can be explained in this way: changes always occur in use. The more frequently a linguistic element is used, the more possibly it changes; the less frequently it is used, the less possibly it changes. Elements that have the least possibility to change have not been in use.

7 The multiple entries of polysemes and homographs are calculated as one entry. Therefore, the statistical number of words (38110) is less than the total number of words (43330).

8 The book calculated the compatible degrees among attributive, adverbial and other grammatical functions but did not calculate attributives and adverbials as modifiers. But only a few words can function as adverbials; an attributive basically represent a modifier.

9 We regard the whole function of a phrase as the function of its head element. For example, 苹果 (apple) in 大苹果好吃 (A big apple is delicious) functions as a subject; the word 去 (go) in 我马上去图书馆 (I will go to library immediately) functions as a predicate.

10 The use of these criteria should eliminate omission and transfer reference. For example, there is omission in 我不 (I do not); we should not classify 不 (not) into predicate words just because it functions as a predicate. 许多 (many) in 许多都坏了 (Many are ruined) is used as a transfer reference; we should not classify it into notional words just because it functions as a subject.

11 The segment such as 一百二十三 (one hundred and twenty-three) is a phrase.

12 ~ X de (的) ⟨noun⟩ refers to the de (的) construction and the construction that the constituent which takes de^2 (的) functions as an attributive.

13 [] denotes the constituent that may not necessarily appear.

7 Conversional words and nominalization

7.1 Conversional words and homographs of different parts of speech

A word that belongs to several parts of speech is a conversional word.

The treatment of conversional words and homographs is interrelated. The following three phenomena are related to conversional words:

A. The same meaning (strictly speaking, the same generalization word) concurrently belongs to several parts of speech. For example, 长期 (long-term), 真正 (genuine) and 临时 (temporary) can only function as attributives and adverbials, concurrently belonging to distinctive words and adverbs. For another instance, 小时 (hour) can be used as 一个小时 (one hour of) and 一小时 (one hour), therefore being treated as a noun that functions as a measure word concurrently.

B. A couple of associated meanings belong to different parts of speech. For example, 典型 (representative) in 一个典型 (one representative) and 很典型 (very representative) has different meanings: the former is a noun, whereas the latter is an adjective. For another example, 通知 (notification) in 通知开会 (notify a meeting) and 写一个通知 (write a notice) has different meanings: the former is a verb, whereas the latter is a noun.

C. Words that have no associated meanings but the same sounds and word forms belong to different parts of speech. For example, 会 (hui, meaning "can") in 会游泳 (can swim) and 会 (hui, meaning "meeting") in 开一个会 (hold a meeting) are homophones and homographs: the former belongs to verbs, whereas the latter belongs to nouns. For another instance, 制服 (zhifu, meaning "uniform") in 一套制服 (a suit of uniform) and 制服 (zhifu, meaning "conquer") in 制服了对手 (conquer one's opponent) are homonymous: the former is a noun; the latter is a verb.

A should belong to conversional words, which we call homonymous conversional words. C should belong to homographs in different parts of speech, and this is not controversial. There are different opinions on how to deal with B. Strictly speaking, a conversional word refers to the same generalization word that has concurrently different parts of speech; therefore, only A belongs to conversional words. But lexicology regards the associated meaning as the different meanings of the same word, and a dictionary treats it as one entry. Our word list also uses such a unit as one entry, and this is comparatively economical (we call it a lexical word, and the unit induced with the identity principle is called a grammatical word). Only A belongs to conversional words in theory, but considering that a dictionary treats associated meaning as one entry and that a computer cannot distinguish A from B in Chinese, we flexibly treat B as a conversional word and call it a heteromorphic conversional word. In order to distinguish between the two kinds of conversional words, we call a homonymous conversional word a conversional word in its narrow sense, which, together with a heteromorphic conversional word, is called a conversional word in its broad sense.

This shows that the conversional word in its narrow sense has something to do with the determination of lexical words.

7.2 What is a real conversional word?

Whether a word belongs to conversional words or not depends on the following three questions:

(1) Whether the word in two positions belongs to the same generalization word (the identity problem).
(2) Whether a word belongs to several parts of speech or their multifunctionality (whether they are transformed at the lexical level).
(3) What classification strategy is used.

If both the lexical meaning and the part of speech are different, then different generalization words actually belong to different parts of speech. Of course, they should be regarded as heteromorphic conversional words. Therefore, Question (1) is not worth discussing. Provided that different generalization words have different parts of speech, they should all be regarded as conversional words. For example, 锁 (lock), 领导 (leader), 科学 (science) and 死 (death) should all be treated as conversional words. After determining the identity, we should determine again whether the various functions of a word differ in parts of speech. We do so according to the method for determining equivalent functions presented in Chapter 6. This method proves that an adjective that takes zhuo (着), le (了) and 过 (guo) does not function concurrently as a verb. It also proves that the transformation of parts of speech at the syntactic level is not their conversion. For example, verbs such as 去 (going) in 去是应该的 (going is obligatory), which function as subjects, do not function concurrently as nouns because they still have the basic functions of a verb, such as taking objects and adverbials. In fact, a large number of verbs can function as subjects. Moreover, we also prove that words such as 研究 (study) and 调查 (investigate) that can be modified by 不 (not), be directly modified by nouns and function as attributives actually have the properties of verbs, nouns and distinctive words. Words such as 干净 (clean) and 新 (new) that can be modified by 很 (very) and directly function as attributives actually have concurrently the properties of an adjective and a distinctive word. Words such as 迅速 (rapidly) and 妥善 (appropriately) that can be modified by 很 (very) and directly function as adverbials actually have concurrently the properties of an adjective and adverb. This problem, which has been solved previously, will not be discussed here. We need to discuss classification strategies.

7.3 Classification strategies and conversional words

7.3.1 Classification strategies

The same generalization word that has the properties of several parts of speech is not necessarily treated as a conversional word in its narrow sense. Whether or not it is treated as a conversional word has something to do with the strategy for classifying parts of speech. We first look at what classification strategies are available.

As shown in Figure 7.1, the properties of two parts of speech can partially overlap lexically. The words in Sphere *a* have the properties of words in Part of Speech A; the words in Sphere *b* have the properties of words in Part of Speech B; the words in Sphere *c* have the properties of words in both Parts of Speech A and B. In theory, the following four classification strategies are available:

I. **The homogeneous strategy**: Starting from the properties of a part of speech, all the properties of the part of speech of a generalization word are treated equally to create a one-to-one correspondence between parts of speech thus classified and their properties. If a generalization word has the properties of several parts of speech, then we treat it as a conversional word. As shown in Figure 7.1, there are two classes of parts

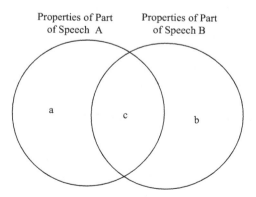

Figure 7.1 Properties of parts of speech

of speech: Part of Speech A (A, C) and Part of Speech B (B, C), where Part of Speech C functions concurrently as Parts of Speech A and B.

The advantage of the homogeneous strategy is that the properties of a part of speech have one-to-one correspondence; its disadvantage is that there are too many conversional words in their narrow sense.

II. **The homomorphic strategy**: Starting from a generalization word, the properties of all its parts of speech are treated equally. As long as the properties of its parts of speech are different, they are classified into different parts of speech. As shown in Figure 7.1, a generalization word is classified into three parts of speech: A, B, C.

The advantage of the homomorphic strategy is that there are no conversional words in their narrow sense; its disadvantage is that there are too large numbers of parts of speech, and that there is no one-to-one correspondence between a part of speech and its properties.

III. **The priority homomorphic strategy**: Starting from a generalization word, we give priority to the properties of a certain part of speech and do not treat as a conversional word a word that has the properties of several parts of speech; instead, we treat it as a priority part of speech, thus creating a correspondence between a part of speech and the properties of a priority part of speech. As shown in Figure 7.1, parts of speech are classified into two classes: A and B. Because the order of priority is different, Class C is grouped into the following two cases:

   (1) The order of priority is: A>B. According to this order of priority, Parts of Speech A and C are grouped into Class A; Part of Speech B is grouped into Class B.

   (2) The order of priority is: B>A. According to this order of priority, Part of Speech A is grouped into Class A; Parts of Speech B and C are grouped into Class B.

In the past, it was often said that "without a change in lexical meaning, there is no change in a part of speech", actually meaning the use of the homomorphic strategy.

The advantage of the priority homomorphic strategy is that there are no conversional words, and that there are not a large number of parts of speech. Its disadvantage is that there is no entire one-to-one correspondence between a part of speech and its properties.

IV. **The consolidation strategy**: A word that has the properties of two parts of speech is consolidated into the one that has one part of speech. As shown in Figure 7.1, a word belonging to Parts of Speech A, B and C are consolidated into the one belonging to one part of speech.

The advantage of the consolidation strategy is that there are no conversional words in their narrow sense, and that the number of parts of speech is small, but its disadvantage is that there are too large numbers of parts of speech, and that there is no one-to-one correspondence between part of speech and its properties.

How should classification strategies be selected?

7.3.2 Selecting classification strategies

There are no right or wrong classification strategies but only good or bad ones. Theoretically speaking, all the above-mentioned four classification strategies are feasible. What classification strategy is to be selected should be decided by taking into consideration the whole grammatical system and the purpose for selecting classification strategies. For example, starting from a practical purpose, the homogeneous strategy should be used for the part-of-speech system for information processing. Namely, we classify into verb-noun conversional words the lexical items that concurrently function as verbs and nouns. The part-of-speech system in this book is not for a specific purpose, and we consider the following two factors in selecting classification strategies:

(1) The simplicity of a part of speech: there are as small a total number of parts of speech as possible and as small a total number of conversional words in its narrow sense as possible.

To reduce the number of parts of speech, it is necessary to use the homogeneous strategy, the priority homomorphic strategy or the consolidation strategy. To reduce the number of conversional words, it is necessary to use the homomorphic strategy, the priority homomorphic strategy or the consolidation strategy.

Why should the total number of parts of speech be reduced? The purpose for classifying parts of speech is first and foremost to meet the needs of people to learn and analyze a language. Too many parts of speech may increase the memory burden and make people unable to have a sound command of the whole part-of-speech system. If the homomorphic strategy is used for all the parts of speech, then words with the properties of verbs, nouns, distinctive words and adverbs should be classified into separate parts of speech. There will be a total of hundreds of parts of speech if classified this way. Such a huge number of parts of speech are obviously beyond the ken of an ordinary person. Because the homomorphic strategy may increase the number of parts of speech, we should avoid it.

Why should the number of conversional words be reduced? The reasons are twofold. First, if a word belonging to two parts of speech is treated as a conversional word, in formulating syntactic rules, we first and foremost need to decide what part of speech the word in a sentence belongs to. Too many conversional words may increase the burden of deciding parts of speech. Second, if most words belonging to two or more parts of speech are conversional words belonging to two or more parts of speech, then words belonging to two or more parts of speech have not yet been differentiated, and there is no need to classify them into two or more parts of speech.

(2) The simplicity of the syntactic rule: the grammatical functions of different words in the same part of speech should be as few as possible.

To make this happen, the use of the homogeneous strategy is needed to treat the word that has concurrently different properties. For example, if the homogeneous strategy is used to treat a word that has concurrently the properties of verbs, nouns and modification words as their concurrent parts of speech, then the following rules may be obtained when constructing syntactic rules with the part-of-speech system:

Noun + verb→subject-predicate
Verb + noun → predicate-object
Verb + verb → combination, predicate-object, predicate-complement, link-verb predicate

However, if the priority homomorphic strategy is used, then the same part-of-speech sequence may produce various results and increase the ambiguity of the syntactic analysis and its level of difficulty as a result. For example:

Verb + verb → subject-predicate, consolidation, attributive-headword, adverbial headword
Verb + noun →subject-predicate, predicate-object, consolidation, attributive-headword
Verb + verb →subject-predicate, consolidation, predicate-object, attributive-headword, predicate-complement, link-verb-predicate, attributive-headword, adverbial headword

The more widely the priority homomorphic strategy is used, the more ambiguous is the sentence thus made, and the less efficiently is the sentence described and analyzed. It may even make the description of syntactic rules with parts of speech meaningless. Therefore, use of the priority homomorphic strategy should be limited.

There is no correspondence in meaning between Chinese parts of speech and syntactic constituents, and a sentence described with parts of speech may be certainly too ambiguous. You may wonder why the use of the priority homomorphic strategy should still be limited. In fact, the lack of a one-to-one correspondence between Chinese parts of speech and syntactic constituents is largely due to the fact that the Chinese grammatical system uses the priority homomorphic strategy to classify parts of speech. If the priority homomorphic strategy were not used to classify parts of speech, then there might be a very strict correspondence between Chinese parts of speech and syntactic constituents. Therefore, lacking a one-to-one correspondence between parts of speech and syntactic constituents cannot explain the reason why the use of the priority homomorphic strategy should be limited.

In addition, under special circumstances, the following should be considered:

(3) Mental acceptability: when one part of speech contains more than one property, it should be in agreement with the human mentality. If the

priority homomorphic strategy is used, then the status of two properties of the same part of speech should be obviously higher or lower, and the first priority is given to the property that has a higher syntactic status.[1] For example, words such as 研究 (study) and 调查 (investigate) that are used concurrently as the two parts of speech of verb and noun should be classified into verb instead of noun with the priority homomorphic strategy, which gives priority to verbs because the syntactic status of a verb is higher than that of a noun.

Factors (1) and (2) are the most basic; Factor (3) is just supplementary. But Factors (1) and (2) are contradictory. The simplicity of a part of speech tends to ruin the simplicity of the syntactic rule. The simplicity of the syntactic rule tends to ruin the simplicity of part of speech. Therefore, in selecting the strategy for classifying parts of speech, we should consider both factors, reducing their total cost to the lowest degree. Under any circumstances, the homomorphic strategy maximizes the total cost of the two factors (the number of parts of speech increases; there is no correspondence between parts of speech and grammatical properties). Therefore, we will not use it. We will only choose the homogeneous strategy, the priority homomorphic strategy or the consolidation strategy.

In fact, different strategies for classifying parts of speech cause a good many controversies related to Chinese parts of speech. Strategies are not right or wrong but only good or bad. Which strategy for classifying parts of speech is the best depends on the specific circumstances.

Then, under what circumstance should the homogeneous strategy or the priority homomorphic strategy be used? Our principles are as follows:

1. If overlapping members take the majority, then we should use the consolidation strategy.
2. If there are comparatively large numbers of words that have two parts of speech or their conditions are identified (namely they can be controlled by rules), then we use the priority homomorphic strategy; if not, we use the homogeneous strategy. We do so because if the homogeneous strategy is used for a large number of words that have two or more parts of speech, a massive number of conversional words may appear. Although the simplicity of the syntactic rule pays off, the part of speech is complicated. Before the syntactic treatment, a massive number of conversional words must be identified; once erroneous identification of conversional words occurs, erroneous syntactic treatment may also ensue. Therefore, when there is a large number of words that function as two parts of speech, we would be better off using the priority homomorphic strategy.
3. If the priority homomorphic strategy is used for a small number of words that function as two parts of speech, although the simplicity of the part of speech pays off, that of the syntactic rule requires too heavy a cost because more syntactic rules are needed to deal with the use of a

conversional word. The use of the homogeneous strategy may simplify syntactic rules, while the simplicity of a part of speech does not require a heavy cost. Therefore, with the total cost considered, we should use the homogeneous strategy. However, if a word that functions as two or more parts of speech can be controlled by rules, then the priority homomorphic strategy is desirable.

In other words, the selection of which classification strategy to use has something to do with the number of words that have concurrently the properties of two parts of speech. This is what Zhu Dexi (1985a) meant: there should not be too many conversional words. We call this principle the systematic principle. What are the bases for the systematic principle? If a word overlapped by two functions belongs to or basically belongs to the same batch, then this means that the two functions do not differentiate in this language, and there is no need to classify the word into different parts of speech. There are no absolute criteria for deciding what proportion of words that have concurrently the properties of two parts of speech is needed to select different classification strategies, but some criteria have a greater tendency than others. In the following, we shall discuss the specific criteria for selecting different classification strategies.

7.3.2.1 *Criteria for selecting the consolidation strategy*

To consolidate words that have the properties of two parts of speech into those that have the properties of one part of speech, the number of words whose parts of speech overlap should not be less than 90% of the total number of words that combine the two parts of speech. In other words, only when the vast majority of words concurrently have the properties of two parts of speech is there no need to classify them into two parts of speech.

The approximately inclusive relation can be regarded as a special case of the consolidation strategy:

As shown in Figure 7.2, if the vast majority of words that have the properties of Part of Speech B have the properties of Part of Speech A, but only a few words that have the properties of Part of Speech A have the properties of Part of Speech B, then we regard Part of Speech B as a subclass of Part of Speech A.

7.3.2.2 *Criteria for selecting the priority homomorphic strategy*

The priority homomorphic strategy is used only when two parts of speech have advantages or disadvantages. The dominant hierarchy of parts of speech is as follows:

Predicate word property > substantive word property > modification word property

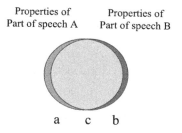

Figure 7.2 The approximately complete overlapping and approximately inclusive relations between two parts of speech

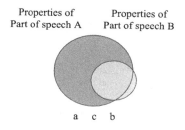

Figure 7.3 The dominant hierarchy of parts of speech (Guo Rui, 1997)

The basis for this hierarchy is combination dominance. The combination of constituents on the left-hand side with those on the right-hand side produces a combined unit whose properties are identical with those on the left-hand side. Namely, the constituents on the left-hand side are the core, for example:

Predicate word property + substantive word property→predicate word property
Predicate word property + modification word property→predicate word property
Substantive word property + modification word property→substantive word property

When the overlapping part accounts for 40% to 80% of the dominant part of speech, it should be included in the dominant part of speech, and only words that are in a weak part of speech should be classified into another independent part of speech.

When the overlapping part takes the majority of the weak part of speech, it should not be included in the weak part of speech.

Part of Speech A   Part of Speech B

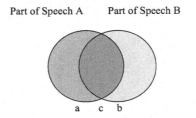

a   c   b

Figure 7.4 The overlapping part accounts for 40% to 80% of the dominant part of speech (Part of Speech A)

Part of Speech A   Part of Speech B

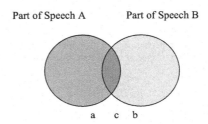

a   c   b

Figure 7.5 The overlapping part takes the minority (<20%)

7.3.2.3 Criteria for selecting the homogeneous strategy

If the overlapping part of two parts of speech has a small number of words that belong to one of them (<20%), then it is desirable to use the homogeneous strategy to classify the overlapping part into conversional words.

Even though the overlapping part takes the majority (51%–90%) of words whose parts of speech are weak, it is desirable to use the homogeneous strategy instead of the priority homomorphic strategy. But if the priority homomorphic strategy has already been used to classify the overlapping part of the dominant parts of speech because it takes a high proportion, then the homogeneous strategy should not be used.

The above-mentioned quantitative criteria refer to general conditions, but in actual operation, the absolute number of the overlapping parts should be taken into consideration. If the absolute number of words that have concurrently two parts of speech is rather big, then they should not be classified into conversional words with the homogeneous strategy. In addition, if the same batch of words has concurrently three or more parts of speech, which classification strategy is to be used must be considered in all respects. Just because of these reasons, in the above-mentioned criteria, we leave the critical proportions 20%–40% and 80%–90% for the two classification strategies. The critical proportions must be dealt with flexibly according to the absolute number of overlapping parts of speech and the number of conversional words. A detailed discussion is presented in the relevant subsections in Chapter 1 of Volume 2.

7.3.3 Classification strategies for the major Chinese parts of speech

In the past, the Chinese grammar circle tended to use the priority homo-morphic strategy. For example, they regarded predicates, attributives and adverbials as the functions of an adjective. Following the above-mentioned new criteria, this treatment should be reconsidered.

The following sections will discuss the selection of classification strategies for the major overlapping parts of speech.

First, let us look at the major overlapping parts of speech:

7.3.3.1 Classifying predicate words and substantive words

When a predicate word overlaps with a substantive word, Zhu Dexi (1985a) proposed three criteria for determining the predicate word that has concur-rently the properties of a substantive word.

1. Functioning as the object of a verb that can take a quasi-predicate as its object, for example, 有 (have), 作 (do), 加以 (conduct), 进行 (carry out) and so on: 有研究 (have study), 有苦难 (have hardship), 进行研究 (con-duct study).
2. Being directly modified by other nouns. For example, 历史研究 (history study), 经济困难 (economy difficulty)
3. Directly modifying other nouns. For example: 研究方向 (research interests). This criterion cannot identify a nominal adjective.

In fact, the third criterion shows the properties of not a substantive word but a modification word. Therefore, the former two criteria are enough to identify nominal verbs and nominal adjectives. Actually, there are only the former two criteria for nominal verbs in Zhu Dexi's *Handouts on Grammar* (1982b).

In Chinese, the proportion between a word that has concurrently the prop-erties of a predicate word and one that has concurrently the properties of a substantive word takes only 19% of the predicate words and 8% of the sub-stantive words, far below the criteria for the consolidation strategy, which should not be used. Neither should the predicate word be regarded as a sub-class of substantive words. The overlapping proportion between predicate words and substantive words should be treated as their conversional words with the homogeneous strategy.

The above data are obtained with the joint investigation of verbs, adjectives and state words within the predicate word. If the verbs, adjectives and state words are investigated separately, then:

Table 7.1 The major overlapping parts of speech

	Multi-functional words	Overlapping proportion	Proportion that overlaps previous words	Proportion that overlaps latter words	Single functional word	Proportion	Functional words	Total
predicate- substantive	2490	6.15%	19.08%	8.33%	37968	93.85%	predicate+ substantive	40458
predicate- distinctive	3895	12.13%	29.85%	16.97%	28207	87.87%	predicate+ distinctive	32102
predicate- adverb	469	3.49%	3.59%	55.70%	12954	96.51%	predicate+ adverb	13423
substantive-distinctive	20081	63.18%	67.17%	87.51%	11702	36.82%	substantive+ distinctive	31783
distinctive-adverb	106	0.88%	0.35%	12.59%	11965	99.12%	distinctive+ adverb	12071
distinctive-adverb	284	1.21%	1.24%	33.73%	23221	98.79%	Distinctive modification +adverb	23505

Multifunctional word	Number	Overlapping proportion	Percentage of verbs	Percentage of nouns
Verb-noun	2381	6.31%	23.12%	8.0%

Words that have concurrently the properties of verbs and nouns still take a rather low proportion among verbs, existing in the critical range between the priority homomorphic strategy and the homogeneous strategy. It is not at all realistic to use the consolidation strategy to treat Chinese verbs as a subclass of nouns; instead, we can use the homogeneous strategy to treat them as conversional words between verbs and nouns, for example, 研究 (research), 生产 (production), 管理 (management) and 学习 (study).

In particular, considering that some words are actually used as nouns far more often than as verbs, it is unreasonable to classify them into verbs. For example, the following table gives the data randomly retrieved from two pages of language data in the Peking University CCL Corpus:

	Properties of verb	Properties of noun
manage	23	55
sleep	2	49

Under this circumstance, obviously it is more reasonable to treat them as conversional words between verbs and nouns.

However, considering that there are a rather big absolute number of words that have concurrently the properties of verbs and nouns, it is acceptable to treat them as verbs with the priority homomorphic strategy. This book still treats them as verbs (nominal verbs) in accordance with Zhu Dexi (1982, 1984b, 1985a, b).

The properties of adjectives and nouns also overlap. Out of 2,355 adjectives, 109 are nominal, accounting for 5% of the total, for example, 平衡 (balanced) and 健康 (healthy). Even though the number is not huge, if adjectives are the only consideration, we can well use the homogeneous strategy to classify them into adjectives concurrently functioning as verbs. But because the priority homomorphic strategy is used for verbs that function as predicates, it is desirable to use the same strategy, not classifying the adjectives into those concurrently functioning as nouns.

7.3.3.2 Classifying substantive words and distinctive words

Too great an overlapping proportion (taking 67% of substantive words) between the properties of substantive words and modification words (distinctive words) indicates that the degree of differentiation between modification words and substantive words is very low. It is advisable to use the priority homomorphic strategy to treat the overlapping part as a substantive word (noun) instead of a conversional word. For example, words such as 木头 (wood), 质量 (quality) and 语言 (language) that can function as subjects, objects or attributives should be treated as nouns instead of conversional words between nouns and distinctive words.

A very high proportion, 87.5%, of words that have the properties of distinctive words have concurrently the properties of nouns. But compared with the properties of nouns, the properties of distinctive words are weak; therefore, it is not advisable to use the priority homomorphic strategy to treat the overlapping parts as distinctive words.

7.3.3.3 Classifying predicate words and distinctive words

The overlapping proportions between the properties of predicate words and distinctive words are not high (6%, 19%, 8%), and the homogeneous strategy should be used to treat them as conversional words between predicate words and distinctive words.

If we investigate separately the verbs and adjectives among the predicate words, the data are as follows:

Multifunctional word	Number	Overlapping proportion	Proportion to predicate word property	Proportion to distinctive word property
verb-distinctive word	3189	29.6%	31.0%	87.4%
adjective (predicate word property)-distinctive word	690	24.5%	29.3%	60.1%

The verbs and adjectives do not take a high total proportion or a high proportion to dominant parts of speech, being in the critical range between the homogeneous strategy and the priority homomorphic strategy. The homogeneous strategy should be used to treat them as conversional words between verbs and distinctive words, for example, 成立 (found), 到达 (reach), 学习 (study) and 研究 (research), and conversional words between adjective and distinctive words, for example, 新 (new), 红 (red), 干净 (clean) and 优秀 (excellent). However, considering that they have a rather big absolute number, and particularly that there are 285 adjectives among the 468 that have the highest word frequency, this book still uses the priority homomorphic strategy to treat them as adjectives.

The very high proportion of the overlapping parts to the weak parts of speech indicates that the specialization degree of a distinctive word is rather low.

7.3.3.4 Classifying predicate words and adverbs

The total overlapping proportion between properties of predicate words and adverbs and the proportion to dominant parts of speech are very low. We therefore use the homogeneous strategy to treat them as conversional words. The very high proportion to properties of adverbs shows that their differentiation degree is rather low.

With the following table, let us look at verbs and adjectives separately:

Multifunctional word	Number	Overlapping proportion	Proportion to verb property	Proportion to adverb property
verb-adverb	131	1.2%	1.3%	39.8%
adjective(predicate word property)-adverb	277	10.3%	11.8%	45.7%

The overlapping proportion between predicate words and adverbs and their proportion to dominant parts of speech are very low. Ideally, we should treat them as conversional words. In other words, we should treat words such as 区别 (distinguish), 继续 (continue) and 重复 (repeat) as conversional words between verbs and adverbs, while treating 认真 (serious), 努力 (laborious), 迅速 (rapid) and 紧急 (emergent) as conversional words between adjectives and adverbs. However, considering that there are 172 adjectives among the 468 that have the highest frequency, taking as high a proportion as 37%, and that words such as 认真 (serious) and 紧急 (emergent) have concurrently the properties of distinctive words, this book treats them as adjectives with the priority homomorphic strategy. To keep the classification strategies consistent, we still use the priority homomorphic strategy to treat words that have concurrently the properties of adjectives and adverbs as adjectives and to treat only the overlapping parts of verbs and adverbs as conversional words between verbs and adverbs.

The very high proportion of the overlapping parts to the weak parts of speech indicates that the specialization degree of an adverb is not high.

7.3.3.5 Classifying noun and adverb

Multifunctional word	number	Overlapping proportion	Proportion to noun property	Proportion to adverb property
noun-adverb	345	2.4%	1.2%	41.0%

The proportion of the overlapping part to the total number of words belonging to nouns and adverbs and its proportion to the dominant parts of speech are very low; therefore, the overlapping part should be treated as conversional words. In other words, words such as 系统 (system), 正面 (front) and 礼貌 (courtesy) should be treated as conversional words between nouns and adverbs.

7.3.3.6 *Classifying distinctive words and adverbs*

Multifunctional word	number	Overlap proportion	Proportion to distinctive word property	Proportion to predicate word property
Distinctive word-adverb	284	1.2%	1.2%	33.7%

The proportion of the overlapping part to the total number of words belonging to distinctive words and adverbs and its proportion to distinctive words are very low. It is, therefore, advisable to treat them as conversional words. The proportion to properties of adverbs is on the high side but does not reach the classification criteria for the priority homomorphic strategy. Moreover, because a distinctive word and an adverb both belong to modification words and have no superior or inferior distinction between parts of speech, thus lacking the preconditions for using the priority homomorphic strategy, it is advisable to use the homogeneous strategy. In other words, words such as 共同 (common), 临时 (temporary) and 长期 (long-term) that can function as attributives and adverbials but cannot function as other constituents should be treated as conversional words between distinctive words and adverbs.

7.3.3.7 *Nouns that function concurrently as measure words*

There are mainly two cases in which some nouns can function as measure words have two: (1) functioning as capacity measure words such as 碗 (bowl), 桶 (barrel), 车 (carload) and 杯 (cup); (2) functioning as action measure words such as 鞭子 (whip), 刀 (knife) and 枪 (gun). Only 109 out of 27,408 nouns can be used in this way, taking just 0.4%. The number is very small, and the conditions for this use can be identified. The former is limited to nouns that denote objects that are often specially used as containers, whereas the latter is limited to nouns that denote objects that are often specially used as a tool. Because these nouns can be controlled with rules, the use of the priority homomorphic strategy does not incur a loss in terms of syntactic rules but pays off in terms of simplicity of part of speech. Consequently, we use the priority homomorphic strategy and do not treat them as nouns functioning concurrently as measure words.

The above-mentioned discussions are carried out against the background that there are no specific syntactic systems. In actual operations, with the exception that it is not suitable to use the homomorphic strategy because it brings about too huge a number of parts of speech, the homogeneous strategy, the priority homomorphic strategy and the consolidation strategy are possible choices. Besides the above-mentioned principles, the selection of which strategy also depends on a matchable syntactic system. For the "lexicon-syntactic structure" in the generative grammar system, it is desirable to use the homogeneous strategy. For example, in the case as shown in Figure 7.6 below, it is possible to treat 顾虑 (worry) and 吩咐 (instruct) (functioning as the objects of 有 (have)) as verbs that function concurrently as nouns. Using the same classification strategy, 木头 (wood) and 质量 (quality) (directly functioning as attributives) should be treated as nouns that function concurrently as distinctive words; 成立 (establish) and 作废 (cancel) (directly functioning as attributives) should be treated as verbs that function concurrently as distinctive words; 调查 (investigate) and 研究 (study) (functioning as the objects of 有 (have) and directly as attributives) should be treated as verbs that function concurrently as nouns and distinctive words. In addition, 干净 (clean) and 新 (new) (directly functioning as attributives) should be treated as adjectives that function concurrently as distinctive words; 危险 (danger) and 温暖 (warm) (functioning as the object of a substantive-object verb, directly as attributives) should be treated as adjectives that function concurrently as nouns and distinctive words; 迅速(rapidly) and 妥善(appropriately) (directly functioning as adverbials) should be treated as adjectives that function concurrently as adverbs; 强烈 (vehement) and 熟练 (skillful) (directly functioning as attributives and adverbials) should be treated as adjectives that function concurrently as distinctive words and adverbs (see Chapter 6).

However, except that 调查 (investigate) and 研究 (research) are treated as verbs that function concurrently as nouns, and that 危险 (danger) and 温暖

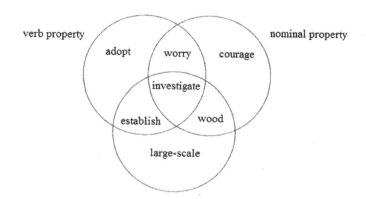

Figure 7.6 The overlapping of verb property and nominal property

(warm) are treated as adjectives that function concurrently as nouns, it is rare to treat them as other kinds of conversional words. The homogeneous strategy does not thoroughly treat words such as 调查 (investigate) as verbs that function concurrently as nouns; what it thoroughly does is, as mentioned earlier, treat as conversional words all the words that function concurrently as several parts of speech. Some scholars emphasize that 调查 (investigate) and 研究 (research) should be treated as verbs functioning concurrently as nouns, but do not treat 成立 (establish) and 作废 (cancel) as verbs functioning concurrently as distinctive words. They neither treat 木头 (wood) as a noun functioning concurrently as a distinctive word nor 干净 (clean) and 新 (new) as adjectives functioning concurrently as distinctive words. This shows that the priority homomorphic strategy is often and commonly used, though nobody realizes that. If we cannot accept that 成立 (establish) and 作废 (cancel) should be treated as verbs functioning concurrently as distinctive words, and that 干净 (clean) and 新 (new) should be treated as adjectives functioning concurrently as distinctive words, then we cannot accept that 调查 (investigate) and 研究 (research) should be treated as conversional words but as verbs. Of course, what classification strategy is used must be in accordance with the syntactic system. This is not a matter of right or wrong but whether a classification strategy is effective or not effective.

7.4 Nature of multiple functions of a Chinese part of speech

The earliest scholar who revealed the multiple functions of a Chinese part of speech is Gao Mingkai. He said that "judging from whatever aspect, Chinese notional words express their many part-of-speech meanings and have no fixed part-of-speech characteristics" (Gao Mingkai, 1960: 38). "The vast majority of Chinese words do not have only one kind of combination properties and can be combined with many classes of words" (Gao Mingkai, 1957: 75).

Gao Mingkai thought that the multiple functions of a part of speech are the reason why a Chinese modification word has no parts of speech. In Chinese, the stem of a word is a lexeme that can be embodied as different variants in the language's syntactic category of part of speech. That is to say, the same Chinese stem or word can have different part-of-speech meanings at different occasions; thus, Chinese has the category of part of speech. But just because these different part-of-speech meanings may be all the different variants of the same word stem, Chinese notional words cannot be classified into nouns, verbs, adjectives and others in accordance with their part-of-speech meanings" (Gao Mingkai, 1963: 49).

Then Zhu Dexi further regarded the multiple functions of a part of speech as an important feature of the Salmon grammar. He (1985b) held that Indo-European languages have a kind of simple one-to-one correspondence between part of speech and syntactic constituent. Roughly speaking, a verb corresponds to a predicate; a noun corresponds to a subject or object; an adjective corresponds to an attributive; an adverb corresponds to an adverbial. But

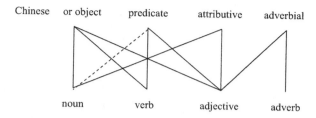

Figure 7.7 The correspondence between a part of speech and a syntactic constituent in English and Chinese

Chinese has no simple one-to-one correspondence between part of speech and syntactic constituent, as shown in the following diagram:

An English adjective mainly functions as an attributive and belongs to substantive modification words, but a Chinese adjective mainly functions as a predicate and belongs to predicate words. The functional equivalence of a Chinese adjective to an English one is the distinctive word that also belongs to substantive modification words. Therefore, the position of a Chinese adjective in the above diagram should be that of a distinctive word; the adjective should be put together with a verb, forming a large category of predicate words.

Moreover, because an English noun can generally function as an attributive, a connection line between nouns and attributives should be added.

The adjusted diagram for the correspondence between a part of speech and a syntactic constituent is as follows:

After adjusting the position of an adjective, the multiple functions of Chinese part of speech decrease because the function of two types of Chinese modification words is still singular, and the multiple functions of a part of speech are mainly reflected in predicate and substantive words.

What is the nature of the multifunction of a Chinese part of speech? It is mainly threefold:

I.   The positions of subject, object or predicate have a rather relaxed selectional restriction on the parts of speech of a word.

We can see that the one-to-many correspondence between Chinese parts of speech and syntactic constituents expresses itself in the fact that a predicate word can function as a subject or object, and that a substantive word can function as a predicate. The positions of subject, object or predicate do not have a strict selectional restriction on the parts of speech of a word. The position of subject or object allows the entrance of both substantive and predicate words. The position of a predicate allows the entrance of both predicate and substantive words.

In Chapter 4.3, we mentioned that 学习 (study), which functions as a subject in 学习很重要 (Study is very important), can take its object or adverbial

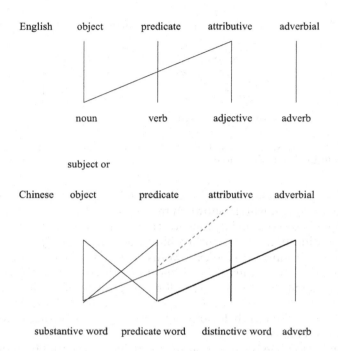

Figure 7.8 The correspondence between a Chinese part of speech and a syntactic constituent

and thus remains a verb. In Chinese, it is very common that constituents with predicate word properties function as a subject or object. We should not think that words that function as a subject or object have changed in their parts of speech.

In the example that noun phrases such as 小王黄头发 (Little Wang yellow hair) function as a predicate, 黄头发 (yellow hair) can still be modified by an attributive 一头黄头发 (a head of yellow hair) and therefore remains a noun phrase.

In Chapter 4.3, we also mentioned that when constituents with predicate word properties function as subjects, their parts of speech may not change but their external expressional functions often have reference meanings. When constituents with substantive word properties function as predicates, their part of speech may remain a substantive word, but their external expressional function often has statement meanings. That is to say, this kind of multifunc-tion of a part of speech is actually caused by changes in its external expressional function. The part of speech does not change; in other words, the selectional restriction of the syntactic position is not strict. In English, the functioning of a verb as a subject, object or attributive requires changes in form by adding expressional function change markers such as "to, -ing, -ed" and so on. The functioning of a noun as a predicate requires the addition of the link verb "be". This shows that Chinese has something in common with English. Namely the expressional function of a word may change and then function as an unconventional constituent. The difference lies in the fact that the changes in Chinese are unmarked in most cases but those in English are marked. Zhu Dexi also said that "the root causes for the two characteristics[2] lie in the fact that Chinese parts of speech have no marked form" (Zhu Dexi, 1985a: 9).

Because of the changes in expressional functions and parts of speech, the loaned part of speech and the theory that the part of speech of a word is based on sentence are reasonable. Simply because there is no distinction between parts of speech at two levels, there is no clear explanation of their relations. Thus we can conclude that Chinese words have no definite parts of speech or none at all.

II. Classifying the parts of speech of a word that has concurrently two or more parts of speech with the priority homomorphic strategy.

The multiple functions of some words are due to their different parts of speech. For example, nominal verbs such as 检查 (examine), 管理 (manage) and 调查 (investigate) have concurrently the properties of a verb and noun. These words can function as predicates and have the properties of a predicate word, but when they function as objects in such phrases as 进行检查 (conduct examination), they show the properties of a noun (being able to be modified by attributives or numerals and measure words) and have no characteristics of a verb at all (not being able to take its object, adverbial, le (了), zhuo (着), guo (过) or complement), therefore, having the properties of a noun. For another example, 干净 (clean), 优秀 (excellent) and 好 (good) can function as predicates and be modified by 很 (very), thus having the properties of a predicate word and being adjectives, but when they function as attributives directly, for example, 干净衣服 (clean clothes), 优秀学生 (excellent student) and 好人 (good person), they no longer have the characteristics of an adjective (not being able to be modified by 很 (very) or 不 (not), and therefore having the properties of a distinctive word. Words like 木头 (wood), 工人 (worker) and 手机 (cell phone) can freely function as a subject or object and be modified by numerals and measure words, thus having the properties of a noun, but when they function as attributives directly, they no longer have the characteristics of a noun (not being able to be modified by numerals and measure words), and actually have the properties of a distinctive word.

The multiple functions of a part of speech such as these are actually due to these words originally having multiple parts of speech. Why should we regard multiple parts of speech as the multiple functions of a part of speech? Other languages such as English also have the phenomenon that one word has concurrently multiple parts of speech, but why is this phenomenon not regarded as multiple functions of a part of speech? This is because the current Chinese part-of-speech classification system generally uses the priority homomorphic strategy and classifies into superior parts of speech words that have concurrently multiple parts of speech. For instance, nominal verbs such as 检查 (examine), 管理 (manage) and 调查 (investigate) that have concurrently the properties of a verb and noun are classified into verbs; words like 干净 (clean), 优秀 (excellent) and 好 (good) that have concurrently the properties of an adjective and distinctive word are classified into adjectives; words like 木头 (wood), 工人 (worker) and 手机 (cell phone) that have concurrently the properties of a noun and distinctive word are classified into nouns.

In other words, such multiple functions of a part of speech actually result from the selection of classification strategies. Strictly speaking, this belongs to the phenomenon that one word has concurrently multiple parts of speech.

As mentioned previously, two Chinese modification words cannot have multiple functions, but in reality, some Chinese words can belong to distinctive words and adverbs concurrently, for instance, 共同 (common), 长期 (long-term), 自动 (automatic), 临时 (temporary) and 真正 (genuine). However, our part-of-speech system uses the homogeneous strategy to treat them as conversional words that belong to distinctive words and adverbs, thus not being treated as the multiple functions of a part of speech.

English also has one word belonging to multiple parts of speech, but English grammar generally uses the homogeneous strategy and therefore has no multiple functions of a part of speech. With only one exception, which is that because a great number of English nouns function as attributives, English uses the priority homomorphic strategy and does not treat them as nouns that function concurrently as adjectives, the multiple functions of a noun are merged.

If Chinese also uses the homogeneous strategy to treat as conversional words that concurrently belong to verbs and nouns, adjectives and distinctive words, nouns and distinctive words, then the multiple functions of a Chinese part of speech may also be greatly reduced. From this point of view, Chinese and English have no substantial difference in language facts; the only difference is their classification strategies.

The reason why Chinese generally uses the priority homomorphic strategy is that it has a rather big number of words that have concurrently multiple parts of speech. In other words, its parts of speech do not have a high degree of differentiation. We shall discuss this issue in some detail in Chapter 3 in Volume 2.

7.5 Nominalization

Nominalization is related to conversional words and will be discussed here.

The debate over nominalization occurred from the 1950s to 1960s. It means that changes take place in the properties of verbs or adjectives in the positions of subject or object, or modified by an attributive. It has different explanations: (1) use as a noun; (2) becoming a noun, or nominalized; (3) already being a noun; (4) nominalization, transformed into an object.

For example, 看下棋 (watch playing chess) and 学习很重要 (study is very important).

Zhu Dexi, Lu Jiawen and Ma Zhen (1961) criticized the idea of nominalization mainly in terms of grammatical meaning and grammatical properties.

In terms of grammatical properties, one of the reasons for nominalization is that verbs and adjectives in these positions have a series of grammatical characteristics of nouns and lose some or all of the grammatical properties of verbs and adjectives. The series of grammatical characteristics means that verbs and adjectives can have anaphoric reference with nouns or pronouns, be modified by attributives and form a coordinate construction together with nouns. The loss of some or all of the grammatical properties of verbs and adjectives means that they cannot be reduplicated and cannot function as predicates. Zhu Dexi et al. demonstrated this as follows:

a. Words of different parts of speech not only have individuality that distinguishes them from each other but also have some commonality. For example, both verbs and adjectives can take le (了). The above-mentioned three points can be regarded as the commonalities of a verb, adjective and noun.
b. The grammatical properties of a part of speech are reflected in a generalization word; not all of its grammatical properties may be achieved in one position. The lost grammatical properties are nothing but those not achieved. Verbs have the properties of 不 (not) ~ and ~ le (了), but they cannot be achieved at the same time.

In terms of grammatical meaning, the reason for nominalization is that in these positions, verbs and adjectives have the meanings of transformed objects, thereby being nominalized. Zhu Dexi et al. demonstrated three levels of transformation into object:

1. The transformation into object with categorical meanings: verbs denote names of behaviors and actions; nouns denote objects; adjectives denote properties.
2. The transformation into object is reflected in the positions of subjects and objects.
3. The transformation into object at the meaning level is represented by 什么 (what) or 怎么样 (how).

The transformation into object at the three levels is not consistent, for example:

(1) 看下棋 (watch playing chess) —看什么 (watch what) (Levels 1 and 2 are not consistent)
(2) 坐着也行,站着也行—怎么样都行 (Sitting is OKay; standing is OKay; whatever is Okay) (Levels 2 and 3 are not consistent)

The transformation into object as nominalization is at Level 2. The inconsistency with the transformation into object at Level 1 cannot prove that there is nominalization.

Zhu Dexi's criticism mainly aims at nominalization but does not really deny the transformation into object. Later on, he changed his point of view, thinking that verbs and adjectives after verbs that take quasi-predicate objects are nominal, for example, 调查 (investigate) and 困难 (difficult) in 进行调查 (conduct investigation) and 有困难 (have difficulty). He called them nominal verbs and nominal adjectives respectively (Zhu Dexi, 1985b).

In the 1990s, a number of scholars raised the nominalization issue once again in the following five ways: (1) Semantic level and syntactic level should be separated; nominalization is thought to be at the semantic level (Hu Yushu & Fan Xiao, 1994). (2) Nominalization is neither acknowledged nor denied, but emphasis is laid on the positions of subject and object, verbs after attributives and changes in the properties of adjectives. Namely, the properties of a predicate word are weakened but the properties of a noun are enhanced (Zhang Bojiang, 1993, 1996). (3) It was held that some verbs and adjectives in the positions of subject or object, or after attributives have already been nominalized, although some of them are still predicate words, the properties of a predicate word are weakened and turn into those of a noun (Yang Chengkai, 1991). (4) The "contradiction" between the headword of endocentric construction and general parts of speech was used to demonstrate that nominalization exists (see Shi Guangan, 1981, 1988). (5) Nominalization is explained in terms of expressional function (see Li Yuming, 1986; Xiang Mengbing, 1991). Respective discussions are as follows:

Hu Yushu and Fan Xiao (1994) proposed that nominalization and nominal object transformation into a noun should be separated; nominalization refers to the transformation of verbs and adjectives into nouns at the syntactic level; the nominal object transformation into a noun refers to the transformation of predicate meanings of verbs and adjectives into the "nominal object meaning" (object meaning). Their argument is that the centers of the semantic structure of a sentence are the verb center and verb argument. The verb center is the center of a predicate; the verb argument is the argument and coordinate-valence constituent. The verb argument has the nominal object meaning or reference meaning. For example: 骄傲使人落后 (Conceit makes one lag behind).

This explanation is still what Zhu Dexi meant by the transformation into object at Level 2. The question is: how does the verb argument denote the nominal object meaning? 坐着 (sitting) in Example (2) can hardly be regarded as having nominal object meaning. For another example:

(3) a   b
干净最重要 (To be clean is the most important).   干干净净的舒服
                                                   (To be very clean
                                                   is comfortable)

教书不容易 (Teaching is not easy)

天 天 练 才 学 得 会 (Learning is done by practicing every day)

(4) 看下棋 (watch playing chess)

打算下棋 (intend to play chess)

考虑参加不参加 (consider whether participating or not)

觉得很好 (feel fine)

The subjects or objects in Examples *b* all have no nominal object meanings, though they are verb arguments.

Although Ways (2) and (3) do not reach entirely the same conclusion, their proof is basically the same. Here we discuss them together. Some scholars hold that changes take place in the positions of subjects and objects and in the properties of verbs and adjectives after attributives. They justify themselves mainly as follows: (1) verbs and adjectives take tense and aspect constituents such as le (了), zhuo (着), guo (过) or complete sentences, namely losing their time meaning; (2) they cannot take modal adverbials such as 大概 (presumably, 也许 (perhaps) and 必定 (certainly); (3) numerals and measure words cannot function as the objects of verbs and adjectives. Hence, they think that verbs and adjectives in the positions of subject and object or after attributives lose some properties of a predicative word and acquire some properties of a noun.

These viewpoints are similar to the nominalization theory in the 1950s and 1960s. Zhu Dexi, Lu Jiawen and Ma Zhen (1961) criticized such viewpoints: not all the grammatical properties of a generalization word may be achieved in one grammatical position. The lost grammatical properties are nothing but those not achieved. This argument is mainly from a logical perspective and does not show that changes take place in the positions of subject and object, and in the properties of verbs and adjectives after attributives, but we cannot deny that changes may take place in their properties. Zhu Dexi (1985b) also admitted that 研究 (research) in 进行研究 (carry out research) is nominal. Then, can the three pieces of evidence proposed by these property change theorists prove that verbs and adjectives in these positions really lose some properties of a predicate word and have some properties of a noun? In our opinion, they cannot. The three pieces of evidence rely on such an assumption: verbs and adjectives that take tense and aspect constituents, modal adverbials and objects made of numerals and measure words reflect the properties of a predicate word. The loss of these characteristics means the loss of properties of a predicate word. We will explain that this assumption cannot be valid.

Evidence One: Verbs and adjectives in the positions of subject and object or after attributives cannot take tense and aspect constituents such as le (了), zhuo (着) and guo (过). This is mainly related to the time meaning of a predicate word. The common thinking is that at this time, verbs and adjectives lose their time meaning. According to Guo Rui (1993, 1997b), the time meaning of a predicate word includes intrinsic time meaning and extrinsic time meaning. Intrinsic time meaning refers to the time meaning decided by the lexical meaning of a predicate word and reflects its intrinsic process structure. The process structure refers to start, continuation and end, and on this basis, verbs are classified into state verbs, action verbs and change verbs. Extrinsic time meaning indicates the relationship between predicate word elements and the external lapse of time. Depending on whether a predicate word element is put into an external time lapse process, it is classified into process and nonprocess elements. Intrinsic time meaning is the inherent property of a predicate word, while extrinsic time meaning is not and is the achieved property in the use of a predicate word. From this perspective, Evidence One cannot prove that verbs and adjectives in the positions of subjects and objects, or after attributives lose their time meaning. In fact, they exist merely in a certain type of special time meaning. Some examples are analyzed as follows:

(5) 假若不幸而无论如何也不调谐,她会用她的气派压迫人们的眼睛,承认她的敢于故作惊人之笔,像万里长城似的,虽然不美,而惊心动魄. (老舍《四世同堂》) (Unfortunately, no matter how hard she tried, if she is not attractive, she may use her imposing manner to attract folk's eyes, letting them admit that she is courageous to dress herself up heart-shockingly like the Great Wall. (*Four Generations in One House* by Lao She)

The adjective 敢于 (courageous) cannot take tense and aspect constituents such as le (了), zhuo (着) and guo (过). In fact, like "is, belong to, feel", "courageous" does not take tense and aspect constituents under any circumstances. This is the restriction on intrinsic time meaning, and no time meaning is lost. These verbs have the infinite construction of a state verb; infinity is their time meaning. Even in the position of predicate, they cannot take tense and aspect constituents. Therefore, the infinity of intrinsic time meaning does not indicate the loss of properties of a predicate word.

(6) 这本书的出版给我们带来了麻烦. (The publication of this book brings us trouble.)

出版 (publication) in this example cannot take any tense and aspect constituents because of extrinsic time meaning. Guo Rui (1997b) thought that the properties of a predicate word can be classified into two types according to its extrinsic time meaning. One type is the process element, that is, the predicate word element observed in the external time process, for example, 他在抽烟 (he is smoking), 他抽了烟了 (he smoked), 他抽过烟 (he has smoked) and 他抽烟呢 (he is smoking). They are usually negated with 没 (no) or 没有 (not have). Another type is the nonprocess element (or property element), for example, 他抽烟 (he smokes), 我抽烟 (I smoke), 你坐下 (you sit down), 猫吃老鼠 (a cat eats a mouse) and 地球绕太阳运行

(the earth turns around the sun). They are usually negated with 不 (not) or its derivative forms 别 (don't), 甭 (needn't). Tense and aspect constituents such as le (了), guo (过), ne (呢) and zai (在) are marked process elements, whereas unmarked elements are usually nonprocess (property) elements. In other words, a predicate word element in the predicate position differs in the process element and the nonprocess (property) element. The property element in the predicate position does not lose its time meaning but is a kind of special time nonprocess. One may insist on the loss of time meaning, but one cannot think that the loss of time meaning is the loss of properties of a predicate word because it cannot be denied that the nonprocess element that functions as a predicate loses the properties of the predicate word. Similarly, verbs and adjectives in the positions of subjects and objects, or after attributives, are often expressed as nonprocess elements (negated with 不 (not)). Their properties of predicate words should not be negated just because they are not process elements. Actually, it is widely acknowledged that verbs and adjectives in the positions of subjects and objects, or after attributives, can still take such adverbials as 不 (not) and 及时 (punctually), objects and sometimes subjects, indicating that they are still predicate words. They do not lose their time meaning and the properties of predicate words, but are expressed as nonprocess elements just as the predicate word elements in imperative sentences, volitional sentences, habitual sentences and universal sentences are expressed as nonprocess elements.

Fundamentally speaking, predicate words (verbs and adjectives) themselves do not have a process meaning but merely express abstract actions, states or attributes, all of which do not have a process meaning. This is just like nouns themselves have no reference meaning but only express abstract objects (Li, 1997). The role played by such elements as le (了), guo (过), zai (在) and ne (呢) in a predicate word element is similar to that played by numerals, measure words and demonstratives in a noun element, making abstract things specific and tangible. Therefore, predicate words that do not take such tense and aspect constituents as le (了), guo (过), zai (在) and ne (呢) are just their true characteristics.

Similar to Evidence One, under the circumstances of Evidence Two, one use of a predicate word is that it takes a modal adverbial. Because the modal constituent is a sentence or a clause, and the constituent that is not in the position of a predicate does not take a modal constituent normally, it cannot be posited that it loses its properties of a predicate word. Fundamentally speaking, a predicate word (verb and adjective) itself does not express any modal meaning, which comes from its use. The true characteristic of a predicate word is that it does not take a modal constituent.

Evidence Three itself does not conform to facts. We can still find some examples that the predicate word in the positions of subject and object takes numerals and measure words as its object:

(7) a. 去一次不够 (Going once is not enough)
     b. 他建议去一趟 (He suggests going once)

However, it is really difficult for verbs and adjectives after attributives to take numerals and measure words as their objects. Conversely numerals and measure word constituents can be put in front of verbs and adjectives (Yang Chengkai, 1991):

(8) a.　*这本书的出版多次 (*publishing the book many times)
　　b.　这本书的多次出版 (many times publishing of the book)

Constituents with the properties of a predicate word in the position of a predicate can also be added to their front with numerals and measure word constituents:

(9) a.　他三天没吃饭 (He did not eat for three days)
　　b.　他一次也没去 (He did not go even once)
　　c.　我多次告诉他…… (I told him many times . . .)
　　d.　我三次去上海,都没有找到他 (I went to Shanghai three times but did not find him)

Should numerals and measure word constituents be placed before or after predicate words? What are the rules? We are not very clear on this. Maybe they are related to pragmatics and focus arrangement. We are sure that from these examples, the front position of numerals and measure word constituents cannot prove that they lose their properties of a predicate word.

Such being the case, the changes in the properties of verbs and adjectives in the positions of subjects and objects, or after attributives, are not real changes in their properties but merely one of the properties of a predicate word. Verbs and adjectives do not lose the properties of predicate words, which are, instead, their true characteristics, namely expressing an abstract action, state or attribute.

Ways (4) and (5) can be discussed together. Shi Guan'gan (1981) thought that because the construction of 这本书的出版 (the publication of this book) is neat and nominal, and that the classification of 出版 (publication) into a verb violates the endocentric construction theory, it should be regarded as a noun. Li Yuming (1986) thought that nominalization is the "positional meaning" reflected by a verb and adjective in their positions of subjects and objects, namely the meaning brought by a grammatical position. Xiang Mengbing (1991) thought that nominalization was actually a reference. There is no contradiction between the headword of 这本书的出版 (the publication of this book) and the parts of speech of the whole construction consisting of a modifier and the word it modifies because the whole construction still has the properties of a verb.

Our points of view are similar to those of Li Yuming and Xiang Mengbing. Namely we think that nominalization is actually a reference, but do not consider it as the properties brought by a grammatical position. Instead, we regard it merely as the temporary properties of a predicate word itself. We neither think that the whole phrase 这本书的出版 (the publication of this book) has the properties of a verb. Its properties are actually nominal. Then how should we explain the contradiction between the headword and the parts of speech of the whole construction consisting of a modifier and the word it modifies? Chapter 4.3 mentions that an expressional function has intrinsic (inherent) and extrinsic (temporary) levels. Correspondingly, a part of speech also has lexical and syntactic levels. 出版 (publication) in 这本书的出版 (the publication of this book) is at the extrinsic level or nominalization at the syntactic level. Though the word 出版 (publication) is still a verb at the lexical level, it is a noun at the syntactic level. The nominality of the whole phrase 这本书的出版 (the publication of this book) is in agreement with the part of speech of the headword 出版 (publication) at the syntactic level, thus not violating the endocentric construction theory. The nominalization of verbs and adjectives in the position of subjects or objects is also the reference at the extrinsic level or the nominalization at the syntactic level. The parts of speech at the lexical level are still verbs and adjectives.

Our points of view are summarized as follows:

"The nature of nominalization" includes the following two cases:

1. The reference of an extrinsic expressional function and nominalization at the syntactic level.
   (10) a. 去不合适 (Going is inappropriate)
        b. 不去不合适 (Not going is inappropriate)
        c. 去广州不合适 (Going to Guangzhou is inappropriate)
        d. 你去不合适 (Your going is inappropriate)
           马上去不合适 (Going immediately is inappropriate)
   (11) a. 社会的公正(是社会进步的基础) (Social justice (is the basis of social progress)).
        b. 社会的不公正(在任何时代都存在) (Social injustice (exists in any era)).
        c. 社会的绝对公正(是社会进步的基础) (Absolute social justice (is the basis of social progress)).
   去 (going) and 公正 (justice) still have the general characteristics of a verb and adjective, and do not change their properties at the lexical level.
2. Some words that have the properties of verbs, adjectives and nouns embody the properties of a noun at the position of subjects or objects. Their functioning as subjects or objects no longer has the general characteristics of a verb or adjective but has the general characteristics of a noun. For example:
   (12) a. 进行调查 (conduct investigation)
        b. *进行不调查 (*carry out no investigation)
        c. *进行调查这个问题 (*conduct investigation of this problem)

    d. *进行他们调查 (*carry out they investigate)
    e. *进行马上调查 (*carry out immediate investigation)
    f. 进行仔细的调查 (carry out careful investigation)
    g. 进行社会调查 (carry out social investigation)
(13) a. 保持稳定 (remain stable)
    b. *保持很稳定 (*remain very stable)
    c. *保持不稳定 (*remain unstable)
    d. *保持稳定得很 (*remain stable nicely)
    e. 保持社会稳定 (maintain social stability)
    f. 保持社会的稳定 (maintain societal stability)

Here, 调查 (investigation) and 稳定 (stability) solely reflect the properties of a noun; thus, we can say that they have two properties of a verb (adjective) and a noun. They can be regarded as changes that have taken place in intrinsic expressional function. In other words, the properties of parts of speech at the lexical level have already changed indeed, but we merely do not treat them as conversional words with the priority homomorphic strategy.

Notes

1 High or low syntactic status mainly depends on the following: (1) after a word is combined with another, with which its integral property is identical. For example, the phrase formed by combining a noun with a distinctive word is a noun phrase because the status of the noun is higher than that of a distinctive word. (2) The direction of change in a part of speech. For instance, most distinctive words change from a noun or a verb; there are few changes in the opposite direction. Therefore, the statuses of a noun and a verb are higher than those of a distinctive word. See Chapter 4.3.3.

2 This refers to the two characteristics that there is no one-to-one correspondence between a part of speech and a syntactic constituent, and that the sentential structural rule by and large agrees with the phrasal structural rule.

8 Conclusions

Because a grammatical position has its selectional restriction on words, Chinese has its parts of speech, and it is necessary to classify them.

There is an intricate correspondence between parts of speech and the distribution of words; therefore, we cannot find any parts of speech that have internally universal, but externally exclusive, distributions. Essentially, a part of speech is not a distributional type; rather, its intrinsic basis is the expressional function and semantic type. In essence, large categories (substantive words, predicate words, modification words) are classes of words classified according to their expressional functions. The basic categories of parts of speech (nouns, verbs, adjectives) are classes that combine semantic types with syntactic functions. Semantic types reflect the categorization of a language and therefore must be taken into consideration in classifying parts of speech. Only in this way can we give a more reasonable explanation for the bases of the selectional restriction of a grammatical position on word. The expressional functions used as the essence of parts of speech refer to the meaning representation pattern of a word, including the four basic types: statements, references, substantive modifications and predicate modifications. Semantic types refer to categorized semantic meanings, such as entity, position, measurement unit, demonstration, behavior, action, attribute, state and so on. Both the expressional function of a word and its semantic type are its grammatical meanings. We classify notional words into 13 parts of speech, each of which has its own grammatical meaning: a noun denotes an entity reference; a positional word denotes a position reference (a place word denotes an absolute space position reference; a time word denotes an absolute time position reference; a locative denotes a relative position reference); a measure word denotes a measurement unit or a grade unit reference. An adjective denotes a property statement; a state word denotes a state statement; a verb denotes a behavior or action statement. A numeral denotes a numerical value modification; a numeral and measure word denotes a quantitative modification; a demonstrative denotes a demonstration modification; a distinctive word denotes a property modification; an adverb denotes a condition modification. The grammatical meaning of a word is the root factor that restricts its distribution, and this is the reason why we can classify parts of speech according to distribution.

Expressional functions can be classified into the intrinsic expressional function and the external expressional function. Correspondingly, we can also classify parts of speech into those at the lexical and the syntactic level. The lexical and syntactic levels often cause changes in a part of speech, indicating that grammar is dynamic. One of the reasons why it is difficult to classify Chinese parts of speech is that Chinese has a predominantly dynamic grammar.

The classification of parts of speech according to the distribution of a word is only a convenient theory. Strictly speaking, the parts of speech of a word are inferred from its distributive characteristics and already exist before "being classified into them".

Although expressional functions are the intrinsic bases for classifying parts of speech, they are not directly observable and therefore cannot be used as criteria for classifying parts of speech. We still use word distribution as a criterion for classifying parts of speech, but do so not purely according to the distributional difference but rather through the "representation-expression" relationship among distribution, expressional function and semantic type (distribution reflects expressional function and semantic type, which are represented as distribution). We use the distribution compatibility and the correlation principle to analyze which distributional differences represent the differences in a part of speech and which do not. In this way, grammatical functions that have equal classification values are collected into clusters, with each equivalent function cluster representing one part of speech. The classification criteria are selected from the equivalent function cluster of a part of speech.

The relationship between a grammatical function and a part of speech is intricate and complicated but has a prototypical connection: a substantive word functions as a subject or object; a predicate word functions as a predicate or complement; a modification word functions as a modifier. Other connections are marked.

Conversional words are mainly concerned with the identity of a word, the multiple functions of a part of speech and the classification strategy. Different generalization words have different parts of speech and, of course, should be treated as conversional words (or homographs with different parts of speech). Whether a part of speech has multiple functions or not is mainly distinguished through distribution compatibility and the correlation principle. If a generalization word has the properties of different parts of speech, whether it is treated as a conversional word or not has something to do with the classification strategy. On the whole, there are four classification strategies: the homogeneity strategy, the homomorphical strategy, the priority homomorphical strategy and the consolidation strategy. The strategy selection should be considered in an all-around way. The principle is to minimize the total costs of part-of-speech simplicity and syntactic simplicity.

Because a Chinese word commonly has multiple functions, Chinese scholars more commonly use priority the homomorphical strategy to classify parts of speech, lest there should be too many conversional words. The so-called "no change in lexical meaning, no change in a part of speech" actually means the use of the priority homomorphical strategy. However, this does not mean that the priority homomorphical strategy has no shortcomings. Because there is no one-to-one correspondence between a part of speech of a word and its grammatical function, the parts of speech classified with the priority homomorphical strategy are not so effective for syntactic analysis. Therefore, in the areas of formal grammar and Chinese information processing, it is advisable to use the homogeneity strategy to classify Chinese parts of speech.

In contrasting the Chinese part-of-speech system with that of another language, the classification strategy should be taken into consideration. The differences in a part-of-speech system, which are caused by using different classification strategies, should not be regarded as the differences in the parts of speech themselves of the two languages. For example, Chinese grammar has the characteristic that "there is no one-to-one correspondence between a Chinese part of speech and a syntactic constituent". To a greater extent, this is actually caused by using the priority homomorphical strategy to classify Chinese parts of speech. As a matter of linguistic fact, if we use the homogeneity strategy to classify Chinese parts of speech, then Chinese will have no such common correspondence between parts of speech and syntactic constituents.

A grammatical position has its selectional restriction on a word, and we actually use it to classify parts of speech. We can say that a part of speech is the basis for syntactic analysis. But because Chinese has no one-to-one correspondence between parts of speech and syntactic constituents, a part of speech may not play such a big role in syntactic analysis as in Western languages such as English. We cannot use the category of a part of speech to write out the quite complete and basically dis-ambiguous phrasal structural rules. How should we look at this? The following are our opinions:

(1) There are two causes for no one-to-one correspondence between Chinese parts of speech and syntactic constituents: (a) The selectional restriction of Chinese syntactic positions such as subjects, objects and predicates on the parts of speech of a word is rather loose. The positions for subjects and objects allow words that have predicate word properties to enter. The position for predicates also allows words that have substantive word properties to enter. (b) Most modern Chinese grammatical systems use the priority homomorphical strategy to classify parts of speech, and thus classify words that function concurrently as several parts of speech into dominant parts of speech. Both causes may make it difficult to describe syntactic rules with a part-of-speech marker.

(2) We should not think that the reason why Chinese words have no part-of-speech distinction is that there is no one-to-one correspondence between parts of speech and syntactic constituents. The observation that a language has no parts of speech actually means that its grammatical positions have no selectional restriction on words, implying that a certain position allows any words to enter. A syntactic constituent is only a grammatical position

that has a rather high generalization level. Although Chinese has no one-to-one correspondence between parts of speech and syntactic constituents, the grammatical position that has a rather low generalization level is quite strict with the selectional restriction on words. We still have to admit that the grammatical position has its selectional restriction on a word. So long as there is selectional restriction, we have to admit that a Chinese word has its part-of-speech distinction. In other words, the distinction may not necessarily be shown in a syntactic constituent, but may well be shown in the main in a rather specific grammatical position, not to mention that a syntactic constituent can show part-of-speech distinctions. For example, a distinctive word cannot function as a complement or a predicate and cannot take an object, a complement or an adverbial, thus distinguishing between a verb and an adjective.

(3) It is a fact that Chinese has no one-to-one correspondence between parts of speech and syntactic constituents, but we cannot distort the fact for the sake of yielding to syntactic analysis. Some people think that once a verb or adjective functions as a subject or an object, it becomes a noun, but this idea is not true to fact.

(4) We cannot count on Chinese to have a completely neat correspondence between parts of speech and syntactic constituents. Even English does not have a complete correspondence. For example, *the* + *adj.* can appear in the position of a subject. But here it remains an adjective because it has an adjective's general properties. For instance, it can be modified by an adverbial and have comparative and superlative degrees.

(5) To overcome the insufficiency of a part of speech for syntactic analysis, we can separate syntactic constituents by attaching conditions. Although different Chinese parts of speech may sometimes occupy the same grammatical position, if looked at in detail, the two have very different structures. For example, verbs and some nouns may function as predicates. But nouns that function as predicates usually denote judgment and are easily distinguished with language sense from verbs that function as predicates. A noun predicate can well be called a quasi-predicate so as to be distinguished from a verb predicate.

(6) Part-of-speech classification can be combined with grammatical characteristic description. Although a part of speech has its limitations for syntactic analysis, we can describe the grammatical characteristics of the words in a word bank in addition to tagging their parts of speech, for example, whether a word can function as subject or be modified by 不 (not) or not, thus offsetting the limitations of parts of speech in syntactic analysis.

The fundamental reason why the four categories of parts of speech classified according to the four positions of expressional functions are universal in the world languages is that the basic work mechanisms of human languages combine statements with references to express meaning and transmit information.

That is to say, a human language expresses its meaning by combining the object-representation constituent with the assertion-representation constituent. It has its division of labor for object-representation constituents and assertion-representation constituents, there being consequently distinctions between nouns and verbs. Furthermore, there is a division of labor among modification constituents, object-representation constituents and assertion-representation constituents. Then a modification word appears as a part of speech. If there is division of labor for object-modification constituents and assertion-modification constituents, then there is a distinction between substantive modification words (distinctive words or adjectives with the properties of a modification word) and predicate modification words (adverbs).

I abandoned the view that distribution is the essence of a part of speech, which I had firmly held for many years, and then proposed the view that the essence is the expressional function/semantic type because my long-time part-of-speech research shows that the former is internally inconsistent and has insoluble internal contradictions. Instead, the latter is internally consistent and can be used as the starting point to determine the classification system and select classification criteria according to the correspondence between distribution and a part of speech, thus making the part-of-speech classification demonstrable and not relying on sense perception to do it. In this way, our attention is focused not on identifying a single distributive characteristic that is internally universal and externally exclusive but on clustering the grammatical functions that have the same classification value through the "reflection-representation" relationship between distribution and expressional function/semantic type, thereby finding the classification criteria. This method is consistent with the form and meaning mutual verification method persistently proposed by Zhu Dexi. In other words, we seek the mutual agreement of form and meaning to a maximal extent and think that only the things that have the mutual agreement of form and meaning exist in language reality and are valuable. From this perspective, the view that distribution is the essence of a part of speech actually holds that a part of speech has only a form, while things that have only forms should be valueless. But a part of speech is valuable. This means that we should change our view and regard the expressional function/semantic type as the essence of a part of speech. The expressional function/semantic type represents meaning, whereas distribution represents form. The agreement between the two is a part of speech. Based on this methodological view, this book strictly uses distributional criteria to classify parts of speech. Therefore, although it asserts that a part of speech is not a distributional type in essence, scholars who adhere to the view that distribution is the essence of a part of speech may rely more heavily on distribution in its classification.

Bibliography

Ai Wen & Jiang Wenqin (1980). Attempt to divide notional words of modern Chinese. *Journal of Wenzhou Normal College*, nos. 1/2.

Arnauld, Antoine & Lancelot, Claude (1660). *Grammaire générale et raisonnée* (trans. Zhang Xuebin & Liu Li). Checked and annotated by Yao Xiaoping. Changsha: Hunan Education Publishing, 2001.

Bai Shuo (1995). *Computer aided discovery of linguistic knowledge.* Beijing: Science Press.

Bhat, D. N. S. (1994). The adjectival category. Amsterdam and Philadelphia: John Benjamins.

Bloomfield, Leonard (1926). A set of postulates for language science. Language, 2(3), 153–164. (Also in Liu Runqing (Ed.). *An anthology of modern linguistic masterpieces*, vol. 1. Beijing: Surveying and Mapping Press, 1988.)

Cao Bohan (1995). *Comments on morphology and parts of speech, issues of Chinese parts of speech.* Beijing: Zhonghua Book Company.

Chen Aiwen (1986). *Research on Chinese parts of speech and division experiments.* Beijing: Peking University Press.

Chen Baoya (1985). Study of syntactic structure. *Journal of Southwest Normal College*, no. 2.

Chen Baoya (1999). *Methodology of Chinese linguistics in twentieth century: 1898–1996.* Jinan: Shandong Education Press.

Chen Chengze (1922/1982). *A draft of Chinese grammar.* Beijing: Commercial Press.

Chen Enquan (1987). Dividing parts of speech in Mandarin. *Journal of Lanzhou University (Social Science Edition)*, no. 3.

Chen Guanglei (1994). *Chinese morphology.* Shanghai: Xuelin Press.

Chen Guanglei (1996). The functions of Chinese parts of speech. *Journal of Shanghai University*, no. 1.

Chen Ningping (1987). Extensions of modern Chinese nouns – studying the boundary between verb and noun in modern Chinese. *Studies of Chinese Language*, no. 5.

Chen Wangdao (1939/1984). From diversity to unity. *Language Weekly*, no. 33. (Also in *Chinese Grammatical Reform Series*. Beijing: Commercial Press.)

Chen Wangdao (1941). Reply to the critique of discussions of Chinese grammatical reform. In *Collected Papers of Chen Wangdao*, vol. 3. Shanghai: Shanghai People's Publishing, 1981.

Chen Wangdao (1943). Study of grammar. In *Collected Papers of Chen Wangdao*, vol. 3. Shanghai: Shanghai People's Publishing, 1981.

Chen Wangdao (1978). *Brief introduction to grammar.* Shanghai: Shanghai Educational Publishing House.

Chen Xiaohe (1999). Study of Chinese parts of speech from the perspective of automatic syntactic analysis. *Language Teaching and Research*, no. 3.

Chen Yi (1989). A discussion on adding words before specialized verbs. *Studies of Chinese Language*, no. 1.

Cheng Zenghou (1988). A review of course in general linguistics. In Hu Mingyang (Ed.), *Selected readings of Western linguistics masterpieces*. Beijing: Renmin University of China Press.

Comrie, B. (Ed.). (1987). *The world's major languages*. London and Sydney: Croom Helm.

Conrad, Конрад Н. И. (1952). On Chinese (trans. Peng Chunan). *Linguistic Issues*, no. 3. (Also in *Studies of Chinese Language*, nos. 9–11.)

Croft, W. (1991). *Syntactic categories and grammatical relations: the cognitive organization of information*. Chicago and London: University of Chicago Press.

Dixon, R. M. W. (1977). Where have all the adjectives gone? *Studies in Language*, *1*(1), 19–80.

Dixon, R. M. W. (2004). Adjective classes in typological perspective. In R. M. W. Dixon & A. Y. Aikenvald (Eds.), 1–49.

Dixon, R. M. W. (2010). *Basic linguistic theory*, vol. 2, *Grammatical topics*. Oxford: Oxford University Press.

Dixon, R. M. W. & Aikhenvald, A. Y. (Eds.). (2004). *Adjective classes: a cross-linguistic typology*. Oxford: Oxford University Press.

Draguno, A. (1958). *Study of modern Chinese grammar: parts of speech I* (trans. Zheng Qingzu). Beijing: Science Press.

Fan Xiao (1990). Functional division of words. *Journal of Yantai University*, no. 2.

Fang Guangtao (1939). Systems and methods. *Language Weekly*, no. 28.

Fang Guangtao (1956). Some fundamental problems in the study of Chinese parts of speech (outline). In *Collected Papers of Fang Guangdao*. Beijing: Commercial Press.

Forey, P. L. (1983). A review of cladistic systematics. In Zhou Mingzhen, Zhang Miman & Yu Xiaobo (Comps.), *Translation collections of cladistic systematics*. Beijing: Science Press.

Fries, C. C. (1952). *The structure of English* (trans. He Leshi). Beijing: Commercial Press, 1964.

Fu Donghua (1938). A proposal for the new system of Chinese grammar. *Language Weekly*, no.16. (Also in *Series of Chinese Grammar Reforms*. Beijing: Commercial Press, 1984.)

Fu Zidong (1956). Division and identification of parts of speech. *Studies of Chinese Language*, no. 3.

Gao Gengsheng (1995). Assumptions on dividing Chinese parts of speech. *Journal of Chinese Linguistics*, no. 6.

Gao Mingkai (1953). Differences in Chinese parts of speech. *Studies of Chinese Language*, no. 10.

Gao Mingkai (1954). Further discussions on differences in Chinese parts of speech. *Studies of Chinese Language*, no. 8.

Gao Mingkai (1955). The third discussion on differences in Chinese parts of speech. *Studies of Chinese Language*, no. 1.

Gao Mingkai (1957/1986). *On Chinese grammar*. Beijing: Commercial Press.

Gao Mingkai (1960). Speech at the May Fourth Scientific Symposium at Peking University in 1959. Linguistic Series, 4th series. Shanghai: Shanghai Educational Publishing House

Gao Mingkai (1963). On parts of speech in modern Chinese research. *Journal of Anhui University*, no. 1, 35–52.

Gao Mingkai & Lin Yongyou (1963). From "nominalization of verbs and adjectives" to parts of speech in Chinese. *Journal of Peking University* (Humanities Edition), no. 2, 49–66.

Givón, T. (1984). *Syntax: a functional and typological introduction*, vol. 1. Amsterdam: John Benjamins.

Gong Qianyan (1997). *The history of Chinese grammar*. Beijing: Language & Culture Press.

Guo Rui (1990). On categorical systems of grammar. In *Papers from the second seminar on modern Chinese grammar*. Huadong Normal University.

Guo Rui (1993). Process structures of Chinese verbs. *Studies of Chinese Language*, no. 6.

Guo Rui (1997a). Types of expressional functions and related issues. *Linguistic Series*, 19th series.

Guo Rui (1997b). Process and non-process: two extrinsic time types of Chinese predicate constituents. *Studies of Chinese Language*, no. 3.

Guo Rui (1999). Part of speech tagging in dictionary of modern Chinese. *Studies of Chinese Language*, no. 2.

Guo Rui (2000). Transformation of expressional functions and functions of Chinese character de (的). *Contemporary Linguistics*, no. 1.

Guo Rui (2005). Re-thinking on conversional words. In *Papers from the 50th Anniversary of Symposium on Parts of Speech Expert Discussion*. Wuhu: Anhui Normal University Press.

Guo Rui (2010). Typology and system of Chinese parts of speech. In *Papers from the 16th Symposium on Modern Chinese Grammar*. Hong Kong: City University of Hong Kong Press.

Guo Rui (2011). Zhu Dexi's study of Chinese parts of speech. *Chinese Language Learning*, no. 5, 13–26.

Guo Rui (2012). Gao Mingkai's study of Chinese parts of speech. In *Essays on Linguistics*, vol. 46.

Guo Rui (2015). Revisions of part of speech tagging in the 6th edition of *Dictionary of Modern Chinese*. *Journal of Chinese Dictionaries*, 1, 167–173.

Guo Rui (2017). System of Chinese parts of speech from the perspective of the Amsterdam model. In *Discussions on Chinese and Japanese studies – the 60th birthday celebration of Professor Yang Kairong*. Tokyo: Asahi Press.

Guo Shaoyu (1979). *A new study of Chinese grammatical rhetoric*. Beijing: Commercial Press.

Guo Xiliang (1996). System of ancient Chinese parts of speech. In Xie Jifeng & Liu Guanghe (Eds.), *Xin Huo Collections*. Taiyuan: Shanxi University Associated Press.

Halliday, M. A. K. (1985). *An introduction to functional grammar*. London: Edward Arnold.

Harris, Z. S. (1946). From morpheme to utterance. *Language*, 22, 161–183. (Also Li Zhenlin (trans.), *Linguistics Materials* (1963), 6th issue.)

Harris, Z. S. (1951). *Methods in structural linguistics*. Chicago: University of Chicago Press.

Hengeveld, K. (1992). *Non-verbal predication: theory, typology, diachrony*. Functional Grammar Series 15. Berlin: De Gruyter Mouton.

Hengeveld, K. (2007). Parts-of-speech systems and morphological types. *ACLC Working Papers*, 2(1), 31–48.

Hengeveld, K., Rijkhoff, J. & Siewierska, A. (2004). Parts-of-speech systems and word order. *Journal of Linguistics, 40*(3), 527–570.

Hengeveld, K. & van Lier, E. (2008). Parts of speech and dependent clauses in functional discourse grammar. *Studies in Language* (Special issue: Parts of Speech: Descriptive Tools, Theoretical Constructs), *32*(3), 753–785.

Hengeveld, K. & van Lier, E. (2010). An implicational map of parts-of-speech. *Linguistic Discovery, 8*(1), 129–156.

Hockett, C. F. (1958). *A course in modern linguistics* (trans. Suo Zhenyu & Ye Feisheng). Beijing: Peking University Press.

Hopper, Paul J. & Thompson, S. A. (1984). The discourse basis for lexical categories in universal grammar. *Language, 60*(4), 703–752.

Householder, F. W., Jr. (1952). Review: methods in structural linguistics. *International Journal of American Linguistics, 18*(4), 260–268.

Hu Mingyang (1992). Prologue for Shi Youwei's call for flexibility. In *Shi Youwei's Call for Flexibility*. Haikou: Hainan Publishing House. (Also in Language Planning (1993), no. 2.)

Hu Mingyang (1995). A survey of modern Chinese parts of speech. *Studies of Chinese Language*, no. 5.

Hu Mingyang (1996a). A review of the study of modern Chinese parts of speech. In Hu Mingyang (Ed.).

Hu Mingyang (1996b). Issues on conversional words. In Hu Mingyang (Ed.).

Hu Mingyang (1996c). A survey of conversional words of verbs and nouns. In Hu Mingyang (Ed.).

Hu Mingyang (Ed.). (1996). *A survey of issues of parts of speech*. Beijing: Beijing Language Institute Press.

Hu Yushu & Fan Xiao (1996). "Nominalization" of verb and adjective. *Studies of Chinese Language*, no. 2.

Jin Zhaoxin (1922/1983). *Studies of Chinese grammar*. Beijing: Commercial Press.

Juilland, A. G. & Elliott, E. (1957). Perspectives of linguistic science. In *Monographs Series on Language and Linguistics*. (Chinese version in Linguistics Materials, 1964, no. 3).

Kotov, A. M. (1986). Functional hierarchy of Chinese syntactic phenomena. *Journal of Fudan University*, no. 6.

Langacker, R. W. (1987b). *Foundations of cognitive grammar*, vol. 1, *Theoretical prerequisites*. Stanford, CA: Stanford University.

Li Jinxi (1924/1992). *Newly published Chinese grammar*. Beijing: Commercial Press.

Li, Y. H. (1997). Structure and interpretations of nominal expression. Paper presented at the 9th North American Conference on Chinese Linguistics, Victoria, Canada.

Li Yuming (1986). A new explanation of "nominalization". *Journal of Huazhong Normal University*, no. 3.

Li Yuming (1996). Status of parts of speech of non-predicate adjective. *Studies of Chinese Language*, no. 1.

Li Zuofeng (1995). *Notional words of classical Chinese*. Beijing: Language & Culture Press.

Liao Qiuzhong (1991). A review of linguistic categorization: typical examples in linguistic theory. *Foreign Linguistics*, no. 4.

Liu Danqing (1991). A view of macroscopic study of grammar from the perspective of Chinese parts of speech. *Jiangsu Social Sciences*, no. 2.

Liu Danqing (1987). Issues of word and non-word in contemporary Chinese dictionaries. *Lexicographical Studies*, no. 5.

Liu Danqing (1994). Preliminary exploration of "Weibo words". *Chinese Language Learning*, no. 3.

Liu Danqing (1996). Correlation between part of speech and word length – the second comment on a series of discussions on phonetic level of Chinese grammar. *Journal of Nanjing Normal University*, no. 2.

Lu Bingfu (1981). Conversional words of verbs and nouns. *Lexicographical Studies*, no. 1.

Lu Bingfu (1992). From parts of speech of "dance" and "inevitable" to distinctions between "suddenly" and "abruptly". *Studies of Language and Linguistics*, no. 1.

Lu Bingfu (1993). *Core-derived grammar*. Shanghai: Shanghai Educational Publishing House.

Lu Bingfu (2010). Considerations of parts of speech and nominalization. In *Papers from the 16th Symposium on Modern Chinese Grammar*. Hong Kong: City University of Hong Kong Press.

Lu Chuan (1991). *Issues of parts of speech in modern Chinese information grammar*. Grammar Research and Exploration, 5th series. Beijing: Language & Culture Press.

Lu Jianming (1980). Grammatical property of "degree adverb + adjective + 'de (的)'" structure. *Language Teaching and Research*, no. 2.

Lu Jianming (1982). A discussion on independent use of adverbs in modern Chinese. *Language Teaching and Research*, no. 2.

Lu Jianming (1983). Distinctions between attributive and adverbial. *Chinese Language Learning*, no. 2.

Lu Jianming (1985). 多 (more) and 少 (less) as attributives. *Studies of Chinese Language*, no. 1.

Lu Jianming (1986). *A tentative discussion on verb as predicate in modern Chinese*. Series of Chinese Language, 2nd series. Beijing: Foreign Language Teaching and Research Press.

Lu Jianming (1987). Study of conditions for inserting adjectives in the middle of numeral-measure word phrase. *Language Teaching and Research*, no. 4.

Lu Jianming (1991a). Phenomenon of referent of Versachlichung in modern Chinese. *Studies in Language and Linguistics*, no. 1.

Lu Jianming (1991b). A brief comment on time words in modern Chinese. *Language Teaching and Research*, no. 1.

Lu Jianming (1991c). *Opinion on intransitive verbs in modern Chinese*. Grammar Research and Exploration, 5th series. Beijing: Language & Culture Press.

Lu Jianming (1993a). *Chinese grammar study in 1980s*. Beijing: Commercial Press.

Lu Jianming (1993b). *On dividing Chinese parts of speech*. *Humanities*, 69th and 70th series, Scientific Institute of Humanities of Yonsei University (Ed.). Seoul: Yonsei University Press.

Lu Jianming (1994). Issues on conversional words. *Studies of Chinese Language*, no. 1.

Lu Jiawen (1982). Criteria and levels of dividing modern Chinese parts of speech. *Zhongzhou Academic Journal*, no. 6.

Lu Yingshun (1998). Dividing parts of speech – the combination of generalized morphology with prototype theory. In *New ideas of language research*. Shanghai: Shanghai Educational Publishing House.

Lu Zhiwei (1938). Chinese monosyllabic words (mimeographed version by Yenching University). In *Monosyllabic Words of Beijing Dialect* (renamed in 1951), Beijing: People's Publishing House.

Lu Zhiwei (1957). *Chinese word formation* (rev. version in 1964). Beijing: Science Press.

Lu Zongda (1955). Dividing Chinese words, *issues of Chinese parts of speech*. Beijing: Zhonghua Book Company.

Lv Shuxiang (1955). Some principles on Chinese parts of speech, *issues of Chinese parts of speech*. Beijing: Zhonghua Book Company.

Lv Shuxiang (1962). On "identification of language units". *Studies of Chinese Language*, no. 11.

Lv Shuxiang (1979). *Issues of Chinese grammatical analysis*. Beijing: Commercial Press.

Lv Shuxiang & Rao Changrong (1981). A tentative discussion on non-predicate adjective. *Studies of Chinese Language*, no. 2.

Lv Shuxiang & Zhu Dexi (1951). Talks on grammar and rhetoric. The People's Daily, June 6 to December 15.

Ma Biao (1994). An attempt to use statistic method to divide parts of speech. *Studies of Chinese Language*, no. 5.

Ma Jianzhong (1898/1983). *Ma's grammar*. Beijing: Commercial Press.

Ma Qingzhu (1991). *Influence factors of dividing parts of speech and their definition principles*. Grammar Research and Exploration, 5th series. Beijing: Language & Culture Press.

Ma Qingzhu (1995). *Reference verbs and declarative nouns*. Grammar Research and Exploration, 7th series, Beijing: Commercial Press.

Magnusson, R. (1954). *Studies of the theory of parts of speech*. Copenhagen: Ejnar Munksgaard.

McCawley, J. D. (1992). Justifying parts-of-speech assignments in Mandarin Chinese. *Journal of Chinese Linguistics, 20*(2), 211–246. (Also in *Study of Functional Grammar of Chinese Language* (trans. Zhang Bojiang). Nanchang: Jiangxi Education Publishing House).

Mo Pengling (1990). Re-understanding issues of parts of speech. *Journal of Nanjing Normal University*, no. 1.

Mo Pengling & Shan Qing (1985). A statistical analysis of syntactic functions of three types of notional words. *Journal of Nanjing Normal University*, no. 2.

Mo Pengling & Wang Zhidong (1988). A preliminary exploration of fuzzy clustering analysis of words. *Journal of Changzhou Institute of Engineering and Technology*, no. 3.

Малдер крылов (1954). Chinese has parts of speech. *Studies of Chinese Language*, no. 6.

Quirk, R., Greenbaum, S., Leech, G. & Svartvik, J. (1972). *A grammar of contemporary English*. London: Longman.

Quirk, R., Greenbaum, S., Leech, G. & Svartvik, J. (1985). *A comprehensive grammar of the English language*. London and New York: Longman.

Ren Ying (2010). Dividing parts of speech: exploring identity of meanings and functions – essence of parts of speech reconsidered. In *Papers from the 16th Symposium on Modern Chinese Grammar*. Hong Kong: City University of Hong Kong.

Rozhdestvensky, IO. B. (1958). *Henri Maspero's view of Chinese grammar*. Translation Series of Language Study, 1st Series (trans. Cao Jing), Department of Chinese, Nankai University (Ed.). Tianjin: Nankai University Press, 1984.

Schachter, P. (1985). Parts of speech system. In T. Shopen (Ed.), *Language typology and syntactic description*. Cambridge: Cambridge University Press.

Shao Jingmin (1995). Analysing coordination valence of disyllabic "v + n" structure. In Shen Yang & Zheng Dingou (Eds.), *Study of modern Chinese valence grammar*. Beijing: Peking University Press.

Shen Jiaxuan (1997). Tagging patterns of syntactic functions of adjectives. *Studies of Chinese Language*, no. 4.

Shen Jiaxuan (2007). Chinese nouns and verbs. *Journal of Sino-Tibetan Languages*, no. 1, 27–47.

Shen Jiaxuan (2009a). My views of Chinese word classes. *Linguistic Sciences*, no. 1, 1–12.

Shen Jiaxuan (2009b). *Half a step forward, re-discussion on Chinese nouns and verbs, essays on linguistics* (3–22), vol. 40. Beijing: Commercial Press.

Shen Jiaxuan (2015). Typology of parts of speech and Chinese nominalisation. *Contemporary Linguistics*, no. 2, 127–145.

Shen Jiaxuan (2016). *Nouns and verbs*. Beijing: Commercial Press.

Shen Yang (1996). Dynamic types of compound words in modern Chinese. In Luo Zhensheng (Ed.), *Study of language and character in computer era*. Beijing: Tsinghua University Press.

Shi Anshi (1980). *A further discussion on dividing Chinese parts of speech*. Language Study Series, Department of Chinese Linguistics, Nankai University (Ed.). Tianjin: Tianjin People's Publishing House.

Shi Anshi & Zhan Renfeng (1988). *Introduction to linguistics*. Beijing: Higher Education Press.

Shi Dingxu (2003). Substantialisation and nominalization of verbs. In *Grammatical Study and Exploration*, vol. 12. Beijing: Commercial Press.

Shi Dingxu (2005a). On referential and asserting properties of verb elements. *Chinese Language Learning*, no. 4.

Shi Dingxu (2005b). The ambiguity of v-n constructions and their disambiguation. *Language Teaching and Linguistic Studies*, no. 3.

Shi Dingxu (2007). Criteria, methods and results of dividing noun and verb. *Language Teaching and Linguistic Studies*, no. 4, 3–12

Shi Dingxu (2009). Issues on dividing Chinese parts of speech. In *Essays on linguistics* (93–110), vol. 40. Beijing: Commercial Press.

Shi Guangan (1981). The part of speech of "publication" in "the publication of this book" under the theory of "centripetal structure". *Newsletter of Chinese Language*, no. 4.

Shi Guangan (1988). Centripetal and centrifugal structures of modern Chinese. *Studies of Chinese Language*, no. 4.

Shi Youwei (1991). *Parts of speech: puzzles of linguistics – a preliminary study of patterns of relational parts of speech*. Grammar Research and Exploration, 5th series. Beijing: Language & Culture Press.

Shi Youwei (1994). Crux of issues of parts of speech and their strategies – a tentative treatment of flexibility of Chinese parts of speech. In Hu Mingyang (Ed.), *A survey of issues of parts of speech*. Beijing: Beijing Language Institute Press.

Shi Youwei (1997). Parts of speech of 出品 (product) and others – a discussion on Chinese parts of speech. *Chinese Teaching in the World*, no. 3.

Shi Yuzhi (1992). *Symmetry and asymmetry of affirmation and negation*. Taipei: Taiwan Student Book Company.

Simpson, J. M. Y. (1979). *A first course in linguistics*. Edinburgh: Edinburgh University Press.

Song Shaonian (1998). Reference and nominalization of predicate constituents of classical Chinese. In Guo Xiliang (Ed.), *Classical Chinese Grammar Series*. Beijing: Language & Culture Press.

Sun Hongkai (1982). *History of Derung language*. Beijing: Ethnic Nationality Publishing House.

Takahasi Yasuhiko (1997). Relationship between noun and locative. *Chinese Teaching in the World*, no. 1.

Tang Tingchi (1992). Chinese parts of speech: basis and function of division. Three series of Chinese Morphology and Syntax. Taipei: Taiwan Student Book Company.

Taylor, J. R. (1989). *Linguistic categorization: prototypes in linguistic theory* (2nd ed.). Oxford: Clarendon Press, 1995.

Taylor, J. R. (1991). Category theory of language, foreign languages and their teaching (trans. Rong Pei). Journal of Dalian Institute of Foreign Languages, no. 6.

Thompson, S. A. (1988). A discourse approach to cross-linguistic category "adjective". In J. A. Hawkins (Ed.), *Explaining language universals* (167–185). Oxford and New York: Basil Blackwell.

Vogel, P. M. & Comrie, B. (Eds.). (2000). *Approaches to the typology of word classes*. Berlin and New York: De Gruyter Mouton.

Wang Hongjun (1994). A view of words and phrases from the perspective of characters and their groups – a discussion on Chinese parts of speech division criteria. *Studies of Chinese Language*, no. 2.

Wang Hongqi (1991). A review of Chinese parts of speech studies. Logical Language Writing Series, 4th series. Beijing: Peking University Press.

Wang Li (1943). *Modern grammar of China*. Beijing: Commercial Press, 1985.

Wang Li (1944). Chinese grammatical theory, *collected papers of Wang Li*, vol. 1, Jinan: Shandong Education Press, 1984.

Wang Li (1955). Issues on whether Chinese has parts of speech. *Journal of Peking University*, no. 2.

Wang Li (1960). Dividing Chinese notional words. Linguistics Series, 4th series. Shanghai: Shanghai Educational Publishing House.

Wang Li (1989). *History of Chinese grammar*. Beijing: Commercial Press.

Wells, R. S. (1947). *Immediate constituents. Language, 23*, 81–117. (Also in Language Materials (1963) (trans. Zhao Shikai), no. 6.)

Wen Lian (1995). Bases and criteria for dividing parts of speech. *Studies of Chinese Language*, no. 4.

Wen Lian & Hu Fu (1954). Discussions on dividing parts of speech. *Studies of Chinese Language*, nos. 2/3.

Wetzer, H. (1996). *The typology of adjectival predication*. Berlin and New York: De Gruyter.

Whaley, L. J. (1996). Introduction to typology: *the unity and diversity of language*. Thousand Oaks, CA: Sage.

Xiang Mengbing (1991). Parts of speech of 出版 (publication) in 这本书的出版 (the publication of this book): re-understanding "nominalization" of verbs and adjectives. *Journal of Tianjin Normal University*, no. 4.

Xiao Guozheng (1991). *A survey of referential uses of object predicate in modern Chinese*. Chinese Language Series, 4th series (ed. Zhang Zhigong). Beijing: Foreign Language Teaching and Research Press.

Xing Fuyi (1981). *Distinctions of parts of speech*. Lanzhou: Gansu People's Publishing House.

Xing Fuyi (1989). Four points of distinction of parts of speech. *Language Teaching and Research*, no. 3.

Xing Fuyi (1991). *Thinking about issues of parts of speech*. Grammar Research and Exploration, 5th series. Beijing: Language & Culture Press.

Xing Fuyi (1997). *Chinese grammar*. Changchun: Northeast Normal University Press.

Xing Gongwan (1956). Morphological method and modern Chinese word formation. *Journal of Nankai University*, no. 2.

Xing Hongbing (1999a). Statistics on uses of modern Chinese parts of speech. *Journal of Zhejiang Normal University*, no. 3.

Xing Hongbing (1999b). *Analysing words whose parts of speech are difficult to divide and tag*. Computational Linguistics Series (eds. Huang Changning & Dong Zhendong). Beijing: Tsinghua University Press.

Xu Tongqiang (1994a). "Character" and Chinese syntactic structure. *Chinese Teaching in the World*, no. 2.

Xu Tongqiang (1994b). "Characteristics" and methodology of Chinese language study. *Chinese Teaching in the World*, no. 3.

Xu Tongqiang (1997). *On language*. Changchun: Northeast Normal University Press.

Xu Shu (1991). *Conversional words and problems in dealing with them*. Grammar Research and Exploration, 5th series. Beijing: Language & Culture Press.

Yang Chengkai (1991). *Parts of speech division principles and "normalization" of predicates*. Grammar Research and Exploration, 5th series. Beijing: Language & Culture Press.

Yang Chengkai (1992). Typological study of generalized predicative objects. *Studies of Chinese Language*, no. 1.

Yang Chengkai (1994). A review of modern Chinese grammatical meta-theory. *Studies of Language and Linguistics*, no. 2.

Yang Chengkai (1996). *Theoretical study of Chinese grammar*. Shenyang: Liaoning Education Press.

Yang Zhenwu (1994). Self-reference and transfer reference. *Research on Ancient Chinese Language*, no. 3.

Yang Zhenwu (1995). "N's V" in modern Chinese and "V of N" in classic Chinese". *Linguistic Research*, nos. 2/3.

Yang Zhenwu (1996). Causes and rules of nominalization of Chinese predicate constituents. *Studies of Chinese Language*, no. 1.

Yin Guoguang (1997). *Studies of parts of speech in Master Lv's spring and autumn annals*. Beijing: Huaxia Publishing House.

Yu Min (1955). Morphological change and grammatical environment, *issues of Chinese parts of speech*. Beijing: Zhonghua Book Company.

Yuan Yulin (1995). Family similarity of categories of parts of speech. *Social Sciences in China*, no. 1.

Yuan Yulin (1998). Analysing Chinese parts of speech based on prototype, *cognition research and computational analysis of language*. Beijing: Peking University Press.

Yuan Yulin (2000). Quasi-axiomatic system of parts of speech in Chinese. *Studies of Language and Linguistics*, no. 4.

Yuan Yulin (2005). Fuzzy division of Mandarin words based on membership degree. *Social Sciences in China*, no. 1.

Yuan Yulin (2009). Realising parallelism between Chinese and English in grammar – on noun/verb and reference/statement, subject/topic, sentence/utterance segments. *Journal of Sino-Tibetan Languages*, no. 3.

Yuan Yulin (2010). *A cognitive investigation and fuzzy division of word-class in Mandarin Chinese*. Shanghai: Shanghai Educational Publishing House.

Yuan Yulin, Ma Hui, Zhou Ren & Cao Hong (2009). *A handbook for dividing Chinese parts of speech*. Beijing: Beijing Language and Culture University Press.

Zhan Weidong (1998). On attributive and headword construction of "np of vp". *Chinese Language Learning*, no. 4.

Zhan Weidong (2009). Three questions on parts of speech: a reflection on learning and using Chinese parts of speech. In *Essays on Linguistics*, vol. 40. Beijing: Commercial Press.

Zhang Bojiang (1993). Constructing "v of n" structure. *Studies of Chinese Language*, no. 4.

Zhang Bojiang (1994). Explaining functions of flexible uses of parts of speech. *Studies of Chinese Language*, no. 5.

Zhang Bojiang & Fang Mei (1996). *A study of functional grammar of Chinese language*. Nanchang: Jiangxi Education Publishing House.

Zhang Gonggui (1983). Relationship between part of speech and sentence constituent with some problems about parts of speech considered. *Journal of Nanjing University*, no. 4.

Zhang Shoukang (1985). *Word formation and morphological method*. Wuhan: Hubei Education Press.

Zhang Yujin (2001). *Syntax of oracle-bone inscriptions*. Shanghai: Xuelin Press.

Zhao Yuanren (1948/1995). *Grammar of Beijing spoken Chinese* (comp. Li Rong). Beijing: China Youth Publishing House.

Zhao Yuanren (1968a/1979). *A grammar of spoken Chinese* (trans. Lv Shuxiang). Beijing: Commercial Press.

Zhao Yuanren (1968b/2002). *A Grammar of spoken Chinese* (rev. ed.). Retranslated by Ding Bangxin. Hong Kong: Chinese University of Hong Kong Press.

Zhou Ren (2015). Reflections on "multiple categories" in Mandarin's parts of speech. *Linguistic Sciences*, no. 5, 504–516.

Zhu Dexi (1956). A study of modern Chinese adjectives. *Studies of Language and Linguistics*, no. 1.

Zhu Dexi (1960). *Speech at the May Fourth Scientific Symposium at Peking University in 1959*. Linguistics Series, 4th series. Shanghai: Shanghai Educational Publishing.

Zhu Dexi (1961). Discussions on "de (的)". *Studies of Chinese Language*, no. 12.

Zhu Dexi (1966). About "Discussions on de (的)". *Studies of Chinese Language*, no. 1.

Zhu Dexi (1979). Syntactic issues related to the verb 给 (give). *Dialect*, no. 2.

Zhu Dexi (1982a). Grammatical analysis and grammatical system. *Studies of Chinese Language*, no. 1.

Zhu Dexi (1982b). *Lectures on grammar*. Beijing: Commercial Press.

Zhu Dexi (1982c). Preface to *Series of Chinese grammar*. In *Series of Chinese grammar*. Beijing: Commercial Press.

Zhu Dexi (1983). Self-reference and transfer reference – grammatical functions and semantic functions of Chinese nominalization marker of de (的), zhe (者), suo (所), and zhi (之). *Dialect*, no. 1.

Zhu Dexi (1984a). Defining centripetal structure. *Studies of Chinese Language*, no. 6.

Zhu Dexi (1984b). *Distinctions between attributive and adverbial and antithesis of nominal and predicate*. Linguistics Series, 13th series. Beijing: Commercial Press.

Zhu Dexi (1985a). *Answers to questions on Chinese grammar*. Beijing: Commercial Press.

Zhu Dexi (1985b). Grammaticised verbs and noun-verbs in modern written Chinese. *Journal of Peking University*, no. 5.

Zhu Dexi (1987). What are objects of study of modern Chinese grammar? *Studies of Chinese Language*, no. 5.

Zhu Dexi (1988). Issues on nouns with verb characteristics in the Pre-Qin Chinese. *Studies of Chinese Language*, no. 2.

Zhu Dexi (1990). A note on distinctions between noun and verb in the Pre-Qin Chinese. In *Collected Papers in Commemoration of Mr Wang Li*. Beijing: Commercial Press.

Zhu Dexi (1991). *Word meaning and parts of speech.* Grammar Research and Exploration, 5th series. Beijing: Language & Culture Press.

Zhu Dexi (1993). A view of nominalization of state adjectives from the perspective of dialect and history. *Dialect*, no. 2.

Zhu Dexi, Lu Jiawen & Ma Zhen (1961). "Nominalization" of verbs and adjectives, *Journal of Peking University*, no. 4.

Index

for classifying parts of speech 95–96; Chinese parts of speech and 82–85; correlations among part of speech, syntactic constituents and **104**, 104–106; discourse function and 91–92; external exclusivity and internal universality and 58–60, 63, 122, 128–29, 144; hierarchies of expressional functions 81–82; intrinsic and extrinsic part of speech characteristics and classification 93–95, 188; lexical item differences and need for classification and 87–88; modification as 78–81; part-of-speech classification system of predicate, substantive, predicate modification and substantive modification words 85–88; patterns of classification 87–88; possible classifications obtained with the two criteria of object and 很(very) 61–63, **62**; relationships among expressional functions 80–81; selectional restriction of grammatical position and 94–95; semantic bases of parts of speech **91**; statement and reference as 77–78, 80–82, 100–103; transformation of 96–104; transformation of (de (的)/di (地) functions in Chinese syntax) 103–104; transformation of (lexical transformation of intrinsic) 97; transformation of (nominalization) 100; transformation of (reference/self-reference and transfer reference) 100–103, *101*; transformation of (syntactic transformation) 97–99, *99*; transformation of (vacant constituents) 99, *99*; universal and rational grammar and 93
extraction 103

finite principle 23–24
functions of a word: materials used to investigate 38–39; words with special uses and 39–40
fuzzy clustering analysis method 11

Gao Mingkai 6, 9, 41–50, 94, 174
Givón, T. 93
God's Truth School 51–52
grammatical function as classification criteria 18, 95, 107; in Chinese parts of speech classification 108–109, 111, 128–29, 154–55; compatibility

of functions and 132–33; compatible degrees among specific grammatical functions of modification words **146**; compatible degrees among specific grammatical functions of substantive words **149**; compatible degrees of main grammatical functions of Chinese notional words **136–38**; correlation between compatible degree and function and word frequency **141**; correlation between number of conversional words and word frequency **142**; correlation between word frequency and compatible degree (substantive word) **150**; de (的)/di (地) 37–38; effectiveness of 123–27, **125–126**, 131; equivalent function clusters as criteria for Chinese notional words classification 143–53; equivalent function determination and compatibility with 132–34, *134*; equivalent function determination methods and rules *134*, 134–35, 139–40, 143; equivalent functions and 131–32; by generalized or specific distribution 119–22; grammatical function defined 114–18; grammatical meaning as reason for 123, 131; lexical meaning and 124; methods of classification by 112–13; morphology and 108–109; selectional restriction of grammatical position and 49–51, 94–95, 113; specific function and general function and 118–19; word formation and distribution and 124–27, **125–126**
Guo Rui 139, 155, 181–82

Harris, Z.S. 114–15
hierarchical classification method 13, 19; colloquial modern Chinese and classical Chinese hierarchies and 24–27
Hocuspocus group of linguists 51–52
Hopper, Paul J. 91
Hungarian, transformation of expressional functions in 96

independent application word property 21
Indo-European languages 6, 33, 43, 46–49, 95, 117, 174
integrity principle: expansion criteria in 21–22; integrity criteria 22
Italian 108

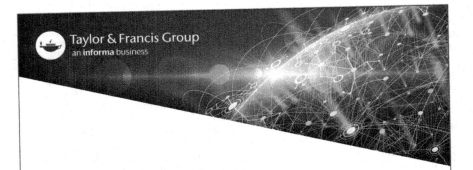